PRAISE FOR PARIS, *PARIS*

"The delightful and insightful essays in PARIS, *PARIS* meld history, atmosphere, and observations on Paris places, Paris people, and Paris phenomena." —*Chicago Tribune*

"Downie is a saunterer, wandering down the narrow ancient streets of the Île de la Cité, picnicking in storied graveyards like Père-Lachaise, observing a seduction at Jardin du Luxembourg with a birder's patience. . . captures the sort of people and places missed by those jetting from starred bistros to hotels with showers." —*Philadelphia Inquirer*

"David Downie's prose illuminates Paris with an unequaled poignancy and passion. He understands and evokes the soul and the substance of the city with a critic's intelligence and a lover's heart. He makes me want to live in Paris again." —DONALD GEORGE, contributing editor, *National Geographic Traveler*

"Downie brilliantly upholds the American expat tradition of portraying the City of Light with an original and endearing touch." —JOHN FLINN, former travel editor, *San Francisco Sunday Chronicle*

"If there is one book I'd read before heading to the City of Light, PARIS, *PARIS* is it. Downie, a longtime Paris resident and roamer, writes with knowledge and verve, pinning down the funny and the sublime as he captures on his canvas the quirks, foibles, and follies, and the peculiar mystery of the people and places, that make up this wonderful city." —HARRIET WELTY-ROCHEFORT, author of *French Toast* and *French Fried*

"When good Americans die, Oscar Wilde wrote, they go to Paris. Don't wait that long. David Downie's new book reflects the city and its light with such power that its title says it twice. PARIS, *PARIS* shimmers with wit and mesmerizes with wisdom. With splendid photographs by Alison Harris, it is, as the French would say, *un must*."   —MORT ROSENBLUM

"Like the guide who leads us through *The Hermitage* and its history in Sokurov's *Russian Ark,* David Downie is the master of educated curiosity. With him we discover Paris, a seemingly public city that is, in fact, full of secrets—great lives, lives wasted on the bizarre; forgotten artisans; lost graves (lost till now); the *'papillons nocturnes'*; and the *'poinçonneur des Lilas.'* I have walked some of the city's streets with him, and reading this book is just as tactile an experience."   —MICHAEL ONDAATJE

Quiet Corners of Rome

Paris City of Night

Food Wine Burgundy

Food Wine Rome

Food Wine Italian Riviera & Genoa

*Cooking the Roman Way: Authentic Recipes from the
Home Cooks and Trattorias of Rome*

*Enchanted Liguria: A Celebration of the Culture, Lifestyle
and Food of the Italian Riviera*

La Tour de l'Immonde

The Irreverent Guide to Amsterdam

Un'altra Parigi (co-author with Ulderico Munzi)

Journey into the City of Light

PARIS, PARIS

DAVID DOWNIE

PHOTOGRAPHS BY ALISON HARRIS

BROADWAY BOOKS

NEW YORK

Copyright © 2005, 2011 by David Downie
Photographs copyright © 2005, 2011 by Alison Harris

Originally published in slightly different form in the United States by
Transatlantic Press, Fort Bragg, California, in 2005.

Library of Congress Cataloging-in-Publication Data
Downie, David.
Paris, Paris: Journey into the City of Light / David Downie;
photographs by Alison Harris.
1. Paris (France)—Description and travel.   2. Paris (France)—Social life
and customs.   3. Paris (France)—Guidebooks.   I. Title.
DC707.D69   2011
914.4'3610484—dc22   2010040397

ISBN 978-0-307-88608-8
eISBN 978-0-307-88609-5

Printed in the United States of America

Text design by Lauren Dong
Cover design by Whitney Cookman
Cover photograph © by Trevillion

10 9 8 7 6 5 4

First Revised Edition

This book is dedicated to

the memory of our dear friend Barbara Bray,

who shared her wit and humor with countless friends and strangers,

filling Paris with life-enhancing light

Contents

PARIS PHENOMENA

Photographs

Of all the books about Paris published each year, not one that I can remember tells you where to find the famous Art Nouveau public toilets in Place de la Madeleine, let alone telling you what to look for in the cemetery of Père-Lachaise. David Downie has a delightful sensibility and the most delighted eye, the most perseverance, and the perfect French, *bien sûr,* and these allow him to uncover secrets. Uncover them he has, the secrets of this fascinating city, and not the ones you'll read about anywhere else. Did you know those ugly brown posts that keep Parisians from parking on the sidewalks are *bittes,* which is slang for what I guess we would call "pricks"? To take this book as a guidebook, walk out with it as he did and follow his path, is to have adventures, and to see a side of Paris anyone could see, but hardly anyone does.

Suppose you aren't in Paris? Or you're in Paris on a rainy day? Just to sit inside and read this book will transport you, for Downie is above all a wonderful, and wonderfully well-read, writer. The essays are delightful as essays, but come fine weather I also recommend following his programs to the letter—a day of looking at the Paris of 1900, for instance. It's still here. You'll eat at Julien, have a coffee at Angelina, go to the movies at LaPagode, look at the Palais des Mirages at the Musée Grévin, the wax museum, where he counsels skipping the wax statues to admire this wonder rescued from the 1900 Exposition Universelle.

Or if 1900 is too recent, try the Paris of Beaumarchais, the playwright who invented Figaro, in the days of Louis XV and XVI. Downie tells you how to get into his historic Hôtel Amelot de Bisseuil, little changed since Beaumarchais's day, to get a glimpse of the remarkable sculpture of the courtyard before the concierge throws you out. You'll learn about the topography of the Buttes-Chaumont, the gorgeous park in the 19th arrondissement, far from the tourist track; it has a bridge by Eiffel and cliffs built to emulate the famous cliffs of Étretat.

What of the man who has served up this delicious array of treats? Something of a gourmet, for one thing, and a fabled cook. I was familiar with his cookbook, *Cooking the Roman Way,* but now I see that the same qualities that make someone love cookery make him love the odd bit of information, the smorgasbord of observations, the taste of the something curious in the scenes before him. Beside a scholar and a gifted *flâneur,* you always want a food-lover to be your guide when possible, and Downie is all three.

And the photographs. Paris must be the most photographed place in the world, from Doisneau to Cartier-Bresson. These beautiful studies by Alison Harris extend that literature with a powerful formal talent. Her camera's loving dissection of details that the busy traveler might not notice makes of this book a splendid object in itself, a sort of bibliophilic gem.

Diane Johnson, Paris

Paris is the kind of city butterfly catchers have trouble netting, tacking down, and studying. Like all great cities and yet unlike any other, Paris is alive and fluttering. It changes with the light, buffeted by Seine-basin breezes. This place called Paris is at once the city of literature and film, an imagined land, a distant view through shifting, misty lenses, and the leftover tang of Jean-Paul Sartre's cigarettes clinging to the mirrored walls of a Saint-Germain-des-Prés café. It's also the city where I and more than two million others pay taxes, re-heel shoes, and shop for cabbages or cleaning fluids.

The tourist brochures and winking websites, the breathless conspiracy thrillers, cinematic fables, and confessional chronicles set in Paris, each offer a view of the city's districts that someone will recognize. Nearly all such views neglect the burgeoning, unexpurgated Paris of last century's housing projects built within and beyond the beltway. For twenty years, my office was in the unfashionable 20th arrondissement. Its windows offered a kaleidoscopic vision of that Paris—a city of Asians, Africans, and Eastern Europeans. I gazed upon their city, walked through it, worked in their midst, but could not know them or it with anything approaching intimacy. The same applies to the gilded 7th arrondissement—a world of old money, old families, old furniture, old objets d'art, and very old, very heavy leather-bound cultural baggage.

The Paris of this book is not a product of the 7th or 20th arrondissements. In its irreverent, erratic way it flutters from one place, person, or phenomenon to the next, touching on aspects of history, alighting on the contemporary, choosing flowers both perfumed and evil-smelling.

The book's emphatic title refers to the Paris of the English speaker, and, in italics, the *Paris* of Parisians. They are cities apart. For a Frenchman, "Paris, *Paris*" sets words at play: *paris* is the plural of *pari,* meaning bet, challenge, risk, wager. Elevate the "p" to upper case and you get a city that's a roll of the dice, a life-wager, a challenge as formidable to meet as Manhattan is to a Mongolian or Miamian.

Beyond its linguistic ambiguity the name "Paris" has a peculiar, pleasing resonance. I often hear it in my head even when I don't actually hear it with my ears, for instance when I ride in the Plexiglas nose cone of the Météor high-speed subway, line number fourteen. I enjoy the subway's swooshing headlong rush down dark tunnels, and the verbal massage the PA system provides.

If you take the Météor from, say, Place de la Madeleine to the Gare de Lyon train station, at each stop you'll hear an unmistakable female voice sing out the stops not once, but twice, with a variation in tone and emphasis. "Pyramides," says the voice of Paris, smooth with self-assurance, before the train pulls into the station. *"Pyramides,"* the voice repeats as the doors slide open, impatient now, a disembodied Catherine Deneuve riding crop in hand.

The change is subtle, not so much marking an accent as a shift to those ambiguous italics. Up and down the futuristic subway's line, the names sing out modulated and *slightly* reformulated. For months, perhaps years, this peculiar duotone subway refrain played in my head without my knowing it, an earworm whispering not station stops but the words "Paris, *Paris*"—words that to me came to signify the great wager, *the* subway stop of my life, where I got off the train I'd been riding aimlessly, and made my stand.

Perhaps because I came to Paris expecting no favors, with few illusions, and with a generous dose of curiosity, I have yet to feel the betrayal some visitors and transitory residents distill into vague resentment. Paris has no monopoly on grumpy waiters, horizontal pollution, or enraged drivers, nor, in my experience, do the elusive, mythical Parisians focus their supposed disdain on any one nationality. I've been privileged to hunt for Paris in many places, with many people, including the occasional Parisian, for more than a quarter of a century. These essays are part of my catch. My vision of the city still blurs from Paris to *Paris* in my daily pursuit of fluttering wings. Happily, I don't want to pin them down, and anyway, Paris always manages to fly away.

PARIS
PLACES

It's the Water: The Seine

The time-worn stones were cold and the ever-flowing stream beneath the bridges seemed to have carried away something of their selves . . .

—ÉMILE ZOLA, *L'Oeuvre* (1886)

No single element of Paris evokes the city's ambiguous allure more poignantly than the Seine. A slow arcing gray-green curve, the river reflects the raked tin rooftops arrayed along its embankments, and the temperamental skies of the Île-de-France. Sea breezes sweep fresh Atlantic air up it into the city. Each day when I step out for my constitutional around the Île Saint-Louis—a ten-minute walk from where my wife, Alison, and I live—I ask myself what Paris would be without the Seine. The answer is simple: it wouldn't.

At once water source and sewer, lifeline, moat, and swelling menace, the Seine suckled nascent French civilization. It made the founding of Paris possible, transforming a settlement of mud huts into a capital city whose symbol since the year 1210 is a ship, with the catchy device *Fluctuat nec mergitur*: "It is tossed upon the waves without being submerged" (and it sounds better in Latin). For centuries this murky waterway has filled Parisians' hearts, minds, and noses with equal measures of inspiration or despair.

Back in the mid-1970s, the low point of Paris urbanism, I visited the city for the first time and was taken aback by the river's chemical stench and the flying suds from its filthy waves quivering over the cars on the just-built riverside expressways. A decade later I willfully forgot such details when I engineered my move here. I was tantalized by the scenes—of dancers on the Seine's cobbled quays, bridges compressed by a telephoto lens—in what might possibly be the worst movie ever made, *Tango*. Never able to tango despite lessons, and aware from the start that I'd duped myself into imagining such a dreamy place could exist, I've been stalking the photogenic quays of Paris ever since. Although I've sometimes felt my passion for Paris ebb, the Seine has flowed along, in its indifference seducing me, a knowing victim, time and again.

Not long ago, after a failed research mission to the National Library on Paris's extreme eastern edge, I glanced down at the river from the Pont de Tolbiac and realized that, despite my wanderings, I'd never actually followed the Seine downstream across the city to the quays of the 15th arrondissement. How long a walk could it be? Without real conviction or particularly comfortable shoes I set off to see how far I could get.

Judging by the smokestacks upstream, the glassy National Library towers, and the floating nightclubs moored in front of them, not to mention the cars dueling on the Pompidou Expressway, it struck me as hard to believe the Seine ever had been a wild river edged by marshlands, where the area's Celtic inhabitants lived. Five thousand years ago that benign river provided France's mythicized forebears—*Nos Ancêtres les Gaulois*—with food, potables, and the protection they needed to build their island-city, which the Romans eventually called Lutetia. Until the 1980s no trace of the Seine Basin's early fisherfolk had been found, but while reconfiguring the formerly industrial Bercy area's warehouses, workmen turned up several Neolithic canoes. The hallowed site is recalled by Rue des Pirogues de Bercy, a street sandwiched between a multiplex cinema and a convention center. City officials quickly latched onto the canoes, seeing in them a symbol of pre-Roman civilization and the solution to an etymological mystery. The canoes jibe with the Celtic-language hypothesis of the origin of "Lutetia": *luh* (river) + *touez* (in the middle) + *y* (house), meaning "houses midstream," an apparent reference to what is now the Île de la Cité and Île Saint-Louis.

Of course everyone knows the unappetizing alternative, which Victor Hugo pointed out in the mid-1800s: in Latin *lutum* means mud, therefore Lutetia was the "City of Mud." As to the etymology of "Paris," the canoes came in very handy. The ancient Celtic word appears to be composed of *par* (a kind of canoe) + *gw-ys* (boatmen or expert navigators). Therefore the Parisii tribespeople were expert navigators with canoes. The Romans dubbed the muddy settlement *Lutetia Parisiorum,* a mouthful that later inhabitants shortened to Lutetia then Frenchified to the euphonic Lutèce. Paris's neolithic canoes are evoked by the dozens of paddle-shaped information panels, designed by Philippe Starck, found in many places around town.

If you believe what the conqueror Julius Caesar wrote in *Gallic Wars,* France's expert canoe navigators (and other warlike inhabitants) savored not only Seine trout, but also human flesh. The fearsome Gauls called their river Sequana, meaning "snakelike," presumably because the Seine meanders on its 482-mile course from its source on the 1,500-foot Langres Plateau in Burgundy to the Atlantic, a torpid yard's tilt per mile. The Romans lost no time humanizing snaky Sequana into a curvaceous water nymph of the same name. In case your mind's eye fails to envision her, a mid-nineteenth-century rendition of Sequana stands in a faux grotto at the Source de la Seine. This watery enclave is near the village of Chanceaux. But the property belongs to Paris: Sequana's fountainhead was claimed for the city not by Caesar but by another emperor, Napoléon III.

By continuing downstream from the National Library on the landscaped left bank, under rows of poplars, past barges, houseboats, and homeless people's encampments, you'll eventually catch sight of Notre-Dame's spire. It marks the center-point from which distances in France are measured. Fittingly, not far from where Notre-Dame stands the Romans built their walled citadel or *civitas* (later bastardized as *la Cité*), ringed by the Seine's natural moat. Then as now the river ran at its narrowest around the Île de la Cité and could be forded when low, which is why Roman engineers first bridged it here.

There was nothing new under the sun in Caesar's day. The Seine's ford lay at the crossroads of older, Bronze Age trade routes, routes that led south to the Mediterranean and west to the English Channel. In time, Lutetia became the crucible where the south's copper and the west's tin met and melded into bronze weaponry. In the fourth century AD, when Julian the Apostate was proclaimed *Augustus* in Paris, the rebellious young emperor elevated Lutetia to the rank of "summer capital" of the Roman Empire, and the Seine became the new Rome's Tiber. In due course, once the Romans had vacated, upriver paddled medieval missionaries and Norsemen of an equally bloody-minded nature, bent on trading, raiding, and proselytizing. And the rest, as they say, is history, a murky tale splayed over centuries and far too slippery to grasp here, with Lutetia becoming "Paris," Sequana morphing into "Seine," and my feet already sore after a mere mile's march downstream.

Since the early twenty-first century even the short seedy stretch of quay fronting the Austerlitz train station has been pedestrianized. You can now walk unmolested by cars along the river's left bank for several miles, almost as far as the Musée d'Orsay. I paused on the Pont d'Austerlitz to reconnoiter and rest my bunions. With several specific episodes of city lore in mind, it struck me that, probably ever since the first Gallic fisherman-cannibal fell afoul of his neighbor hereabouts, the Seine has been the favorite accomplice of murderers, and a convenient channel for the lifeblood of adulterers, warriors, revolutionaries, royalists, and massacre victims.

Take, for instance, Isabeau of Bavaria, luckless bride of mad King Charles VI. Around 1400, in a fit of jealousy, he had one of her admirers sewn into a cloth sack and tossed into the river (from where the Pont Louis-Philippe now stands, on the Right Bank). And what about the Saint Bartholomew's Massacre of 1572, when the Seine famously ran red? It did so again during the Revolution, as illustrated by eighteenth-century chronicler Jean-Louis Mercier's account of Louis XVI's execution at Place de la Concorde. Mercier tells of an onlooker who dipped his finger into the sovereign's blood as it ran toward the river, pronouncing it particularly salty. Victor Hugo, no stranger to prose in full flood, preferred the sewers to the Seine for many uplifting scenes in *Les Misérables,* though he did finish off his misguided police inspector, Javert, in the river's maelstrom.

As I ambled downstream, I tried to remember how many times in Georges Simenon's novels Inspector Maigret fished bodies or their parts from the Seine, into whose depths Maigret stared daily from his office on the Quai des Orfèvres. The silver screen has certainly upheld the ghoulish-river tradition. People are pushed or fling themselves into Sequana's arms with alarming frequency, as in the otherwise forgettable *Paris by Night.* Relatively recent history has also seen the river run *rouge*: in October 1961, during the Algerian War, the infamous Nazi collaborator Maurice Papon, then prefect of the Paris police, ordered hundreds of Algerian demonstrators to be beaten or bound and dumped into the

Seine. The crime was denied for decades, and Papon, protected by everyone from De Gaulle to Mitterrand, remained free until 1999. A plaque on the Pont Saint-Michel records the event. It was placed there in 2001 by mayor Bertrand Delanoë.

But I suspect most contemporary visitors to Paris couldn't give a flying buttress about the morbidity of moviemakers, literati, historians, and statisticians, who note that in an average year about fifty people fling themselves into the river hoping to end their lives. Like me, when I'm in a good mood, they imagine the Seine as a romantic setting, with pairs of lovers twining. That was precisely what I saw ahead, midstream, in the shade of a spreading sycamore, on the upstream tip of the Île Saint-Louis. The sight reassured me that, on the river's edge, there's something for everyone. There's the Tino Rossi sculpture garden, for instance, with built-in sand pits and convenient statuary for insouciant dog-walkers. There are concrete-lined heat sinks for sun-seeking optimists, amphitheaters for tango enthusiasts, footpaths for red-faced joggers, and many an isolated stretch where anglers wet a line or clochards a wall.

Day and night, the river buzzes with *bateaux-mouches,* speakers blaring and floodlights glaring, gaily conveying millions of merrymakers each year on a magical Paris mystery tour.

But how much of the Seine's glamour is carefully staged illusion? When in a sardonic frame of mind, induced, as was now the case, by the press of bodies around Notre-Dame, I often think of the river's curving sweep as seen from a satellite: an eyebrow raised at all romantic notions of Paris, starting with my own. Romance? Two hundred years ago Napoléon I, ever the poet, dubbed the river "The highway linking Paris and Rouen." Thanks to inspired twentieth-century planners, the Seine is still a highway, paved with asphalt on both sides, and girded by commuter train rails underneath the left embankment. Industrial barges and tour boats churn up the dark waters between.

Twenty-five million tons of freight, much of it toxic, transits on the river yearly. The effluent and garbage of the capital and upstream Seine Basin have flowed across Sequana's bosom since the days of Lutetia. That paragon of romantic bridges, the Pont des Arts, linking the Louvre to the Institut de France, was long where street sweepers dumped their loads. So foul was the Seine by 1970, the statistical baseline for reclamation efforts, that it was pronounced "nearly dead." Of the dozens of fish species pre-industrial fishermen once snared in their nets, scientists could find only three remaining. The situation has slowly improved, with bottom-feeders such as torpedo fish making a comeback, though in the early 1990s then-mayor Jacques Chirac was a trifle premature when he tossed trout and salmon into what was still a sump. The fish promptly went belly up. Granted, a few escapees from the Canal Saint-Martin do cross Paris now and again, swimming as fast as their fins will take them to Le Havre and the sea. In 2010 one lucky angler famously fished out a plump, healthy hatchery salmon—and practically made front-page news.

Today, with the river's quays and bridges a UNESCO World Heritage Site, few Parisians suspect that Sequana is on a respirator: six oxygen-pumping plants hidden along the banks keep floundering fish species alive. Still fewer people notice the submerged garbage-catching barriers discreetly emptied by trucks or barges. And hardly anyone thinks of the hundreds of employees working around the clock to keep the river tidy, police it, control its flow, and purify its water. This is not done merely to please environmentalists or the tourism board. The fact is eighty percent of Paris's drinking water comes from the Seine. The turgid flow is treated in four plants at the rate of three million cubic meters daily then piped into the homes of unsuspecting residents. I recall the day I heard rumors that, on average, by the time the Seine reaches my kitchen sink it has been through five human bodies. Try telling that to an enraptured visitor at a riverside café.

Parisians shrug off such reports. They seem to acquire a taste for chlorine and kidney-filtered water. With that pleasant thought in mind I gulped an espresso and a glass of Seine then descended a stairway to the riverbank, just downstream of Place Saint-Michel. I was in time to see the Brigade Fluvial, stationed near the Pont des Arts, struggle into wetsuits and brave the waters. I prayed to Sequana that these fluvial firemen were inoculated against every known water-borne disease and heavily insured. Ditto the Seine police, who fly by on speedboats, their sunglasses flashing, apparently having the time of their life. If only their dream duties did not include dealing with the successful suicide victims, and the many, many others who try but fail.

Despite the widely reported death of Jacques Chirac's trout and salmon, many Parisians continue to dream of fishing and swimming in the Seine, so much so that Paris's port authority and long-serving mayor Delanoë are studying the feasibility of creating inner-city bathing beaches. Delanoë got his toes in the water in summer 2002 with an initiative called *Paris Plage,* as in "beach." He ordered that the Right Bank expressway be closed temporarily, and had outdoor cafés, sun umbrellas, and portable swimming pools planted on the tarmac. The initiative is now a regular summertime event, and the expressway is also closed from mid-morning to early afternoon on Sundays, transforming the pitted asphalt into an enchanted Yellow Brick Road. But no one so far has been foolhardy enough to scatter sand on the riverbanks and dive in.

As I shuffled now over the handsome, modern Solferino footbridge to the Right Bank quays flanking the Tuileries, I paused to take in the seductive views, and had to admit that a sandy strand somewhere hereabouts wouldn't be bad. Once the water was clean enough for a swim, however, there would remain the minor detail of the Seine's yearly floods, which tend to wreak havoc and would possibly sweep away the mayor's beaches.

Earthquake-prone California lives in fear of "the big one." But

Paris dreads a repeat of the 1910 flood, whose height and extent are remembered around town by small plaques. Were it not for the reservoirs, dams, locks, and embankments perfected following the 1910 deluge, in the dry season the Seine would be a muddy trickle, while in rainy months it would slosh as far as the Bastille, Odéon, and Opéra neighborhoods. A replay of 1910, termed a "Parisian Chernobyl" by police and municipal authorities, would cost billions of euros and shut down the city for months.

Floods would be nightmarish indeed, but occasional high water can be a boon, providing walkers with a blissful respite between marks on the meter stick. Moderately high water means cars can no longer use the expressways, while pedestrians can still pick a path between the puddles. Traditionally, Parisians gauged the river's height by Le Zouave (it rhymes with suave), a giant statue of a soldier. Le Zouave juts from the Pont de l'Alma and when Sequana caresses his neck, the city is in trouble. Happily, the river was barely licking the statue's boots as I crept by on the Pont de l'Alma. I switched back to the Left Bank and sauntered along the stretch of quay in the Eiffel Tower's shadow.

Feet throbbing, I limped onto the Allée des Cygnes, a narrow, half-mile-long island anchored midstream. It joins the tiered bridge of Bir-Hakeim to that of Grenelle, thereby uniting the bridges' respective monuments to hope, pride, or self-deception, depending on your interpretation of history and your worldview. At Bir-Hakeim a 1949 plaque reminds readers that "France never stopped fighting" in World War II. Downstream at Grenelle a thirty-foot Statue of Liberty faces west, turning its buttocks to Notre-Dame. On the Allée des Cygnes itself I saw no swans, but spotted many peacocks in designer sportswear. They lazed on benches, and appeared to be enjoying the unusual views of 1950s to 1970s highrise architecture.

Another quarter-mile downstream at Javel (as in *eau de Javel,* or bleach, produced here starting in the 1770s) the Seine flowed melodiously beneath the ironwork Pont Mirabeau. In the rushing mainstream I could hear Guillaume Apollinaire's wistful refrain of time and love slipping by, the one every French high schooler memorizes: *Sous le pont Mirabeau coule la Seine et nos amours faut-il qu'il m'en souvienne la joie venait toujours après la peine . . .*

But I hadn't walked three hours to weep tears of nostalgia. The goal I had been advancing toward was near: a giant bronze nymph, symbol of the river, affixed to the Pont Mirabeau. On the railing above her head is a crown in the shape of a turreted citadel, and the device *Fluctuat nec mergitur*. The sculpture's décolleté suggests that the sculptor was more interested in his model's bounteous *seins* than in the Seine. I gazed down into her corroded but smiling eyes and recognized Sequana.

A Day in the Park: The Luxembourg Gardens

[Y]ou shall meete some walkes & retirements full of Gallants & Ladys, in others melancholy Fryers, in others studious Scholars, in others jolly Citizens; some sitting & lying on the Grasse, others, running, & jumping, some playing at bowles, & ball, others dancing & singing; and all this without the least disturbance . . .

—JOHN EVELYN'S diary, April 1, 1644

"The gardens shall be open from sunrise to sunset all year, but never before seven a.m." So reads one of the nine articles of the Règlement du Jardin du Luxembourg, that most sublime of Paris parks that greens the Left Bank between the Latin Quarter and Montparnasse. Like countless enthusiasts who've visited the gardens in the past four centuries, I've stood at dawn before the wrought-iron gates waiting for the keepers of the castle to let me in. On warm summer evenings, when the sun and moon meet in the canopy of horse-chestnut trees west of the Palais du Luxembourg, I've hidden in the shadows, savoring the dusky light, until the guards have ushered me out of those tall, uncompromising gates.

You are denied sunrises and sunsets at the Luxembourg (and the pleasures of the night) but little else worth mentioning. In their own way, the gardens are a perfect world: sixty acres of terraced woods and walks, fountains and pools, with sweeping perspectives along alleys of surgically clipped trees. There's an old-fashioned music stand, two quaint cafés, a restaurant, and several snack bars. City and country embrace to seduce you. A day spent loitering here teaches you more about Paris and its inhabitants than many a scholarly tome.

Some Parisians make a science of studying people's behavior in the Luxembourg gardens. A friend of mine once boasted that he could tell the time of day by the breathlessness of the before-work joggers, the ruddiness of the lunchtime loafers, and the decibel levels of the babies, maids, and beaming young mothers out for an afternoon stroll. I challenged his boast but had to admit that, though I'd been to the gardens many times (they're only a half-hour's walk from where I live), I'd never actually spent a day there. And I resolved to do just that.

I arrived at the park from Place de l'Odéon one spring morning and walked straight to a wooden kiosk. A handful of these are scattered around the gardens. Displayed are a map and a poster showing the species of trees—elm, sycamore, ginkgo, giant sequoia—that grow here, with names in French and Latin, for the benefit of budding botanists. You also find a brief history, in four languages, of the Luxembourg palace and its grounds.

Legend has it that the gardens stand over the ancient Roman encampment of Emperor Julian the Apostate (AD 331 to 363). But there's no trace of it. From Julian's day to the eleventh century, the area was farmed. The farms are also long gone. In the 1200s, Louis IX—known as Saint Louis—gave part of the neighborhood to the Carthusian monks. Alas, the monastery is gone, too.

As for the flower-spangled, sun-washed gardens we know today, their life began in the early 1600s as a green garland adorning the palace built by architect Salomon de Brosse for Henri IV's widowed queen, Marie de Médicis, née Maria de' Medici, a Florentine. She wanted an Italian-style palazzo to remind her of the Pitti Palace back home. Instead, she wound up with rusticated stonework grafted onto the archetypal Île-de-France château, surrounded by formal French gardens.

Jostled by joggers, I strolled from the kiosk to the Fontaine de Médicis and sat beside it. This oblong pool is flanked by twin ranks of tall sycamores draped with ivy bows, a living garland motif. No matter what the season, it's cool and damp here. The moody setting seems to attract a soulful breed of visitor. On one side of the pool sat a solitary young man pretending to read *Le Monde.* Across from him posed a comely young woman, the real object of his attention. She looked wistfully at the white marble sculptures of Acis and Galatea enlaced rapturously in the fountain's grotto. Above them lurks the menacing Polyphemus, a greenish bronze monster twice their size. The young woman's eyes swept over the pool to the ivy garlands, to the half-opened newspaper, and finally to the young man's handsome face. Each time her gaze fell upon him, *Le Monde* trembled.

My thoughts returned to the luckless Marie de Médicis, who so loved this fountain. She moved into her palace in 1625 while the plaster was still wet and was expelled from France shortly thereafter by her thankless son Louis XIII. The name of the Duc de Tingry-Luxembourg, the property's former owner, was revived, and Marie de Médicis's was forgotten. The palace then passed through the hands of the Duc d'Orléans, the Duchesse de Guise, Louis XIV, and several less illustrious heirs. The only notable incidents in the gardens during these centuries seem to have been the visits of Watteau, who painted many a sensual canvas here, and the late-night summertime orgies of the Duchesse de Berry. She had all the gates but one walled up so she could frolic "with the sort of abandon that requires accomplices and not witnesses."

I was just about to leave Marie's fountain when along came a teetering octogenarian, led unsteadily by her young grandson. "Where are the goldfish?" demanded the boy, waving a stick. "They must be at the other end," whispered the woman. They shuffled along together, side-stepping the nervous young woman and attracting the attention of the man reading *Le Monde*. He folded his newspaper then edged around the pool. "Aren't you Sylvie?" he asked. She said a friend of hers was named Sylvie. Perhaps they'd met at Sylvie's house? "Yes," replied the eager young man. "That's it . . . Shall we have a coffee? It's damp by this fountain." And the two walked awkwardly toward the park café in a nearby grove of flowering horse-chestnut trees.

Meanwhile, there were no goldfish to be found at either end of the fountain. The elderly woman and her grandson headed toward the so-called Great Octagonal Pool—the garden's centerpiece—facing the rear of the Palais du Luxembourg. I followed, settling into an armchair to sniff the sea of flowers and watch the world go by.

It's hard to imagine this place as a prison. Yet during the Revolution's darkest days, the grounds were sealed and hundreds of royalists and sympathizers interned. Guests included Danton, the painter David, and Tom Paine (who had the effrontery to vote against the execution of Louis XVI). Paine spent many a day wandering the gardens' alleys, looking for a way out, and by luck escaped the guillotine. Few others did.

Revolutionaries also ransacked the palace. A series of monumental paintings by Rubens depicting the life of Marie de Médicis that had hung here for more than a century were packed off to the Louvre, where you may admire them to this day.

Since then, with brief interruptions, the building has housed the French Senate. The grounds were expanded under Napoléon I, who destroyed the Carthusian monastery, and were reduced in the 1860s under Napoléon III, who ordered his prefect, Baron Georges-Eugène Haussmann, to rebuild the neighborhood from scratch. Haussmann would have paved the gardens over had not twelve thousand angry citizens poured into the streets to stop him. Instead he moved the Fontaine de Médicis to its present location and ran a road or two across the grounds.

But Haussmann and his team did bequeath the park its handsome round music stand, gingerbread cafés, beekeeper's bungalow, and most of the compound's other charming nineteenth-century elements. For years my favorites were the battered green metal garden chairs, about which I developed a theory long ago. Each of the four distinctive types of chair seemed to have its own personality and attract people of corresponding character. Some chairs were upright and grave, others slung back at a suggestive angle, still others had generous round seats decorated with delicate pinhole patterns and armrests shaped like arabesques. These I thought of as grandmother chairs, and sadly they have disappeared. They were comforting and weathered, appealing to thoughtful, mature strollers with a nostalgic twinkle in their eyes.

On weekday mornings, when the gardens aren't too crowded and there are plenty of chairs to go around, you can still guess what kind of person will choose what kind of chair, where. Sun gods and goddesses lope down the gravel lanes then drape themselves over the low-slung variety, usually in the vicinity of the *orangerie,* a heat sink dotted with orange trees and outsized potted palms. Chess players favor a combination of one upright, armless chair (for their boards) faced by armchairs. They set up in the grove of paulownia trees and in spring play under a rain of mauve blossoms. Amorous couples prefer secluded lanes, leaning two armless chairs side by side. The empty chairs, left as arranged by their last occupants, tell of trysts, duels, and roundtable talks.

From my comfortable old armchair by the octagonal pool, I watched as children played with weathered wooden sailboats, prodding them with long wooden sticks. A sinister-looking man of middle age with a radio-controlled submarine chortled as his U-boat prowled just below the surface.

The wizened woman who rents the sailboats displays dozens of the battered little craft on the cart she wheels out rain or shine. She is known to be fierce, defending her boats from the abuse of rambunctious children. Every once in a while, a submarine or powerboat rams a sailboat and she flies into a rage.

Children often misuse the wooden sticks she supplies and take a poke at the pool's enormous old carp. Witness the fish-hunting grandson I'd seen earlier at the Fontaine de Médicis: the boat woman has summoned a park guard and ordered him to subdue the child and confiscate his stick.

As the grandmother and her chastened grandson slunk off, I remarked to a neighbor in an upright chair that the *gardien* was perhaps too strict.

"Monsieur," my neighbor remonstrated, "the rules must be enforced." A chorus of Gallic voices agreed. "Rules, rules, rules," echoed the stiff chairs.

With that mild reproach coloring my cheek, I stole away to the park café, installed myself under the leafy horse-chestnut trees at a wobbly metal table, and soothed my pride with a sandwich and a beer. The beer was cool and refreshing, the sandwich tough as rubber and the prices extortionate. Still, a brass band was playing under the music stand's canopy, the sun slanted through the budding grove, and I couldn't help enjoying myself.

I hadn't been there five minutes when a battalion of *gardiens* appeared for their break. Paunchy and of indeterminate age, the men ordered rough red wine and soon it was flowing like the Médicis fountain. The *gardiens* wear dark blue uniforms with brass buttons and matching képis. In winter, they wrap themselves in dark blue overcoats or heavy black capes and look like avenging angels. They carry walkie-talkies and whistles and are not shy about using either. Peep-pee-EEP—get off the lawn! Peep-peep-pee-EEP—don't pick the flowers! Put away that camera—no photos allowed with a tripod!

Some afternoons, the birds can't compete with the *gardiens*'s shrilling. But now, as they ate and drank and smoked luxuriantly, they seemed entirely human. Every kingdom must have its rules and someone to enforce them.

Later, as I wandered around the romantic English garden west of the main esplanade, I reflected upon this simple fact. Without the *règlement,* would the Luxembourg lose its magic? As it is, no one pilfers the pears grown by botanists on the pocket-size orchard's espaliered trees. Or throws smoke bombs at the beehives kept by the Société Centrale d'Apiculture, whose courses on beekeeping, devised to bring Parisians into contact with nature, have been a fixture since the 1860s. Were they allowed on the lush yet delicate lawns, would the gleeful thousands of students from the Lycée Montaigne facing the park soon wear the grass thin? One nineteenth-century chronicler remarked that so many high school and college students have always come here that if the trees were full of parrots, the parrots would speak Latin—though the current language of choice seems to be Franglais, that admix of French and English, spiked nowadays with Arabic.

Not far from a bronze statue of a stag and deer, and the busts of a score of forgotten men, famous in their day, stands a marble sculpture of Watteau posed beside a buxom demimonde. He seems pleased, at home, as do the drunken Silenus, falling off his mule, and the ecstatic Pan across the esplanade, whose lithe figure when glimpsed from the palace appears artfully framed by the Panthéon.

I took another turn around the grounds, this time to admire the monuments to Baudelaire, Verlaine, Gérard de Nerval, and Delacroix. These weren't military men or industrialists. Demigods, poets and artists, like guardian spirits, have always inhabited this park. At their feet, children spin on an old merry-go-round, pedal antique tricycles made to look like horses and royal carriages, or roar at the antics of Guignol and Gnafron at the park's eternal puppet theater. Ponies troop up and down, followed by zealous road-apple sweepers armed with worn brooms. Businessmen and bus drivers unknot their ties and troubles and play bowls in the shade of spreading sycamores.

As I drank in this cheerful spectacle, the bells of nearby Saint-Sulpice tolled four o'clock. Soon the gardens were swarming with perambulators, *poussettes, cochecillos de niño, carrozzine,* and whatever else the au pairs and young mothers choose to call a baby carriage in the Babel of languages they speak. Could it be the day-care centers had just closed? At length scores of starched-looking matrons from the luxurious apartments bordering the park were chatting away with immigrant maids and young bourgeois babysitters.

The words of Louis-Sébastien Mercier, written more than two hundred years ago, sprang to mind: "This peaceful garden is free from the extravagance of the city, and immodest and libertine behavior is never seen nor heard . . . the garden is full yet silence reigns." In truth, there is more joyous laughter in the Luxembourg nowadays than reverential silence, and I'll bet there always has been.

Before I knew it, the sun was dipping into the trees and the whistles of the *gardiens* had begun to blow. Children froze in their games. Lovers released their passionate embraces. Chess players stopped their clocks. And slowly, reluctantly, we took our leave as dusk spread above. I watched from outside the gates as gardeners, rarely seen by day, set to work with shovels and rakes, readying the Luxembourg for dawn.

A Lively City of the Dead: Père-Lachaise Cemetery

I rarely go out, but when I do wander, I go to cheer myself up in Père-Lachaise.

—HONORÉ DE BALZAC, in an 1819 letter

A fascination with death, what the French call *nécrophilie,* takes many forms, one of them so common it afflicts some two million individuals who each year enter the hallowed gates of Père-Lachaise cemetery in Paris's 20th arrondissement. Hilly, wooded, with winding paths knotted around crumbling tombs, this is without doubt the most celebrated monumental city of the dead in Europe. Surprisingly it stands within the limits of the sprawling French capital. It also happens to be about 150 yards as the raven flies from the office I rented for twenty years, which is why I became a Père-Lachaise habitué. I love many things about the place: the greenery, the lack of cars, the expansive views from looping gravel lanes and, of course, the sepulchral monuments. Père-Lachaise quietly merges ancient and modern death cults, thereby assuring itself perennial status on the top-ten list of Paris tourist sights. Peak attendance nowadays is on the newly fashionable Halloween, an Anglo-Saxon holiday, and on November 1 and 2, the traditional All Saints' and All Souls' days. But the procession to Père-Lachaise of curious funerary pilgrims knows no season and braves all weather.

Amid the cemetery's hundred lush acres stand faux Egyptian pyramids, mock Greek or Roman temples, and neo-Gothic chapels erected during the heyday of Romanticism two hundred years ago, when the cemetery opened for business. These are my favorite monuments, and their setting is wonderfully evocative. Moss-grown, lichen-frosted, and shaded by venerable, voracious vegetation, the graveyard's first tombs were made in imitation of the antique, specifically of Rome's tomb-lined Via Appia Antica. They too are now antiques—proof that time can render true what begins as falsehood.

Scattered among these proto-memorials are Second Empire neoclassical piles worthy of Paris's notorious 1853-to-1870 prefect, Baron Georges-Eugène Haussmann. Fewer in number but more remarkable are the eerily delicate Art Nouveau fantasies from the turn of the nineteenth century. The modernist Le Corbusier–style slabs salted around are devoid, like that worthy Swiss genius, of any perceptible humor or humanity. Each tomb faithfully mirrors the times in which it was conceived. There are even a handful of postmodern pastiches—a cat's cradle of Plexiglas, steel, and stone, for example—expressing the confused brutalism of recent decades.

The cemetery's upper third marches across a plateau crowned, outside the cemetery's walls, by Place Gambetta. In keeping with the precepts of the 1850s when this section was developed, the layout is a deadening, dull grid. Had it been easy, or even possible, Baron Haussmann's minions would have done in the 1850s to Père-Lachaise what they did to Paris as a whole: tear up the meandering alleys and asymmetrical tombs, replacing them with an efficient checkerboard of plots for the disposal of the dead. But the modernizers failed, much to the relief of nostalgic lovers of Vieux Paris such as Victor Hugo, or Joris-Karl Huysmans. In his 1880 *Croquis parisiens,* Huysmans lashed out against the "tediousness" of Haussmann–style symmetry, seeing in the higgledy-piggledy Père-Lachaise and its rural surroundings "a haven longed for by aching souls. "

Ironically, the thousand-plus seditious Communards massacred by Napoléon III's troops amid Père-Lachaise's tombs in 1871 are buried in the cemetery's symmetrical Second Empire section. Haussmann, enemy of Communards and old Paris alike, wound up in Division 4, an older, less symmetrical area. He lies not far from such utterly un-Haussmannlike free spirits as Gioacchino Rossini and Alfred de Musset. Subversive Colette, lover of women and weaver of intrigue, is practically his neighbor, fifty yards away. There is no such thing as justice, poetic or otherwise, in death, the great equalizer.

What has preserved unpredictable Père-Lachaise from the compulsive straighteners such as Haussmann is a legal concept that, like religious faith, defies logic and in so doing attempts to deny the temporal nature of human life and institutions. That concept is the *concession à perpétuité,* literally a concession granted forever by the city of Paris to families who own plots at Père-Lachaise. This was a novelty in the late 1700s, when the plan to create cemeteries outside Paris was hatched. Until then nearly everyone was thrown into common graves: only important churchmen, nobles, and the very rich rated individual burials, usually inside a church, under the paving stones.

But new ideas on hygiene arising from the Enlightenment's

scientific advances, plus a renewed familiarity with the burial practices of the ancient Romans, led Paris's administrators to ban inner-city cemeteries and under-floor burials in favor of sites beyond the city walls. The immediate stimulus for these reforms, however, came from the collapse of the cemetery of the Innocents (in the square of the same name near today's Les Halles shopping center). When the bones and rotting corpses of millions of Parisians—about seven hundred years' worth—burst through the graveyard's walls into the surrounding neighborhood, administrators scrambled. They built the catacombs in abandoned quarries. Later, in 1804, they inaugurated the Cimetière de l'Est. "Eastern Cemetery" is the official name of Père-Lachaise to this day.

It may be hard to credit but in 1804 the site stood beyond Paris's walls in rolling countryside. Known by various names, including Mont-Louis, the area had been covered since at least the Middle Ages by woods, vineyards, orchards, and market gardens. In the mid-1600s Jesuit father François d'Aix de la Chaise, better known as Père Lachaise, became Louis XIV's confessor. An ambitious, worldly fellow, Lachaise eventually prevailed on the monarch to help him buy Mont-Louis and turn it into the country resort of Paris's Jesuit brothers. Included in the deal was a nice little château for Lachaise's personal use, perched at the hill's highest point. The Jesuits were evicted in the 1760s and Mont-Louis passed through the hands of several private owners. Paris's municipal authorities eventually bought it and created a graveyard to serve the city's eastern arrondissements. Later still, the same authorities demolished Père Lachaise's château. Since about 1820 a chapel has stood on the site.

What's in a name? François d'Aix de la Chaise isn't buried in the cemetery that bears his name (he reposes beneath the church of Saint-Paul, in the Marais). Apparently, when it first opened, the clinical-sounding Cimetière de l'Est didn't seem like the ideal place to bury loved ones. For this reason the site's earliest developers hit upon the scheme of calling it Père-Lachaise, to give it a hallowed, Jesuitical ring. Then as now religiosity was an effective marketing tool. The cemetery was not consecrated ground under the Jesuits and is not consecrated today. By law French municipal graveyards must welcome all sects, creeds, and religions, as well as agnostics and atheists.

These same developers used another clever marketing ploy to promote the cemetery. It involved relocating the tombs of a few famous dead, so that potential clients would be able to say, "Well, if Père-Lachaise is good enough for abbots and royalty it's good enough for me." The first celebrity corpses whisked to the cemetery were in fact those of the luckless abbot Abélard and his pupil Héloïse, the twelfth-century lovers whose tragic tale of emasculation (his) and enforced separation (mutual) was the rage among early 1800s Romantics. Abélard and Héloïse's towering neo-Gothic tomb, still one of the most spectacular in Père-Lachaise, is the highlight of Division 7, the cemetery's oldest section. For similar promotional reasons, Louise de Lorraine, widow of King Henri III, was shifted to Père-Lachaise from the convent of the Capucines, perhaps in a bid to entice Royalist customers. (Her tomb was later dismantled.) To make intellectuals and artists feel welcome, Molière and La Fontaine were disinterred from the Saint-Joseph and Innocents cemeteries, respectively, and placed in new tombs in Division 26, high on a hill. Never mind that the bones of both playwright and author had been mixed with those of other skeletons in a common grave; their tombs are in fact cenotaphs, since no one can be sure whose remains they hold.

Soon after these transfers, another celebrated playwright was dug up and moved to Père-Lachaise: Caron de Beaumarchais, author of *Le Mariage de Figaro*. His original grave in the garden of his townhouse on what is now Boulevard Beaumarchais stood in the way of progress, so the move was both convenient and necessary.

Though business was slow at first the twin ploys of the Jesuit's name and the famous transplanted skeletons eventually worked. By the 1810s Père-Lachaise had become *the* resting place for families of high social standing or aspiration, those, in other words, with the money to buy a perpetual concession and build a monumental tomb. People spoke of the cemetery's most desirable neighborhoods, paralleling them to Paris's *beaux quartiers*. That explains why the roster of nineteenth- and twentieth-century marquee names with a slice of Père-Lachaise is a *Who's Who* of France.

Among my favorite residents are botanist-agronomist Antoine-Augustin Parmentier of potato fame (his tomb is surrounded by potato plants), essayist Louis-Sébastien Mercier (author of *Tableau de Paris* and *Le Nouveau Paris*), military heroes Maréchal Ney and Kellermann (both rate a Paris street in their honor), not to mention Chopin, Balzac, David, Gustave Doré, Oscar Wilde, Guillaume Apollinaire, Amedeo Modigliani, Marcel Proust, Edith Piaf, Gertrude Stein, and Yves Montand. Just about every distinguished poet, writer, musician, composer, statesman, military hero, doctor, actor, playwright, scientist, blueblood, industrialist, and plutocrat of the past two hundred years lucky enough to have died in or near Paris is buried here. Montparnasse's celebrated cemetery pales, ghostlike, in comparison.

But it's not merely the one million illustrious occupants of the seventy thousand tombs strewn picturesquely along ten miles of paths veining the cemetery's panoramic parklands that draw visitors to this preternaturally Parisian necropolis. There is an additional, intangible attraction I notice each time I wander here: the cult of the dead, the fascination, sometimes morbid, that the living feel toward the related phenomena of death, time passing, and collective memory. This fascination takes many forms, and Père-Lachaise accommodates them all, embracing the rites of conventional Catholics, Jews, Muslims, Buddhists, Zoroastrians, and adepts of black magic. Even believers in the transmigration of the soul are well served. For the delectation of Spiritists there is the flower-strewn sepulchral monument, perpetually besieged, dedicated to Allan Kardec, father of this curious creed. His tomb is in Division 44 near the crematorium and every time I pass it,

Kardec's followers are there by the dozen. They lay hands on the tomb and, they claim, communicate with their master.

Nature and the elements play a big part in the Romantic spell Père-Lachaise casts on visitors. Magnificent trees sprout from graves, consuming them one particle at a time. Ravenous roots and trunks bear up bits of stone, iron, or bone. The most astonishing sepulcher-devouring tree I know is an arm-span-wide purple beech on the Chemin du Dragon (in Division 27). Its gray, elephantine roots have been delving for decades into the Duhoulley family plot. They have obliterated at least one other tomb and are inching toward its neighbors.

If you fancy a frisson, take a look at the imposing sepulcher in Division 8 of Étienne Gaspard Robertson (1763–1837), a magician. Winged skulls, like demonic cherubs, perch at each corner of the massive tomb. Adepts of black masses swear the skulls swirl into the air with Robertson on moonless nights. In keeping with the symbolism of superstition, there are real, live feral cats and owls in many a ruined family chapel. Some nest in the boughs of ancient horse-chestnut trees. They scurry and flap in the twilight as they feed off the countless rodents that day-trippers seldom see. I have had the honor of seeing the rats and cats, owls and bats, having, on several occasions, been among the last visitors escorted out at nightfall.

Friends still ask me what it was like to work in an office practically in the cemetery's back yard. I tell them the truth: I went to Père-Lachaise almost daily, to stroll and meditate, and I still cross Paris at least once a week to do the rounds of my favorite graves and monuments. In this Honoré de Balzac (buried in Division 48) is my mentor. In the 1810s and '20s the sardonic novelist noted that he wandered among the tombs regularly to cheer himself up. It is cheering, in a way. I find nothing bizarre about eating lunch on a bench among the sepulchres when the weather is nice, for instance. But most people I know recoil at the thought of a picnic at Père-Lachaise.

Innocent picnicking is one thing, I retort. Scavenging for souvenirs is another. Just as visitors to Paris's catacombs sometimes emerge with skulls or tibia tucked into their packs, a certain kind of souvenir-hunter combs Père-Lachaise searching for ceramic wreaths, stone heads, brass ornaments and, of course, bones. One egregious example of mindless souvenir hunting revolves around the cemetery's most problematic resident: James Douglas Morrison, the "Jim" carved on scores of trees and tombs.

Jim was none other than the celebrated lead singer of the Doors, who died in Paris of a drug overdose in 1971. From the start his grave attracted attention, much of it unwelcome. However, not long after the release of Oliver Stone's movie *The Doors,* the numbers of rowdy Jim-worshippers swelled into the thousands. Many vandalized Morrison's and other, nearby tombs. Someone even managed to break off and steal Morrison's stone bust, probably at night.

Why bother? For the same reasons the Grand Tour travelers of the eighteenth century looted the cemeteries of Rome, Naples, and Athens, perhaps. It may well be that for some benighted souls such trinkets represent a means of possessing the past, stopping time or climbing back through it to another age.

"One day these hills with their urns and epitaphs will be all that remains of our present generations and their subtle contrivances," wrote a prescient Étienne Pivert de Senancour in the early 1800s. "They will compose, as Rome was said to do, a city of memories."

In French the word *souvenir* indicates both objects and memories. Despite the eternal ambitions of the *concession à perpétuité,* though, nothing lasts forever, neither urns nor epitaphs nor even the memories associated with them. Who remembers Pivert de Senancour, for that matter, author of the deathless *Reveries sur la nature primitive de l'homme,* or fellow writer Benjamin Constant? Madame de Staël's longtime lover, the acclaimed author of *Adolphe* and dozens of other works, Constant died fabulously famous in 1830, drawing one hundred thousand mourners to his funeral.

Who remembers François Gémond, whose obelisk (in Division 25) is the tallest in Père-Lachaise? And what of Félix Beaujour (1765–1836)? His phallic stone tower in Division 48 rises from a rusticated stone drum to dizzying heights and is surely one of the world's most astounding funerary monuments. The stones still stand but most of the men and women and their deeds have been forgotten.

Each year dozens of tombs collapse, exposing generations of coffins stacked vertically underneath. The roofs of chapels give way. Trees fall in storms, crushing tombstones and statuary. Iron rusts and stones flake into nothingness. Families, too, disappear. If the city authorities deem a tomb abandoned—usually because it is unsafe to passersby—its owners have three years to respond and make repairs. If they fail, the city revokes the concession, removes what remains of the tomb, and resells the land.

Eternity? The going price for a repossessed plot at Père-Lachaise is under ten thousand euros. That does not include work needed to make the site buildable, or, naturally, the cost of a monument. Private firms or family members must maintain the tombs and plots. The city of Paris merely sweeps and repairs the paved streets and gravel lanes, and plants the pansies or chrysanthemums in the cemetery's many raised beds.

Death goes on, you might say, but then so does life. Among the monuments, oblivious children play. Lovers entwine on hidden paths, unwittingly reenacting the passion of Abélard and Héloïse. Elderly gentlemen sit in the sun, reading *Le Parisien, Le Monde,* or *Le Figaro,* while widows, always outnumbering them, polish the granite gravestones or feed the stray cats. And then of course there are the tourists, most of them clutching maps as they trip from tomb to tomb many, doubtless, wondering why they are here and what it all means in the grand scheme of things. Père-Lachaise is a lively city of the dead indeed and it's likely to remain so, perhaps not for eternity, but for a long, long time.

François's Follies: Building Afresh in a Museum City

The idea that Paris in a century or two could become the privileged enclave of Japanese tour operators is a thought that makes Mitterrand bristle.

—LUC TESSIER, Director of the Coordinating
Body of the *Grands Projets,* 1988

"Pharaoh," "emperor," and "king" were favorite titles given former president François Mitterrand. Admirers and detractors alike also called him "Tonton" for his avuncular charisma, or "La Grenouille," because he looked startlingly like a frog. Mitterrand's presidency lasted from 1981 to 1994. But his heritage as a builder lives on. Like a pharaoh, he commissioned a pyramid (at the Louvre) and a Great Library of Alexandria (the Très Grande Bibliothèque, at Tolbiac). With Napoleonic imperiousness he ordered a triumphal arch (at La Défense) and one-upped Napoléon III with a bigger opera house (at La Bastille). To prove he could subsume his presidential predecessor, he adopted the unfinished projects of Valéry Giscard d'Estaing: La Villette, the Musée d'Orsay, the Institut du Monde Arabe.

Anyone who thinks Mitterrand's so-called *Grands Projets* are old news should rethink: not only do Parisians have to live with them daily, a condition known by some as "collective sore eye." The heritage of Mitterrand's genius continues to gall into the current century. His international conference center planned for the Quai Branly near the Eiffel Tower only got under way after he died. His successor Jacques Chirac torpedoed the plan and commissioned the Quai Branly museum instead. A comic-strip supertanker or cargo ship with rust-red, canary yellow, and ochre shipping containers jutting from one side, the egregious complex excogitated by star-architect Jean Nouvel houses controversial African, Asian, and global multiethnic, multicultural collections. But this fiasco is not Tonton's fault. His credits lies elsewhere.

With something approaching awe and horror I watched Mitterrand's follies coalesce and had the good fortune to scramble through many while under construction, and interview their prime movers. Not long ago I revisited the president's main offspring. Have they, as Mitterrand hoped, saved Paris from becoming a "museum city" cut off from its suburbs? Have they lastingly boosted the prestige of French architects, while indelibly impressing Mitterrand's name in the history books?

Métro line 1 links the troika of sites that were closest to Mitterrand's heart: Bastille, Louvre, Grande Arche. For the sake of chronology and convenience my first stop was the Louvre. Mitterrand's earliest and most ambitious operation was transplant surgery on what had become a dusty, dreary place whose decline threatened Gallic *gloire* and *histoire,* not to mention tourism revenues. After visiting Washington's National Gallery, Tonton highhandedly hired its designer I. M. Pei to create Le Grand Louvre. No architectural competition was held, a technical illegality. Mitterrand briefed Pei to respect the Louvre's historic components. His solution was the now-familiar seventy-foot (twenty-two-meter) pyramid of glass and crisscrossed steel that rises above an underground entrance, theater, shopping concourse, and parking lots.

Like most Paris denizens, I was not thrilled by Pei's proposal. But I recall my bafflement when critics claimed the pyramid would "deface" the Napoléon Courtyard's façades. A historicist's hodgepodge, they were as kitsch in their day as the pyramid was in the 1980s. In reality, at issue was the Socialist president's perceived defiling of a royal enclave. As some pundits put it, Mitterrand marked it as a dog might.

Swept by crowds from the Métro station into the Louvre's subterranean maw, I couldn't help marveling now at Pei's success in hitching high art to consumerism. Where the weary masses of old once deciphered turgid texts or strained their eyes on the museum's badly displayed and unloved treasures (most of them looted in the days of earlier French kings and emperors), here were smiling hordes stuffed with exotic delicacies from the merry-go-round of Louvre restaurants, casting beatific glances at skillfully lit artworks before loading up on reproductions, CDs, designer sportswear, computers, and gadgets.

Pei's entrance was conceived to simplify the Louvre's labyrinth. Experts claim it takes less time than ever to reach the Mona Lisa (still the goal of ninety percent of visitors). Persnickety regulars at first grumbled about a crass Grand Louvre for beginners, and militated for a reopening of doors in the museum's many wings. But they soon learned to slip in through the Pavillon de Flore, via whatever temporary exhibition is being mounted there, skipping the subterranean feeding frenzy.

Early on boosters said the pyramid would blend into the cityscape. They were right. As Pei predicted, the glass panes reflect changeable skies. They also collect soot, despite frequent scrubbings. Cosmetic concerns aside, I saw nary a grimace now as I shuffled with thousands from sculpture courts (where cars once parked) through restored Renaissance rooms and lavish Second Empire salons (formerly the Finance Minister's office), to excavated medieval bastions. Back outside, I took a table at Café Marly and watched visitors dance in feathery water sprays or soak their feet in the fountains flanking the pyramid. Attendance has risen from 2.5 million in the early 1980s to nearly 9 million today. What better sign of approval might a monarch desire?

Laid out in 1670 by Louis XIV's royal architect Le Nôtre, the so-called Triumphal Way runs west from the Louvre's Cour Carrée through the glass eye of the pyramid and nearby Carrousel Arch, across the Tuileries and up the Champs-Élysées, under the Arc de Triomphe, straight across town to La Défense, crowned by Mitterrand's Grande Arche. My subway train covered the distance in twenty minutes. Even though from La Défense's highest point I couldn't see back into central Paris, I knew the Triumphal Way, alias the "Power Axis," was there, also extending east from the Louvre to the Bastille.

Unexpectedly the Grande Arche is the sole Mitterrand project to have garnered near total support at the time of building. It actually improves La Défense, a paragon of architectural mediocrity bristling with mirrored-glass skyscrapers and studded with concrete apartment bunkers. The absence of cars, and recent landscaping, are the saving graces of this Moscow-meets-Manhattan satellite city.

As I queued under the Grande Arche in the windy vortex comically termed a "piazza," then rode to the roof in a glass-bubble elevator, I recalled watching back in the late '80s as the viewing deck was poured into place at a height of more than 300 feet (100 meters). Building the arch required much engineering wizardry. The vistas from on high aren't nearly as spectacular as those you see from the Eiffel Tower, but if you're into cannon-shot perspectives you won't be disappointed.

Arch designer Johan Otto von Spreckelsen adroitly poised his bauble 6.30 degrees askew, mirroring the skew of the Louvre's Cour Carrée without blocking the Power Axis. In theory a super-human bowler could roll a ball through the arch's wind-tunnel piazza to the grubby panes of Pei's pyramid. At a distance of twenty-some years this sounds like manual self-pleasuring, but it long preoccupied Tonton's planners.

A nitpicker might carp about the arch's smog-stained Car-rara cladding, the threadbare carpets inside, or the prison-camp aesthetics of the rooftop terrace. Even arch devotees cannot help noting that the suspended canvas windbreaks called "Nuages" look less like the hovering clouds Von Spreckelsen had envisioned than a tattered and stained Bedouin tent. They simply don't work. Wind or not, the arch is standing up to time's weathering, and it seems a pity that Von Spreckelsen died before it was completed.

A lesser archway, this one clad with sparkling dark granite, graces the entrance to the Bastille Opéra at the historic axis's east-ern end. Of all Tonton's arch-follies it has aged the worst and de-spite constant upkeep looks, though barely into adulthood, like a shabby, overweight old cocotte who sometimes wears a hairnet. The netting comes and goes, depending on the danger level. It was in place for a decade or more to prevent the shoddily anchored gray granite cladding of the building from falling onto passersby. Millions of euros were thrown at the problem in the 2000s and by 2010 most of the perilous parts of the exterior had been replaced.

The reasons for the Bastille fiasco are now clear. In a rush to make a July 13, 1989, bicentennial celebration deadline, but de-sirous to appear fair this time around, Mitterrand held a "blind" competition for the project. Everyone in Paris soon knew that the president's choice was remote-controlled by associates who mis-takenly believed they had identified star-architect Richard Meier's opera-house mockup. The fruit of this cock-up is Canadian-Uruguayan Carlos Ott's $350 million monstrosity. It measures nearly half a mile (800 meters) around and 150 feet (48 meters) high. "People don't like my opera house because they say it's ugly, it's fat, it doesn't have any gold or red velvet inside, and it looks like a factory," a red-faced Ott told me in 1989. "And all those things to me are compliments!" Ott has received many compliments since *Newsweek* first compared his masterpiece to "the alien mother ship that spawned the public toilets."

However, as I bustled into the behemoth with droves of elegant opera aficionados and enjoyed a tear-jerking performance of *La Bohème,* I had to admit that the main auditorium is a formidable resonating chamber (Ott had help designing it). The blue-gray granite walls, oak flooring, and black velour seats that seemingly disappear when the lights go down are as handsome and functional today as the building's outside was, is, and always will be ridiculous.

A ten-minute walk farther east and I came upon Mitterrand's unsung Ministry of Finance complex. When built it was Europe's longest continuous building, a seeming leftover from Stalin's USSR. It goosesteps in an "L" from the Gare de Lyon to the Seine at Bercy. I remember the spiel co-architects Paul Chemetov and Borja Huidobro gave the press in the late 1980s. The Bercy Métro-viaduct, they said, with its double set of white stone arcades, inspired their concept. Too bad the inspiration penetrated only as far as the architects' highly active vocal cords.

Detractors quickly dubbed the $500 million trifle "futuristic," "Stalinesque," and "nightmarish." Its defenses include a moat and a cubical citadel of glass (for private ministerial meetings). A hive buzzing with six thousand pen pushers, honeycombed with identical, modular offices, the complex sports color-coded signage devised to get drones through a synapse-stunning thirty-five kilometers of corridors. That's twenty-three miles. When I first toured the building in 1989 my embarrassed PR guide lost her way on the sixth floor of Building C, panicked, and had to call for help. Little has changed, though nowadays Bercy is smog-stained and seems less futuristic or "intelligent," as it was once called (meaning one hundred percent computerized). I walked through it now and was comforted to learn that the air-conditioning still turns off when windows are opened. In-house mail continues to arrive via something called "Télédoc," a ceiling-mounted electronic shuttle system. The minister flies in by helicopter (there's a landing pad on the roof) or splashes in by speedboat (to a high-security dock on the Seine). With synthesized voices the elevators tell visitors what floor they're on. And countless people still get lost.

Before leaving, I peered from a window at the Palais Omni-sports across the street from the ministry. This semi-subterranean, pre-Mitterrand 1980 sports stadium boasts multicolored tubular metal frames, glass walls, and a steeply pitched roof covered with turf. The building is proof that grass can grow at a sixty-degree angle. Parisian kids claw their way up it and slide down. Some graffiti-aficionados are less gentle. Years ago I noticed that some-one had physically torn out chunks of turf to form the characters "¥" "€" "$," thereby demonstrating a yen for yen (¥), euros (€), and dollars ($). YES! The people most likely to read this cryp-tic message were of course the bigwigs in the ministry building. Strangely, I realized now that the "YES!" could still be made out. The grass, like the permanently ailing economies of Europe, has never quite recovered from the savaging.

While enjoying a restorative dose of caffeine at a café outside the ministry's moat, I asked the barman how the fortress complex had changed the neighborhood. Local businesses are profiting, he chortled. Real estate values have risen. "And who cares if it could be in Moscow," he asked, jerking his thumb eastward. "The TGB is worse!"

Upstream I crossed to the Left Bank at Tolbiac and stood be-fore the Incan plinth on which the National Library rises amid a forest of construction cranes. Local redevelopment is still under way after a quarter-century of jackhammering. The library's catchy official name is "Bibliothèque de France, Site François Mitterrand." But everyone calls this one-billion-plus-dollar marvel the TGB (Très Grande Bibliothèque), a play on the acronym for the TGV high-speed train. Whatever you call it, the library is *folie de grandeur* incarnate.

Subtle? From the Seine embankment the library's four, three-hundred-foot towers of glass, designed to mimic open books on end, look like flying wedges poised atop a dance floor almost a thousand feet long. The wonderful brashness of it is startling, making the TGB possibly the world's defining set piece of post-postmodernism.

Can kitsch be dangerous? I skittered on buckling planks of tropical wood in the windswept shadows of the towers. A search among caged holly trees rattling in the wind revealed an entrance; fortunately I'd been here before and vaguely remembered the way. The site's hidden heart is a glassed-in subterranean garden the length of two football fields, accessed via a tilted, moving sidewalk. Reportedly Mitterrand envisioned this as the twenty-first-century cloister of a neo-medieval monastery, inspired by Umberto Eco's 1980s bestseller *The Name of the Rose* (later a Hollywood block-buster starring Sean Connery). Set in a monastery, the tale was still the rage at the time Mitterrand's courtiers came up with the TGB plan. The French government actually contemplated hiring Eco as a consultant. Like the caged hollies, the gardens' hand-some red pine trees double as contemporary bondage art, girded by steel cables so they won't crash through the windows.

Wind is not the only problem at the TGB. I still haven't gotten used to genial young architect Dominique Perrault's underground reading rooms, or his cleverness in storing books in glass towers, where retrofitted wooden panels block daylight. The original plan was worse: conveyor belts were to cross an open courtyard, exposing books to rain and sun. I stood now in the western atrium and had plenty of time to take in the view of leaking ceilings and plastic buckets extending almost seven hundred feet east. Hours can go by while you get a computerized pass then summon a book from a tower into a reading room half a mile away. Best of all is trying to exit: if your returned loan hasn't been scanned back

into the system, as happened to me, you can't get out. Red lights
flashed. The turnstile wouldn't turn. Librarians and security
guards leapt into action. Then Big Brother pushed a button somewhere and finally I was free to go.

Detractors have had so much fun running the TGB into the
ground that, standing in it again after an absence of many years,
I actually felt protective of the library's bigness, coldness, and in-
efficiency. Gone are the early days when TGB employees held
strikes against "inhumane working conditions" and a "fundamentally flawed computer system." Certainly, the computerized
miniature train that retreives books still sometimes goes off the
rails, despite years and millions of dollars' worth of fine-tuning.
But strides have been made. The library's other minor flaws—the
leaks, diseased trees, cavernous architectural deadends, stifling
air, dank—are nothing another billion euros and a few more decades of work can't fix.

Most of all, thousands of French university students seem
to love the TGB. It mirrors the spirit of our time, one bright
young lady told me as we stood in line together at the snack bar.
Proof of the students' approval was obvious once I stepped onto
the smoking deck, an outdoor enclosure at treetop level inside
the cloister. Future Ph.D.s dressed almost uniformly in black
gulped plastic cups of coffee, posed and puffed, looking much
like Jean-Paul Sartre and Simone de Beauvoir might if dressed
in twenty-first-century garb, with piercing and tattoos, and electronic equipment appended.

Why Simone de Beauvoir? The archetypal French intellectual,
a trailblazing feminist writer whose life-partner was the supreme
philanderer-philosopher Jean-Paul Sartre, de Beauvoir smoked
and drank herself to an early death. Accordingly, the recently
completed suspended footbridge linking the TGB to the Bercy
gardens across the river is named after her. It's an elegant span.
Depending on your point of view, and the way the light falls, the
swaying Passerelle Simone de Beauvoir evokes a length of DNA,

a wooden whale diving and surfacing, a centipede, or one of those delicious sea creatures Frenchmen devour while murmuring the poetic name *cigale de mer*—locust lobster.

From the smoking deck I leaned into the wind, bouncing across the Seine on the lobster bridge, turning and swaying back, all the while marveling at the construction cranes still dancing overhead. Since the mid-1990s those cranes have been in action, and for just as long, some Paris newspapers and magazines have been touting the TGB's nascent surroundings as "the new Marais" or "nouveau Quartier Latin"—meaning they will soon be hip, lively, and desirable places to live, work, and shop. Wishful thinking? True, the apartment houses are filling up with intrepid yuppies. A department of the Sorbonne—dubbed "Site Tolbiac"—has moved in (a decade late). A few hard-hitting contemporary art galleries have migrated, with their Marais minimalists and outer-arrondissement rebels, to Rue Louise Weiss and Rue des Frigos, across the tracks from the TGB. But few others have followed, and some galleries have given up waiting and have moved back to the Marais. Office towers, a research institute, additional upmarket housing, and a greenbelt over the rail yards are still being built. When will they be finished?

I asked a cheerful construction foreman. He repeated a line I'd heard on my first visit to the library in 1998, and again in 2000, 2005, 2008, and 2010. It may even have been spoken by the same construction foreman: "Tolbiac won't be finished for another thirty years!" When pressed he admitted the job might get done in another twenty. This sounded like lifetime employment in an age of global insecurity and institutionalized recession. The developers' slogan, confirmed the foreman, is still "Paris Awakens in the East." Perhaps, I quipped, someone should brew stronger coffee.

Compared to the empty lots, railroad tracks, 1970s architectural triumphs, abandoned industrial sites, and defunct warehouses that formerly stood here, almost anything would be an improvement. Almost.

Down on the riverbank, I strolled along the landscaped Allée Arthur Rimbaud, wondering if the tormented poet of *The Drunken Boat* had liked the kinds of weepy, willowy trees planted here, and what he would have made of the TGB. One bonus of the riverfront re-conversion that Rimbaud, a walk-aholic, would surely have hailed is that you can now hike from the promenade bearing his name to the Latin Quarter on the Seine's banks entirely unmolested by cars. That's no mean achievement in a city as automobile-obsessed as Paris. Rimbaud, also an unrepentant party boy, would doubtless further enjoy the quayside hot spots fronting the TGB, which were not envisioned by Mitterrand. Moored there were half a dozen drunken boats—home to floating cafés, restaurants, and nightclubs.

My explorations of Mitterrand's megalomania had a surprisingly happy ending in the 19th arrondissement at La Villette, four Grands Projets in one. Three times the size of the Pompidou Center, the old meatpacking plant west of the Ourcq Canal has been the world's biggest science museum since it opened in 1986. No beef here, I reflected as I hoofed through this Emerald City of high tech. Cast as the Wizard of Oz, Mitterrand hijacked but couldn't completely reconfigure the project after drubbing Giscard d'Estaing at the polls, and it is Mitterrand's name that you see writ large on a bronze plaque in the cavernous main hall full of electronic gizmos.

I crossed the canal and found the doors open to the reconverted 1860s glass-and-ironwork cattle auction hall. Now an expo and concert venue, the Grande Halle evokes Victor Baltard's dearly departed Les Halles, and, as with Giscard d'Estaing's equally successful Musée d'Orsay and Institut du Monde Arabe, try as he might not even Mitterrand could spoil it.

Not content with surrogate fatherhood at La Villette, Tonton commissioned the Cité de la Musique, a silly name for the national music conservatory and instrument museum. Architect Christian de Portzamparc subsequently won the prestigious Pritzker Prize and is perhaps the sole Frenchman to have fulfilled Mitterrand's hope of global glory. (Flamboyant, fashionable Jean Nouvel is well known nowadays, and also won the Pritzker, but how many serious scholars of architecture would place him in the Hall of Fame is a question worth asking.) De Portzamparc also designed classy Café Beaubourg facing the Pompidou; its counterpart here felt like a grand piano turned inside out. Like the other Grands Projets, De Portzamparc's buildings show precocious signs of gritty wear. The superfluous metal superstructures that metaphorically "bridge" the abutting Péripherique beltway and the bathroom-tile façades seem hopelessly mired in a postmodernist aesthetic. Yet the curving indoor "street" playfully evokes an inner ear, and the museum's displays and live music are a harmonious delight.

Before heading home I took a turn around the Parc de la Villette, a deconstructionist's dream its Swiss-born American architect Bernard Tschumi termed "an urban park for the twenty-first century," meaning it rejects the notion of a refuge. Tschumi's quintessentially twentieth-century, misguided idea is itself now widely rejected, but his "discontinuous building," a sequence of twenty-six whimsical "garden follies" painted fire-engine red and set along cobbled footpaths, lawns, and the Ourcq Canal, are intriguing. In this Tschumi's success is unquestionable: a refuge from the city the park isn't. Cars and trucks thunder by on the abutting beltway, and riverboats chuff past. The follies merge jungle gym, firehouse, and lifeguard station. Despite "keep off" signs, kids gleefully scaled the wheel rims of Claes Oldenburg's outsized *Buried Bicycle,* a sculpture seemingly meant to be appropriated. Others hunted frogs in a bamboo-stippled marsh, unaware of their prey's resemblance to a certain former president, the man who had this park built. It struck me that none of those happy children had lived through Mitterrand's murky reign, and probably not a one would recognize his name.

Island in the Seine:
Île Saint-Louis

If you walk along the streets of the Île Saint-Louis, do not ask why you feel gripped by a sort of nervous sadness. For its cause you have only to look at the solitude of the place, at the gloomy aspect of its houses and its large empty mansions...
—HONORÉ DE BALZAC

A spectacular stone gangplank leaps across five arches to link Paris' Right Bank with an unsinkable luxury liner midstream in the Seine. The gangplank is the Pont Marie, an early 1600s bridge. The ship is the Île Saint-Louis, an island measuring less than half a mile from tip to storied tip but packed with history, mystery, and atmosphere. Peopled primarily by rich, retiring islanders, its narrow streets are lined by dozens of landmark townhouses and ringed at water level by cobbled quays stippled with poplars. The cathedral of Notre-Dame on the noisy Île de la Cité squats within shouting distance, across a wide footbridge that doubles most of the year as a stage for mimes, fire-eaters, and stand-up comedians. On the isle's opposite side, beyond the Pont Marie, the Marais spreads its fashion boutiques, art galleries, and mansions, fanning eastward to Place des Vosges and the Bastille.

At first glance the physical distance isolating Île Saint-Louis from mainland Paris may seem negligible, yet the island manages to preserve a peculiar identity, defined more often than not by mixed metaphor. To some it's Mount Olympus, where writers and artists from Voltaire and Restif de la Bretonne to Théophile Gautier, Charles Baudelaire, Camille Claudel, Dos Passos, and the inevitable Hemingway have lived, worked, and loved. The envious call it a self-contained, self-satisfied biosphere for native bluebloods and transplanted plutocrats. Property values and rents are among the city's highest. The Rothschilds long lorded it over the island's upstream end from the gilded salons of the Hôtel Lambert, built in the early 1640s by royal architect Louis Le Vau and, as befits such a manse, surrounded by high walls few mortals ever breach.

To most Parisians, though, the isle has long been perceived as a cruise ship in both shape and spirit, floating free between the Right Bank–Left Bank political divide, so much so that in 1935 cosmetics queen Helena Rubinstein knocked down a 1640s mansion to build herself a vaguely Art Déco pile with a giant transatlantic porthole window at 24 Quai de Béthune. Former French president Georges Pompidou and his fashion-plate wife Claude, alias "the godmother of French art," also lived in the building, perhaps to be close to their friends the Rothschilds. Nancy Cunard, of the shipping fortune, occupied number 2 Rue Le Regrattier, and Ford Maddox Ford's *Transatlantic Review* published Pound, Conrad, Cummings, Stein, Joyce, and others at 29 Quai d'Anjou.

Rejecting nautical references, my wife thinks of the island as an open-air cloister, its sunny side facing south to the Latin Quarter, its northern side lichen-frosted, cool, and shady. That makes sense: like a cloister, much of the time the isle is quieter and moodier, its quays more secluded, than just about anywhere else in town, the result of the locals' political muscle, which has helped maintain an ingenious system of one-way streets and bridges designed to thwart all but the savviest of cabbies.

Habitués saunter over seeking not bustle and must-see monuments but an eddying, slow Seine churned by riverboats and dotted with seagulls, ducks, and the occasional lost Canadian goose. There are benches shaded by sycamores and weeping willows, lazy anglers of uneatable bottom fish, sunbathers and moon gazers, picnickers and pairs of lovers tangled atop the parapets.

Quiet? Perhaps not in hot weather, when partying youngsters and overexcited bongo drummers beseige the quays. This new-found animation might be catching: the once-dusty Polish library, with Chopin memorabilia, has been given a lick of paint, but its operating hours are relaxed and, frankly, few set foot in it. The church of Saint Louis en l'Île used to be remarkable only for its gilt clock. Now it has a functioning three-thousand-pipe organ specially designed for baroque music. You practically have to beg to get into the Hôtel de Lauzun, a townhouse owned by the city, for a view from on high. Add in a handful of cafés with outdoor terraces facing Notre-Dame or Saint-Gervais, a travel bookshop run by a colorful woman who seems to love to turn away customers, an unusual fishing and fly-tying establishment called La Maison de la Mouche ("the fly house"), a few cozily pricey hotels and undistinguished restaurants that cater to the compatriots Hemingway disdained, and that's about it. Except, naturally, for Berthillon ice cream, and the chocolate shops, bakeries, butcher shops, and sellers of "antiques," gadgets, and junky souvenirs—all on the downstream end of the island's spinal-column street, now the haunt of sports-shoppers, those marathon inspectors of window displays.

Admittedly, in this street, in 2003, former three-star chef Antoine Westermann of Strasbourg's Buerehiesel opened a chic restaurant, Mon Vieil Ami. It and it alone has managed to regild the island's culinary reputation. The famous, some might say notorious, Nos Ancêtres les Gaulois, the archetype of pseudo-Gallic kitsch, is a block away and serves fare whose operative descriptor is "Gaul."

It's precisely the unrushed, backwater-ish quality of the island's residential perimeter and crossroads that make l'Île appealing. A stroll around this metaphorical luxury liner's deck is often the twilight highlight of my day, and not simply because I live a few hundred yards east of the Pont Marie and its mainland Métro station—no grubby subway has ever sullied the Île Saint-Louis itself. For one thing this is big-sky country with low buildings, a wide river, and sea breezes blowing up from Le Havre. The best views in town of Notre-Dame's buttressed back, and the Pantheon's massive dome, are through the leaves of the trees lining the Quai d'Orléans. There are architectural details galore: carved keystones, masks, rusty mooring rings, stone garlands. The Right Bank's turreted, statue-encrusted Hôtel de Ville, alias city hall, seems much more than an 1870s fake when glimpsed at dusk from the island's Quai de Bourbon, named not for sour mash but for the royal dynasty that produced the bigwig pre-Revolutionary series of kings named Louis, including number XIII (1601 to 1643).

It was this otherwise unremarkable monarch who, in 1614, gave developer Christophe Marie and his partners the go-ahead to build the Pont Marie and transform the island from cow pasture to aristocratic playground. Marie devised the novel grid of streets girded by stone embankments. As I do my daily shuffle around this early masterpiece of real estate speculation, hands clasped behind my back, I spot the same regulars, pedigrees on each end of the leash, circling slowly, lifting their eyes or legs to the mossy old mansions. They weave warily among the hordes of ice-cream pilgrims slurping cones on the island's busiest cross streets, Rue

des Deux Ponts and Rue Saint-Louis-en-l'Île. Among gastronomes and guidebook authors the Île Saint-Louis is celebrated
today more for its luscious Berthillon *glaces et sorbets* than for its
architectural or literary past, much to the chagrin of islanders
with genealogical trees as complex as the spreading old sycamores
knotted around my favorite spot, the isle's downstream prow.

That past is written in stone, made easy to read for nonspe-
cialists by plaques mounted on about half the landmark townhouses, nearly all of them designed in the mid 1600s for royal tax
collectors and others with a license to steal. The plaques provide
names and birth dates, followed by a few pithy words that can
lead you a merry romp through the history books. Here's what
you find at number 22 Quai de Béthune, facing the Latin Quarter: *Hôtel Lefebvre de la Malmaison, conseiller au Parlement, 1645.
Baudelaire y vécut 1842–43.* Deciphered, the plaque tells you the
mansion's name (Hôtel Lefebvre de la Malmaison), the owner's
occupation as councillor at Parlement, the construction date, and
the fact that poet Charles *Les-Fleurs-du-Mal* Baudelaire lived here
in the mid-nineteenth century. The façade doesn't stir the imagination, exception made for the curious bat-like creature with a female, human head, poised over the main door. Yet you can't help
wondering if it was within these walls or at Baudelaire's other
island abode, among the hashish-smokers of the Hôtel de Lauzun, that the tormented genius penned the lines *Luxe, calme et
volupté*—luxury, peace and sensuous indulgence—so often associated with the paintings of Matisse. Is it a coincidence, you might
ask, that while here, or perhaps while remembering his time on
the Île Saint-Louis, Baudelaire wrote of the mythical island Cyth-
ère, sad and bleak, an "Eldorado of all the old fools"?

Baudelaire wasn't talking about a Cadillac but rather referring
to Voltaire's imaginary golden paradise in *Candide*. It's a two-fold
reference: Voltaire also lived on the island, in the 1740s, ensconced
with his lady friend the Marquise du Châtelet in the longtime
Rothschild residence, the Hôtel de Lambert. There's no plaque to

this effect on the palatial, 43,000-square-foot townhouse. Nor is there anything to indicate that from 1949 until his death in 2004, the once-flamboyant and later reclusive Alexis von Rosenberg, Baron de Redé, lover of the wealthy Arturo Lopez-Willshaw and soul mate of the Baroness Marie-Hélène Rothschild, lived in the mansion's magnificent second-floor apartment, among precious antiques and artworks. *Le baron* would famously flit along the "Gallery of Hercules," whose priceless paintings of the scantily clad hero had been done by royal artist Charles Le Brun. Meanwhile the other baron—Marie-Hélène's husband, Guy—was often absent, and Lopez-Willshaw's wife-of-convenience, Patricia, was busy, as one reporter put it, with "her own romantic distractions."

In keeping with its Thousand-and-One-Nights ambience, the latest chapter of the *hôtel*'s history features a Qatari prince. In 2007, Abdullah Bin Abdullah Al Thani bought the landmark, gift-wrapped in red tape, for the equivalent of eighty-eight million dollars, planning to spend nearly as much again on restorations and improvements. It was the "improvements" that led him into a legal labyrinth from which he only began to emerge in 2010, much enlightened.

Baudelaire's own romantic distractions included installing his mulatto mistress and muse Jeanne Duval, alias the Black Venus, nearby at 6 Rue Le Regrattier. Scratch the surface and seamy stories well up all over the island.

At number 15 Quai de Bourbon, facing the church of Saint-Gervais, the painter and poet Émile Bernard (1868–1941) lived and worked. He founded the Pont-Aven Group of Symbolists. The plaque doesn't tell you that in his studio, under the gilt beams, court painter Philippe de Champaigne labored in the mid-1600s, his official residence two doors upstream at number 11.

Sculptor Camille Claudel, Rodin's protégée and mercurial lover, had a ground-floor studio from 1899 to 1913 at number 19 Quai de Bourbon. Islanders still grimace when recalling that,

for several months after the movie *Camille Claudel* came out, the
sidewalks were impassable because of the mobs paying homage to
the mad artist, who died in an asylum. You can't get into the studio, but you can see one of the sculptures she made here, *Maturity,*
an allegory of human mortality, at the Musée d'Orsay.

Another curiosity exhumed from the history books is that the
1659 townhouse capping the Quai de Bourbon goes by the name
"House of the Centaur," because of the pair of low-relief sculptures on the façade showing Hercules fighting Nessus, the savage
mythical beast, half man, half horse. For years Madame Louise
Faure-Favier held her literary salon here, hosting poet Guillaume
Apollinaire, painter Marie Laurencin, writer Francis Carco, and
poet Max Jacob, Picasso's penniless friend. The centaurs overlook
a pocket-size park, which is a popular picnic and panoramic spot.
Alison and I come here often for the view. The mansion's current
occupants apparently enjoy entertaining. On more than one occasion we have watched as society women in *gowns* and gentlemen
in tuxes mingled under a second-floor ballroom's painted ceiling.

It was this kind of wordly tableau that inspired eighteenth-
century author Nicolas-Edme Restif de la Bretonne to invent a new
literary genre, the nighttime prowl, writing about it from 1786 onward in *Les Nuits de Paris ou Le Spectateur nocturne,* a rambling account of 1,001 nights on Paris's streets. His ramblings often started
from the Île Saint-Louis (he lived nearby). Taking nighttime walks
around the island, with a magic-lantern show of interiors, is my
preferred form of voyeurism.

Another, equally fun by day or night, is to poke around the
shady courtyards of the island's largely impenetrable mansions.
Electronic coded locks called Digi-codes keep the rabble out. But
I've discovered two methods to subvert them: wait outside and when
someone leaves, confidently stride in, or, two, follow local mail carriers with passkeys on their rounds, starting about ten a.m. Stealth
and subterfuge transform innocent exploration into an adventure.
They once got me into number 15 Quai de Bourbon after years

of cat-and-mouse with the concierge. Hidden in the wide cobbled courtyard I discovered a stone staircase with elaborate ironwork railings. On the roof above rises a two-story gable fitted out with a pulley—presumably to hoist furniture or intruders like me.

By systematically testing the island's doors I've found a few that are nearly always open. The best belongs to the Hôtel de Chenizot, at number 51 Rue Saint-Louis-en-l'Île. Giant griffins uphold a balcony over the studded door. Step in and at the back of the first crumbling court you see a low-relief Rococo floral burst. Keystones carved with heads peer down at you. The rusticated sections of the mansion date to the 1640s. The taller additions are from 1719, when Jean-François Guyot de Chenizot, a royal tax collector from Rouen, redecorated. The building then spiraled downward, becoming, in succession, a wine warehouse, the residence of Paris's archbishop, a gendarmes' barracks, a warehouse again, and a moldering apartment house. Today the leprous plaster hides the requisite sweeping staircases and a rear court with a weathered sundial. Though parts of it have been scrubbed, atmosphere still oozes from the place like wet mortar between bricks.

There is a third method I have mastered for penetrating the isle's inner sancta: take a guided tour. This can turn mystery into mere history, but it's the only way to get inside the sole townhouse whose interior is accessible to the public, the Hôtel de Lauzun. Here you actually taste a crumb of the upper crust's lifestyle under the Bourbon Louis—numbers XIII to XVI. The building's history is lavished upon you, like it or not, by a loquacious cicerone. A potted version of it might run as follows.

Charles Chamois, a military architect, designed the Hôtel de Lauzun in 1657 for a stolid cavalry commissioner named Grüyn. But no horses are to be found: Grüyn's boar's-head coat of arms shows up on fireplaces and wall decorations. Much racier a character, the Duc de Lauzun lived here from 1682 to 1684, shacked up with Louis XIV's first cousin, alias La Grande Mademoiselle. That's why the Lauzun name stuck.

Surprisingly the townhouse has survived almost intact, naturally without anything the heirs could un-nail and sell, meaning period furniture and original paintings. However, the venerable Versailles parquet creaks satisfyingly underfoot. Several tons of gold glitter from delicately decorated beams and walls, and when light pours through the many-paned windows the effect is blinding. Baudelaire and Théophile Gautier slummed here in the 1840s when the gilding had gone black—no doubt in part because of the hash fumes spewed by adepts of the Club des Hachichins (pronounced Ha-She-Shans). Baudelaire's hashish-induced hallucinatory poetic visions—of nude women and cloudscapes—apparently derive in part from the mansion's music room, a salon garlanded with dreamy plasterwork damsels.

Love Conquers Time was the title given to a second-story ceiling decoration but alas, it has succumbed to the centuries. The catalogue of short-lived unions enacted beneath it, and in the island's many other similar townhouses, suggests au contraire that Time Conquers All. That's not a bad motto for the Île Saint-Louis, though I can think of an even better one, given the isle's ostensibly unchanging qualities—its stony mansions and merry-go-round of wealthy inhabitants. It's a saying coined by French wit Alphonse Karr in 1849: "The more things change, the more they stay the same."

Montsouris and Buttes-Chaumont: The Art of the Faux

Let us stroll in this décor of desires, this décor filled with mental misdemeanors and with imaginary spasms . . .
—LOUIS ARAGON at Buttes-Chaumont, *Paris Peasant*

The leaves of the horse-chestnut trees overhanging the sidewalk broke into a sudden jig. Smoke and steam shot through them, puffing up over the tops of the hedges along the street where we were strolling, outside the historic park of Montsouris in Paris's 14th arrondissement. Alison poked her head through the hedge and beckoned me to follow. I heard a swish and a chug and saw an old black steam engine dive into a tunnel under the park, on the tracks of the Petite Ceinture—theoretically an abandoned railway. A ghost train? I'd read somewhere that back in the nineteenth century those tracks had linked in a loop the outer edge of Paris. I'd also read that they were used occasionally by train buffs to exercise vintage rolling stock.

By the time Alison and I had ambled across the shady, landscaped curves of Montsouris and dug into our picnic on a lakeside bench, we'd forgotten about the train. The quacking ducks and shifting light, the luxuriant greenery and human parade passing by lulled and enchanted us. There were students from the nearby Cité Universitaire campus and the usual selection of au pairs, plaster-spackled workers in blue dungarees, and tourists shod with running shoes. The gingerbread Pavillon de Montsouris, a restaurant filled with hoity-toity Parisians in their Sunday best, seemed plucked from the proverbial Impressionist painting. So too the oversized prams, the fancy picnic hampers, and the awkward 1870s statuary dotted around us on freshly mowed lawns and raked gravel paths. Exception made for the tourists and joggers, and the cars parked outside the gates, much was as it might have been when the park was built atop abandoned quarries almost a century and a half ago, by Napoléon III's planners.

Mont Souris means "Mouse Mountain." I couldn't help chuckling at that as we circled the flower-edged knolls covering about forty acres of prime real estate. It seemed an unlikely moniker for the site of an ancient Roman burial ground originally strung along the road leading south from Paris to Orléans. Among the sepulchral monuments once stood the tomb, now lost, of a supposed giant: the gravestone measured about twenty feet long. The giant's name has come down to us twisted from something now forgotten to Ysorre, Issoire, or possibly the mousy-sounding Souris. "Issoire" lives on in the Avenue de la Tombe-Issoire, a nearby traffic artery.

From the Middle Ages to the late 1860s windmills rose among the ruined tombs and quarries. Nowadays the modest heights of

Montsouris sport the parabolic antennae of Paris's meteorological station. From the park's belvedere we gazed down and saw a flash of steel—a train rattling over the RER regional express subway tracks. The railway, originally linking Paris to suburban Sceaux, has been here since the inception of Montsouris as a park. The engineers who landscaped the neighborhood used the quarries and the lay of the land to route the trains through almost unnoticed. Those of the Petite Ceinture ran through tunnels even farther underground.

It was the thought of those tunnels that reminded me of the steam train we'd spotted earlier that day. A penny dropped in my head, a rusty handle turned, and I recalled a similar scene in another of my favorite time-tunnel parks, also built on abandoned quarries, Buttes-Chaumont. The event had taken place ten, maybe fifteen years ago, when I'd first stumbled upon the lush Buttes-Chaumont on the opposite side of town in the 19th arrondissement. There too I'd heard a steam train rumbling below, hidden by trees. Irrationally I now wondered if the ghost train we'd seen earlier could possibly be circling Paris, and if we could intercept it across town.

I took Alison by the hand and rushed down Montsouris's snaky paths to the RER station. We transferred at Gare du Nord then trotted from the Ourcq subway stop to the northern entrance of Buttes-Chaumont. Panting and sweaty like the droves of joggers on the park's paths, we found the footbridge over the Petite Ceinture. Did we see the old black steam train conveniently chuff by? Of course not. But as I leaned on the bridge's iron grilles catching my breath amid swerving perambulators, swinging picnic baskets, and bourgeois families seemingly whisked along behind us from Montsouris, I was glad to have been so impulsive. Though the scene around us was in living color—a riot of blossoms and garish outdoor casual wear—my mind's eye focused on a sepia-tinted image from the Second Empire circa 1865.

In it there were brand new boulevards lined by balconied

buildings, and as many smokestacks as church towers on the surprisingly familiar horizon. It was an image my brain had clicked on and dragged from the novels of Zola and Balzac, the poetry of Baudelaire, the photography of Charles Marville—official photographer to Napoléon III and Haussmann. Welling up from it I could almost smell the electrifying greed of the Second Empire's new bourgeoisie, a perfume powerful enough to overwhelm the cabbage-scented misery of the hundreds of thousands of peasants pouring into town, seeking their fortune amid the smokestacks. How might it have felt to wake up in Paris one day in the 1860s to discover a new city had mushroomed overnight, with not only new roads and buildings and parks like Montsouris and Buttes-Chaumont, but also a new soul, a new way of living—the birth of the modern?

Alison tugged my hand. It was too hot to stand around waiting for a steam train that might never appear. We sought shade on the far side of a lake. A graceful suspension bridge spanned the greenish waters. Stone pinnacles shot up from the center of the lake. An airborne colonnaded temple nested atop one of them, at least a hundred feet above the groups of rowdy teenagers rowing in leaky boats around us. A waterfall rumbled in a grotto, setting mist adrift through gaps in the cliff face. A colorful kaleidoscope of neighborhood children played in channels of rushing water that spilled from rockeries. Sun-baked codgers pulled big, lazy bottom-feeders from the lake, dangled them in front of goggling toddlers, then tossed them back into the water. Swans and geese cruised by, honking and snapping at flotillas of stale bread. We cooled our heels in the shady stream, safely out of the swans' reach, and Alison wondered out loud how many city kids and hot, tired adults like us had sought refuge in the park over the years.

I had a vague notion of the Buttes-Chaumont's history, gleaned from park panels, guidebooks, and French literature. I knew, for example, that the site had been called *Chauve Mont*—bald mountain—because the gypsum and clay in the soil kept vegetation from growing, so that when it was turned into a park tons of horse manure and topsoil had to be brought in. I remembered that the same team of planners, architects, and designers who built Buttes-Chaumont worked their magic on the Bois de Boulogne, Bois de Vincennes, Montsouris, and about two dozen city squares, at more or less the same time—the 1860s zenith of the Second Empire. Romantic English and exotic Asian gardens were in vogue then, and that would explain the park's sinuous paths, I now reasoned, as well as the strategically positioned copses of trees and rock outcrops. Like anyone who's read any French history, I'd come across stories, most of them inaccurate, of the *Gibet de Montfaucon,* a gallows built on a rise somewhere near here, where countless men and women were hanged from the Middle Ages into the Renaissance. And of course there were the tales of the bloody repression of the Communards, who fought the emperor's counterrevolutionary Versaillais troops at Buttes-Chaumont in 1870, were slaughtered by them, and were buried or burned en masse on the Butte's lawns.

But as we sat in the shade and dangled our feet in the stream the violence the park has known was nowhere to be seen, heard, or felt. Caged peacocks called from atop a grassy knoll, children squealed, teenagers exchanged bodily fluids, and I thought I caught the hissing of the old steam train echoing out of the cutting below Rue de la Crimée. But I was too dazed and content to climb the rise and have a look.

The heat, the summery garden scents, and the murmuring water lulled me into a state of reverie. That dazed sensation followed me home and, having engendered a powerful curiosity about the park, drove me to crack open several reference books on Paris, the Second Empire, and Buttes-Chaumont in particular. I soon discovered some curious facts. For instance, the park's pinnacles were created to emulate the cliffs of Étretat, a favorite resort of the Second Empire's upper classes (and of its painters, including Monet). My reference books also confirmed that the pinnacle-top temple is an exact replica of the Temple of Cybele in Tivoli, near Rome, dedicated to a goddess of the hearth. I learned that the suspension bridge stretches one hundred twenty feet across and thirty-five feet above the lake, and that the other, shorter bridge linking the temple to the park's upper section is known as the Suicide Bridge. Jilted lovers long favored its tempting seventy-foot free-fall. Another nugget of information I came upon is that Gustave Eiffel built one of the park's least remarkable bridges. As to statistics, various sources agree that amid the twenty five acres of lawn, the 3.2 miles of paved road, and 1.5 miles of winding paths, there are approximately 3,200 trees. My estimate would be that there are about thrice that many shrubs, something on the order of 10,000. Among the vegetation sprout many sculptures—some innocuous, some ludicrous—plus a hodgepodge of neo-Gothic, neo-Renaissance, Sino-English, and faux-Swiss park buildings typical of late-1800s eclecticism.

Though Baron Haussmann was in charge overall of the remake of Second Empire Paris, the real hero of its parks was Jean-Charles-Adolphe Alphand, an engineer and public works designer, flanked by landscaper Édouard André and architect Jean-Antoine-Gabriel Davioud. The big parks they created were linked by the ultramodern Petite Ceinture steam railway, and were conceived as more than mere rehab projects. The depleted quarries of Buttes-Chaumont, for example, had become the garbage dump of Belleville, to which the area then belonged, as well as an open-air slaughterhouse for horse-butchers, and the lair of murderers, robbers, and literary heroes like Arsène Lupin, the gentleman thief.

Ostensibly the reason Napoléon III commissioned his men to build Buttes-Chaumont, Montsouris, and the city's other green spaces was the International Exposition of 1867. But these "democratic oases" as they were called were first and foremost an experiment in social engineering, what surrealist writer Louis Aragon in his bizarre book *Paris Peasant* called "artificial paradises." The new parks of the brave new Paris were as essential as the *grands boulevards,* the train stations, and the smokestacks, thought Aragon and others. They were safety valves for the age of patriarchal capitalism, which depended on immigrant labor. Every leaf, every landscaped knoll and babbling watercourse was calculated to outdo Nature. By spending a few hours in the park, the theory went, the worker-bees of the empire, most of them transplanted French provincials or starveling Italians, would better bear the stress of the factory, the overcrowded city, the loss of beloved forests and fields. So, these soothing parklands were in reality tools of exploitation, an antirevolutionary opiate?

Buttes-Chaumont is only a half-hour's walk across the Ménilmontant and Belleville neighborhoods from Père-Lachaise cemetery in northeastern Paris, one of my favorite stomping grounds. So, having satisfied my bookish curiosity about Napoléon III and his diabolical amusement parks, I took my usual cemetery stroll and eagerly trotted back to the Buttes to have another look. To me it is the most astonishing, picturesque, and alluring of the city's artificial paradises. I wanted to view it again, with knowing eyes. Would this proto-Disneyland dreamed up by a dictator be as seductive now as I'd found it on earlier visits, when uninitiated into the emperor's secrets?

"Let us stroll in this décor of desires, this décor filled with mental misdemeanors and with imaginary spasms," wrote the playfully cryptic surrealist Aragon from the Buttes-Chaumont. "Décor" is the right word: as I stood again in the grotto near the thundering cascade I could see that the stalagmites were poured from cement, like the faux-wooden railings on the faux-stone pathways. But they were covered with fresh moss and seemed so worn and weathered that I couldn't help finding them endearing.

From Cybele's panoramic temple I took in the jumbled view, with Montmartre's kitsch cupolas to the west and the housing projects of Pantin on the northeastern horizon. It was not a view calculated to please tourists, but I found it intriguing nonetheless, another example of social engineering, this one dreamed up by 1960s-'70s French president Georges Pompidou. Glancing down at the placid lake around the pinnacles' base, I noticed in its ugly concrete bottom a tangle of water pipes.

Was the curtain being drawn back on the Wizard of Oz, I wondered ruefully?

Down the cast-concrete steps I clambered, through faux-caves, settling eventually on an old green bench near a garrulous group of fishermen.

"No, we do not catch sardines," one of them quipped when I started to make conversation about the fishing. "We catch gudgeon, carp, and pike and we know some of them by name, like we know the swan, whose name is Jojo by the way."

The fishermen chuckled at these apparently oft-recited lines. They knew the fish as well as they knew each other, they explained, because they bought them from a fish farm and stocked the lake yearly and were the only anglers legally entitled to dangle hooks for the bottom-feeders therein.

More artifice, I sighed, realizing that the poor dumb fish keep biting the same fishermen's bait day in, day out, hooked and released, until the day they die of old age. But as I circled the lake on carefully plotted paths with temple-topped perspectives engineered to be dazzling whether glimpsed from high or low, and as I sipped a drink at the gimcrack café designed by a dictator's minions, I felt a growing kinship not only with the duped immigrant workers of yesteryear who came here to rest up after their slave labors. The fact is I felt like the gudgeon, carp, or pike stocked by the fisherman. Maybe, I thought, sipping my coffee, maybe it's precisely because Buttes-Chaumont, Montsouris, and the other Second Empire parks I love are so utterly artificial, so wantonly faux, that I'll keep falling for their sepia-tinted charms hook, line, and sinker for as long as I live in Paris, the world capital of illusionism.

Going Underground

Through me you enter the city of pain
Through me you enter suffering eternal
Through me you go among lost souls . . .
　　　—Engraved upon the gateway to Hell, Dante, *Inferno*

It all started with two apparently unrelated subterranean events. The first was a routine damage-control visit to our basement—the *cave*. Records indicate our Marais building got its façade in a 1784 remake of the neighborhood, near Saint-Paul's, but that the structure dates to about 1630, with foundations and cellar from further back, poised atop the long-demolished priory of Sainte-Catherine-du-Val-des-Écoliers, founded in the thirteenth century.

You need a chopstick and a key to open our cellar door. Then you descend a steep, moldering staircase into centuries past, into the chalky, muddy underbelly of Paris—what Victor Hugo called "Lutetia, City of Mud," a reference to the ancient Gallo-Roman city that stood here. I struck a match, sizzling cobwebs as I went, wrenched open the rotting wooden door to our section of cellar, and dug out a preindustrial candlestick holder. In the flickering candle flame I spotted a crack in the masonry I'd never noticed before. I could see nothing beyond, of course—the darkness was absolute. But I imagined an infernal world.

The main Roman road from Lutetia to Melun—nowadays Rue Saint-Antoine—runs a few hundred yards to the south of our building. The priory had stood here five hundred years, from twelve-something until the 1770s. Neighborhood oldtimers had told me of hidden passageways fanning from our cellar to catacombs, quarries, and long-gone fortresses.

"There's another Paris under Paris," intoned one neighbor, a paleontologist, echoing Hugo, the bard of buried Lutetia. The paleontologist's words, recalled as I stood in our cellar, sent a pleasurable chill down my spine.

I snuffed my candle and plunged through a time tunnel into the Gallo-Roman city, then burrowed onward and upward to the malodorous Middle Ages, then to the days of Baron Haussmann and Jean Valjean (fugitive hero of Hugo's *Les Misérables*), slowly resurfacing with Occupation-era French Resistance fighters and their underground networks, before clawing metaphorically back to the comforts of our banal present day. I re-lit the candle and dragged some suitably decomposed junk from the cellar to the garbage.

Not long after this first fantasy voyage, while strolling under the arcades of Place des Vosges near our building, I decided to step into a cluttered shop I'd passed a thousand times but had only visited twice. The affable owner, Pierre Balmès, a specialist in antique timepieces, reminded me that he'd opened for business in 1949. While moving in he had made a curious discovery. The square's identical pavilions were built, he'd said, between 1605 and 1612—everyone knew that. But few realized Place des Vosges's northern flank sits over the cellars of the Hôtel Royale des Tournelles, erected in 1388, destroyed in 1563 by order of Queen Catherine de Médicis. "I was sweeping the cellar floor," Balmès recounted, "when I noticed what looked like a trap door . . ." The door led to another vaulted stone *cave* below it, choked with historical debris.

My mind boggled at Balmès's words. Could his cellar be linked to the one under our building, a mere two hundred yards away as the mole burrows?

A kind of feverish curiosity seized me. Wherever I went in following days I peered down not up. I peered into stairwells, and into churches to see if they had a crypt, into road works, drains, and wells. Slowly I began assembling a list of underground sites, a mental mole's map of Paris, including but not limited to classics like the sewers and catacombs.

On that list are nightclubs, supermarkets and shopping centers, a reservoir, the Senate building, movie theaters, the Opéra, swimming pools, crypts, wells, burial grounds, quarries, wine cellars, half a dozen museums, department stores, rivers, subways, secret passageways, a canal, dozens of train lines, a fabulous Art Nouveau public bathroom, and more.

Let's get one thing straight: I have never been a devotee of the underworld. But two things continue to fascinate me about subterranean Paris. There's the physical layer-cake of civilizations, a millennial mille-feuille of Gallic, Gallo-Roman, medieval, Renaissance, and more or less modern constructions, with associated lore.

Perhaps even more intriguing, though, are the people I've encountered who are obsessed by this buried metropolis. Take, for example, the thousands of (mostly young) Frenchmen and women who spend countless hours on their hands and knees delving into the 175 miles of Paris's abandoned limestone quarries, a subterranean cityscape as porous as the proverbial Swiss *fromage* (Victor Hugo, better than I at simile, compared it to a sponge). Parisian cave mavericks are known as *cataphiles*—lovers of catacombs. Because the quarries have been off-limits since 1955, *les cataphiles* are pursued in an endless game of cat-and-rat by a special police squad, the Brigade de Dispersion et d'Intervention en Carrière (BDIC), whose members are nicknamed *cataflics*—catacomb cops.

Decked out in survival gear, complete with rubber boots, waterproof packs, and powerful flashlights, *cataphiles* will do just about anything to get into the intestine-like quarry passages and watery chambers a hundred feet or more below the city's surface, a mole's paradise where the weather, light conditions, and temperature—50 to 55 Fahrenheit—never change. They throw drug parties, conduct spooky chthonic rites, play at Phantom of the Opera or at Jean Valjean escaping the gendarmes. They carve tables and chairs or entire subterranean theaters from the live rock walls, create art galleries, hold secret meetings, and screen movies, tapping into the city's underground power grid for their electricity. Wherever bones have fallen into the lightless tunnels from the cemeteries above—at Père-Lachaise or Montparnasse, for instance—hardcore *cataphiles* crawl undaunted over mounds of moldering skeletons. Skulls are favorite trophies.

I've long wondered whether the *cataphiles* are misunderstood Romantics or certifiable loons. Whichever, they're sometimes extremists who belong to rival bands and wear costumes—including Nazi uniforms. Most have cryptic nicknames. They often cut through the metal bars or drill through the cement blocks and walls installed by *cataflics* over the 388 known quarry entrances, many of them in abandoned railroad tunnels. They sometimes use dynamite to blow open new access holes. To elude the *cataflics* or other *cataphiles,* they toss smoke bombs then disappear into the labyrinth. Some get lost for hours or days. Some get hurt. Some have no doubt died underground, like Philibert Aspairt. In 1793 this doorman at the Val-de-Grâce convent descended into the cellars to fetch a bottle of liquor; he turned the wrong way and was found eleven years later under what's now Rue Henri Barbusse. The spot has been a *cataphile* pilgrimage site ever since.

Mystery, danger, disobedience, a yearning for things lost, hidden, dead—this is what motivates many of Paris's peculiar cave people, anomalies in the Internet age, and therefore somehow remarkable if not endearing.

But as a former longtime commandant of the BDIC told me one day, those thinking of joining a band of *cataphiles* for a foray should know that some cynical veterans also use their smoke bombs to frighten and disorient *touristes,* meaning first-time visitors. As in fraternity-style hazings, newcomers are sometimes stripped of their flashlights and clothes, then left to whimper in the impenetrable darkness. "In case that isn't enough to discourage you," added the commandant's successor, when I spoke to him, "there is always Mother Nature." Bona fide claustrophobia is unpleasant, but it's nothing compared to leptospirosis, a potentially lethal illness carried by germs in rat urine. Before venturing into Lutetia's muddy bowels, therefore, savvy *cataphiles* get immunized against it. "Be warned," say the *cataflics,* sounding like the soothsaying damned in Dante's *Inferno.*

Most casual underground thrill-seekers—meaning people like you and me—start and end their visit to subterranean Paris at Les Catacombes. You might better spend your time reading a page or two of *Les Misérables,* or looking at Félix Nadar's sublime 1861 photographs of this bizarre realm (Nadar actually invented flash photography to immortalize Paris's sewers and catacombs). A better place to begin an underground itinerary is the unsung Crypte Archéologique, beneath the square facing Notre-Dame cathedral. This admittedly tame display of ruins, jazzed up with clever spotlighting, nonetheless provides a potted history of Paris from pre-Roman times forward. You see maps and mockups of the city as it spread from the Île de la Cité outward, a history written in rubble. There are Roman roads and the rooms of Roman houses, medieval staircases and wells, and an egg-shaped section of nineteenth-century drainage tunnel. A hodgepodge, the crypt hints at the true buried treasure of this ancient, palimpsest city: an understanding of the past and a perspective on the present.

You can continue a Roman-to-medieval visit at the Musée de Cluny, built atop Imperial-era baths (the cold, warm, and hot rooms are still there, in ruins, plus plenty of archaeological finds). Within a few hundred yards of the crypt and Cluny are several centuries-old Left Bank cellars open to the public. The most easily accessible lie under the celebrated (or notorious) Caveau de la Huchette and Caveau des Oubliettes, both nightspots. Here you descend into atmospheric jazz dens, under venerable vaults where unspeakable horrors—torture, imprisonment, and execution—were once daily occurances. At La Huchette there's even a skeleton on view, and a well-worn chastity belt. A quarter-mile west, another chastity belt lurks in the buttressed basement of Le Relais Louis XIII restaurant, which is built atop the defunct Grands Augustins convent, an institution whose members were presumably familiar with such contraptions.

In my desultory pursuit of information relating to Paris's underbelly, I have discovered that many of the Latin Quarter's hundreds of *caves* were formerly linked by secret passages, some leading into abandoned Roman quarries beneath the Montagne Sainte-Geneviève, which is now crowned by the Panthéon. In the Second World War both Nazis and Résistance fighters scurried through these passageways, and in the 1950s and '60s moviemakers showed their "underground" films here—a dauntingly close ordeal according to friends who participated and lived to tell. Nowadays among young Parisians the term "underground"—in English—once again means subversively cool, hip, or trendy, in part because the clandestine film screens of old started up again in the early 2000s, organized by a mysterious band of vaguely anarchistic sometime-*cataphiles* with a quirky political agenda.

In the hit parade of infra-Paris sites, the Louvre's Carrousel area offers the subterranean spectacle of Charles V's moat and walls—a seductive alignment of round tower bases and inclined ramparts. For the aesthetic experience, however, my favorite dens are underneath the Hôtel de Beauvais and the Marais historical society's sixteenth-century headquarters, the Maison d'Ourscamp, both in Rue François Miron. The Gothic vaulting and elegant columns originally supported several parts of a now-demolished thirteenth-century abbey. In each of the two cellars is a well, a common feature of Paris houses before the arrival of Baron Haussmann and his waterworks engineer, Eugène Belgrand, in the mid-1800s.

To grasp the revolutionary aspects of Belgrand's sewers and water supply try imagining a filthy, disease-ridden Paris where groundwater and the Seine were contaminated, waste flooded the streets, and thousands died every year from water-borne diseases. Victor Hugo may have lamented the passing of this soulful, pestilential city, but not Nadar, whose black-and-white photos show Belgrand's spacious conduits in all their stunning symmetry. Today they're much as they were when built in the 1850s—orderly, clean, utterly unromantic yet redolent of a sickly sweetness Hugo would have loved, for the streets of his Vieux Paris were legendary for their stench of decomposing cabbage.

Let's be honest, it helps to be a historian or an engineer to enjoy the sewers. Nowadays only a quarter-mile section of them under the Quay d'Orsay is open to the public and only on foot (when I first visited Paris, visitors toured the sewers in rowboats). But your average sewer-goer is too baffled and nauseated to study the museum displays, which range from gumboots to computers, or appreciate the ingeniousness of the gravity-flow tunneling, the tunefulness of the gurgling gutters, and the beauty of the brownish cascades. Surprisingly, many of Belgrand's 150-year-old devices are still in use, including giant wooden balls that rumble through the system's 1,300 miles, crushing muck as they go. To me this revolting spectacle conjures up images of the big night-marish ball in the cult 1960s TV series *The Prisoner,* and like its star, I long for escape.

Nadar took some of his most ghoulish images not in the sewers but in Les Catacombes, in 1861. They capture that most sublime moment of Haussmann's modernization of the city: the stacking of the bones of some six million dead, many of them transferred here starting in 1786 from the cemetery of the Innocents, near what is now Les Halles. Unlike those of Rome, Paris's catacombs are an ossuary, created for practical reasons: to empty the Innocents of a decomposing cargo that had burst through walls to poison the surrounding neighborhood.

The catacombs provide proof, if any were needed, that our modern age has no monopoly on perversity. Toward the end of the Ancien Régime the ossuary became a rendezvous of depraved aristocrats. The Comte d'Artois, later King Charles X, held torch-lit *fêtes macabres* here with ladies in waiting from the court in Versailles. The site was officially opened to tourists only in the 1870s, after Haussmann had sanitized it. Nadar's photos show workers sorting and stacking the bones dumped here from a dozen graveyards (all Paris's inner-city cemeteries were eventually cleared), building decorative retaining walls with femurs, tibia, and skulls and tossing smaller bones behind.

Accessing the catacombs is still a daunting experience. A descent down the spiral staircase that worms a hundred feet beneath Place Denfert-Rochereau, the main entrance to the site, is guaranteed to leave you dizzy. Claustrophobics need not apply. You enter a mile-long maze of tunnels that zigzag toward what nineteenth-century commentators, paraphrasing Dante, dubbed "the realm of the dead." As you march single-file over slippery stones, preceded and followed by hundreds of fellow visitors, it's little comfort to know that sections of these ancient former quarries have collapsed as recently as 2010. You squelch over mud, wondering when the lights or ventilation might fail, and, if you're like me, asking yourself what you're doing here in the first place, gaping at millions of weirdly displayed age-mottled bones.

Evidently I belong to a squeamish minority. Almost two hundred thousand tourists a year besiege the catacombs, loving them to death with cameras flashing and boots resounding. If ever there was a time you could quietly contemplate this disconcerting sanctuary's significance—the backbreaking work of underpaid miners, the technical genius of Enlightenment thinkers and engineers, the anonymity of six million forgotten ancestors—that innocent time is long gone. As I clambered out of the caves a security guard was checking backpacks. A stolen skull stared forlornly from a table, and a youngster with a stupid grin was doing his best to talk himself out of trouble. "Happens all the time," sighed a guard when I asked. "You've got to wonder . . ."

After the catacombs, the life-enhancing qualities of the subterranean Canal Saint-Martin can only come as a relief. You board a riverboat at the Arsenal marina, abutting the Bastille, then putter leisurely toward La Villette under several miles of vaults conceived by Haussmann—who else? But the first, the great Emperor Napoléon deserves some credit, too. He had the canal built as an open waterway. The relentless Baron covered the canal to thwart riotous Parisians who, he feared (based on the 1830 revolution) might use it again as a defensive moat. Happily, nowadays tour boats and pleasure craft cruise the canal and there is no echo of its bloody past.

Another sublime subterranean spot is the basement of the Bazaar de l'Hôtel de Ville—the BHV department store—an unrivaled Aladdin's cavern of hardware, now equipped with its own subterranean café-restaurant, Bricolo. And under Place de la Madeleine hide what may just be Paris's most beautiful Art nouveau *toilettes publiques,* with carved wood panels, brass and mirrors, floral frescoes, and stained-glass windows in each *cabinet.*

Here, once you've awakened the sleeping *Madame Pipì* (i.e., the bathroom attendant), you may tidy up like a real fin-de-siècle lady or gentleman.

Of course the greatest and most useful thing in Paris's underground world is the Métropolitain, inaugurated in 1900. Its deepest stations are at Abbesses, halfway up Montmartre, and Cité, on the island of the same name. However, as if to prove that earlier centuries can't claim all the glory, the Météor line running from Madeleine past François Mitterrand's National Library is a staggering wonder of the subsoil, a postmodern folly, as symbolic of our times as the sewers or catacombs were of theirs. Glass escalators lower you into cavernous halls, then down to the platforms, where glass barriers prevent passengers from falling onto the tracks. Météor is driverless. Its path crosses the Marais. Whenever I ride it, I make a point of checking, irrationally, for traces of Paris history buried not far from our dusty, moldy cellar.

Place des Vosges

Sitting among old armor, and old tapestry, and old coffers, and grim old chairs and tables, and old canopies of state from old palaces, and old golden lions going to play at skittles with ponderous old golden balls, they made a most romantic show, and looked like a chapter out of one of his own books.

—CHARLES DICKENS after meeting Victor Hugo
in his Place-des-Vosges apartment, 1847

The Marais's centerpiece Place des Vosges isn't the biggest or the grandest of Paris squares, but it seems to me the most alluring. Under its arcades the noise of traffic fades—well, on three of four sides anyway—replaced by the splashing of fountains. Pigeons and sparrows duel over the steep slate roofs of the square's thirty-six identical pavilions. Their brick and stone façades, never shaded by other buildings, catch the shifting light of the Paris sky. People stroll by, peering into shop windows. Waiters weave among café tables set out under the vaults. In the square's center, safe behind iron grillwork, children oblivious to the backdrop play in sandboxes while au pairs chat on double-sided benches.

Place des Vosges draws me in at least once a day and in all seasons, for the simple reason that Alison and I live about two hundred yards west of it. Sometimes, especially on a rainy night, the square feels like our cloister, a place of reflection and meditation. Sit in summer under the scented linden trees as the sun goes down and the street lamps flicker into life and you'll feel not only the linden blossoms' sticky weeping, but also your sensibilities tingling. Or, on a winter's day, wander from shop to well-lit shop under the arches while the rain pours down on the rest of the world, and ponder the ephemera of consumerism.

Architects and art historians will assure you that Place des Vosges offers France's best example of early seventeenth-century urbanism. Essentially it's a cross between Italianate Mannerism and late-Renaissance Dutch styles, neatly combining a gracious piazza and four sets of row houses. The proportions are on a human scale, with four stories raked skyward, a succession, from ground level up, of arches in rhythmic rows, tall French windows, and rectangular dormers or porthole-shaped *oeils-de-boeuf* on the roof. Time and the elements have conspired with the foibles and fantasies of man to round the square's hard edges and skew what had been intended as perfect symmetry.

Unlike the bustling, coldly beautiful Place Vendôme or Place de la Concorde, famed for their hotels, clubs, and ritzy jewelry shops, Place des Vosges has always been animated and lived in, and ultimately that is what makes it a likeable spot. Madame de Sévigné, the seventeenth-century queen of epistolary literature and high-society gossip (now read exclusively by French high schoolers), was born on the square's south side. Across the way,

Marion de Lorme, the courtesan of kings, distributed her favors, if we must be polite. On Place des Vosges's northern flank the pious Armand Jean de Vignerot du Plessis, Deuxième Maréchal-Duc de Richelieu, seduced a catalog of lovers that reportedly included every noble lady then resident in the square's pavilions. Piety and licentiousness walked arm-in-arm, just as it does today.

The duelists, the gamblers, and the glittering Grand-Siècle pomp of the place—originally named La Place Royale—inspired Pierre Corneille's now unreadable comic play, also named, somewhat predictably, *La Place Royale*. Even when the square hit its nadir just after World War II, its badly lit arcades and grubby backcourts provided the setting for Georges Simenon's murder mystery, *L'Ombre Chinoise* (later turned into a cult movie).

"It was Montgomery's lance that created Place des Vosges," wrote Victor Hugo with typical aplomb. From 1832 to 1848 Hugo lived at number six and his apartment is now an embalmed house-museum. Decrypted, Hugo's line means that Gabriel de Lorges de Montgomery, captain of the French sovereign's Scottish Guards, accidentally killed King Henri II here in 1559. The two were jousting in front of the Hôtel Royal des Tournelles, which stood more or less where Place des Vosges stands today. Montgomery's lance pierced the king's visor, eye, and brain. Understandably, Henri II's widowed queen, Catherine de Médicis, came to hate the royal residence, and eventually had it demolished. For decades the former main courtyard did service as a horse market. It was populist King Henri IV (famous for coining the expression "a chicken in every pot," and for sleeping in a different damsel's bed every night), flanked by his minister the Duc de Sully, who in 1605 hit upon the idea of turning the horse market into a piazza—an Italian novelty unknown in Paris at the time—lined by money-spinning weavers' works and boutiques. Here the court could stroll and make merry far from the Machiavellian intrigues of the Louvre (or so Henri IV thought). About two centuries later, during the French Revolution, the name was changed from Place

Royale to Place des Vosges, to reward the first administrative
département—Les Vosges—that paid taxes, thereby recognizing
the revolutionary regime.

Heavy carriage doors, nowadays often locked, hide courtyards, some groomed into pocket-size formal gardens, others dotted with statues. In several there are workshops, art galleries, or
fashion boutiques, and these are the easiest to breach. Since this
is a particularly toney address, you're likely to encounter well-fed
movie stars, politicos, and other nouveaux on the threshold of
L'Ambroisie, among France's most expensive and pretentious
multiple-starred restaurants, located at number nine. Starveling
models saunter out of Issey Miyake's fief of fashion headquartered
nearby at number five.

Like any poor little rich boy, the square has its problems,
though none seems life-threatening. Locals complain about the
rush-hour traffic on the north side, a through street, and about
the ever-swelling number of tourists on weekends. Some years
ago one long-time resident I met, a dealer in antique Japanese art,
closed her boutique and retreated to a by-appointment-only showroom in a rear court. Too many visitors were handling her fragile
collections, she told me with a shiver of disgust. The square's bête
noire for decades was a self-styled antique dealer who spilled his
ragbag of merchandise under the arcades (but that was nothing
new—the first ban on flea market–style displays dates to 1758).

Then there are the itinerant bangle-hawkers, organ grinders,
and sour-mash Dixieland bands that besiege the square daily to
the delight of some locals and the horror of most others. Pierre
Balmès, the expert on antique timepieces who opened his shop
here in 1949, had observed the remake. "Sometimes I miss the old,
run-down Place des Vosges," he told me one busy Saturday. "It
was so peaceful and quiet." Alas, the gentle Balmès' hour tolled,
and his magical time-tunnel shop is now yet another gallery selling merchandise that falls under the much-abused rubric, "art."

The one blight against which all residents united back in the 1990s is the tour bus. After many an administrative battle, buses were limited to disgorging their hordes on the north side of the square before moving to less scenic quarters. There's talk every few years of creating a car-free zone here and in the surrounding Marais; on Sundays many streets are now off-limits to the vehicles of nonresidents. A permanent pedestrian island might not be a bad idea, as long as a Montmartre-style elephant train isn't part of the deal and the car-free area is big enough to thin merrymakers to acoustically acceptable levels.

"I'd like this to be my kingdom," a thirty-year resident told me several years ago as we stood on his second-floor *étage noble* balcony. The square's original aristocratic residents always lived on the *étage noble,* and my host, perhaps unwittingly, emphasized how privileged I was to enter the hallowed halls of his multimillion-euro apartment and enjoy a glimpse of how the other half lives. "In an ideal world no one else could live here or come in but me," he confessed unself-consciously, "and that just goes to show you how attached one becomes." He reminisced about how, in the early 1990s, he and other property owners had asked the powers-that-be to lock up the park and hand out keys to residents only—a scheme that had provoked public outrage (including my own) and much wringing of hands. The square seems to breed such undemocratic sentiments, inspired, perhaps, by the dramatic views from on high. It's as if the architects had drawn their plans with condescension in mind.

There are several public entrances (five to be precise), but there is only one proper way to approach Place des Vosges the first time around: take Rue de Birague. An unremarkable street, narrow by modern standards, it used to be called Rue Royale. Kings, courtiers, and countless red-blooded parvenus have rolled up it in the past four hundred years. What I do to get the right perspective is sidestep the occasional passing car and take regal strides up the middle of the street. Framing its northern end is the Pavillon du Roi, built by Henri IV for his own use and therefore considerably larger than the square's other pavilions. Through two of the three arches supporting it (the third was made into a stairwell hundreds of years ago) you get a keyhole view of the square beyond. If, like me, you're shortsighted, as you near the king's pavilion its fluted stone pilasters, lacy ironwork balconies, and the crossed swords, lyre, and sculpted "H" of Henri IV will come swimming into focus. Luckless old horny Henri, immortalized in bas-relief, gazes out from the far side of the archway onto the square he didn't live to see completed.

An assassin killed the king as he left the Louvre, in 1610. Two years later the stammering eleven-year-old Louis XIII, a king whose renown rests largely on his subservience to the powerful Cardinal Richelieu, inaugurated the square instead of Henri IV. By then Richelieu had built his own corner pavilion at what is now number twenty-one. Louis XIII promptly retreated to the Louvre and never lived in the Pavillon du Roi. But his court did indeed take over Place Royale. The Duc de Sully, Henri IV's right-hand minister, saw how the wind was blowing and eventually moved into a residence on Rue Saint-Antoine. He lavishly remodeled and expanded it, which is why it's been known ever since as the Hôtel de Sully. The gorgeous groomed garden and *orangerie* are accessible from 5 Place des Vosges.

Overnight, the Marais mushroomed with townhouses, a vogue that lasted until the end of the seventeenth century (when the Saint-Germain and Saint-Honoré neighborhoods became the rage). It's for this reason that Place des Vosges's creation has long been attributed erroneously to Louis XIII. The park in the square's center is named after him, and so too is the architectural style of the square's buildings. Even its centerpiece equestrian statue represents a smiling Louis, his whiskbroom moustaches erect. Poor Henri IV has only a banal boulevard in the Marais to glorify his name, and a fine equestrian statue elsewhere, on the Pont-Neuf, which he also had built.

Some history-mad locals get worked up about such perceived injustices. Not a few are thankful for the screen of century-old horse-chestnut trees that hide the hated Louis XIII's statue. Stendhal, with a slash of his quill, called the king's mount an overgrown mule, not a horse. Truth be told, what enraptured visitors see today is an artless nineteenth-century copy of the original bronze, which was melted down during the Revolution. If you ask me, the second-rate statue is one of the square's endearing imperfections, like the clunky nineteenth-century bird-bath fountains, or the weathered "brickwork" that on closer inspection turns out to be cheap trompe-l'oeil plaster applied to wood. A generous admirer might describe this old harlot of a square as a study in layered eclecticism.

Every few years, in the name of architectural purity, some pious perfectionist lobbies the city to get rid of the statue and the fountains, uproot the trees, and knock down the Louis Philippe–period grilles and shepherd's-crook street lamps—none was around in the early 1600s, after all. These militant purists would restore the square to death in order to bring back its original unimpeded architectural perspectives. They're unlikely to succeed. In Paris, tampering with living layers of history is a tricky business. Here it would involve destroying one remarkable stratum to get at another. Up to now restoration and repair work have been cosmetic. About forty years ago the park's ailing elms were replaced with linden trees that are carefully pruned to preserve perspectives and views. More recently, the lawns were reshaped and the fountains replumbed and equipped for nighttime illumination. Since the early 1960s the French government has paid for two-thirds of the cost of mandatory repairs to façades and roofs. In exchange a few residents have been made to close up unsightly skylights, or remove recent dormers and gables that saw nary a

Henri or Louis, nor Napoléon for that matter. So the pavilions' exteriors now look much as they did in 1612.

Given its age and the number of cataclysmic social events that have occurred around it—the storming of the Bastille, the Glorious Revolution of July 1830, the Industrial Revolution, two world wars, and rampant real estate speculation—it's a miracle Place des Vosges has survived at all. People often say that poverty preserves and prosperity destroys. The postwar building boom threatened not only the square but also the entire Marais neighborhood around it. The bulldozers were stopped a few minutes past the nick of time, in the 1960s, by then culture minister André Malraux, who declared the neighborhood a historical monument. But the poverty-prosperity dictum's opposite is also true: the 1789–to–Second World War chapter of Place des Vosges history is a chronicle of corrosive decline. Factories sprang up in courtyards. Pavilions were dismembered, their aristocratic interiors junked (luckily a few were preserved and remounted at the nearby Musée Carnavalet, Paris's city history museum). If vast sums hadn't been spent on the square in recent decades it probably would have collapsed.

Most of the friends I take to visit Place des Vosges wonder out loud about the people who live behind those handsome, impenetrable façades. If you wander aimlessly along the park's grilles of an evening you can catch tantalizing glimpses of painted ceilings, of rare and valuable pictures hanging high upon a wall. But this is not just a bastion of the wealthy, I discovered some years ago. Henri IV's 1605 building code set the architectural theme and also specified that pavilions had to be owned by single families—presumably very good, old families worthy of the royal square. That unusual law remained in force as late as the 1960s, so there are still a few single-family pavilions, purchased in the 1800s or early 1900s when the square was dilapidated. Some pavilions were split long ago into cheap, rent-controlled apartments. Others are occupied to this day by the descendants of once-rich dynasties now living in genteel penury, their cluttered apartments lifted from a Zola novel. I'll never forget the time I visited one, and was led from floor to sagging floor by the pavilion's unwashed, unshaved, ornery owner, who scowled out of the broken windowpanes and cursed his inheritance. "You think it's beautiful," he shouted over and over. "You like the view? I hate it here, I hate it . . ."

Many impoverished heirs have sold off apartments piecemeal over the past forty years. Properties worth peanuts a few decades ago now fetch staggering sums. *Étage noble* flats are the most valuable at up to seven million dollars.

Other pavilions have been "nationalized" and taken over by an elementary school, the Victor Hugo museum, and an Ashkenazim synagogue, which explains the numbers of small children, the tourists clutching copies of *Les Misérables,* and the more or less constant flow of Jewish wedding parties hamming it up for photographers under the linden trees or in front of the fountains.

In the Place des Vosges social hierarchy, inhabitants still fall into whole-pavilion or single-apartment categories. To some pedigreed clans, former culture minister Jack Lang, with his *étage noble* digs, is a *petit arriviste*—a social climber. Trendy denizens abound, though as one self-consciously fortunate resident told me, it's inaccurate to call the square "fashionable." "Fashion is facile, easy to acquire and superficial," he quipped with a regal wag of bejeweled fingers. "Place des Vosges is complex, expensive—a kind of cloister."

On several occasions I visited the apartment of one of Paris's most successful and controversial art auctioneers, the affable scion of a family that has owned an entire pavilion since the early 1800s. His two-story apartment is littered with priceless antiques and artworks. It is also haunted, he told me, deadpan, by the ghost of Concino Concini, Maréchal d'Ancre, a nobleman murdered in 1617 by the Baron de Vitry, the pavilion's first owner. The auctioneer leads a resolutely modern lifestyle. He had his beamed ceiling repainted by a Senegalese artist. The dining room looks like something out of Jules Verne, with a curious, curved sheet-metal ceiling. "I like mixtures," he told me.

The auctioneer spoke convincingly of restoration, fashion, purity, and eclecticism, and pondered what it means to live today in a monument, dripping with history. "I even like the little nineteenth-century park there with its slightly worn, old-fashioned look and *bouquet* of chestnut trees," he declared at last, with the easy brashness typical of his trade. He used the word "bouquet" on purpose. "It's a naïf—a sort of Henri Rousseau," he continued. "But I think it's beautiful all the same." As if echoing his words, a nattily dressed nanny appeared from the arcades below and swerved into the park, her blue baby carriage scattering pigeons and autumn leaves. A charming naïf it was, I agreed, framed by a masterpiece.

Belly Ache: Les Halles Redux (Again)

The worst of late twentieth-century Modernity . . .
—*New York Times*

L es Halles, the historic market district nicknamed "The Belly of Paris" since the mid-1800s heyday of novelist Émile Zola, will evolve in coming years from its 1970s incarnation. Into what, no one is yet sure. A public architectural competition held in 2004 ostensibly to bring the complex up to European Union safety standards proved unsatisfactory. Fanciful designs by star-architects Jean Nouvel and Rem Koolhaas lost. No one "won." Described by the *New York Times* as a "toothless architectural figurehead," the relatively unknown David Mangin has since then courageously wrapped his gums around a "supervisory" role. Under the watchful eye of mayor Bertrand Delanoë, Mangin is charged with the remake of the subterranean Forum des Halles shopping mall, adjoining park, and RER commuter train station.

But after years of studies and politicking, work set to get under way in 2010 was repeatedly sandbagged, sometimes by planning commissions or courts, sometimes by outraged neighborhood associations. This entertainingly unpredictable roller-coaster provided me with the excuse to revisit the neighborhood yet again with fresh eyes and a determinedly light step.

When it was still a wholesale market, roughshod Les Halles employed upwards of thirteen thousand around the clock, including hundreds of the famously scurrilous *forts*—bruiser porters who to be certified had to haul four hundred forty pounds of freight on a hand-truck across the hangars, about five football fields in length. Les Halles today is a colorless expanse of mirrored buildings reflecting cement. With a budget of one billion dollars and a timeline of many years, the remake is no minor urban renewal scheme.

The entire Les Halles neighborhood covers only twenty-five acres, but few Paris places are freighted with heavier symbolic baggage. Victor Hugo set the riot scenes here in *Les Misérables,* and every French writer or poet worthy of note since has at least nodded in Les Halles's direction. When Georges Pompidou's Gaullist government brazenly removed Les Halles's wholesale market to suburban Rungis in 1969 then demolished the market's iron-and-glass "Baltard pavilions" two years later, an estimated three hundred thousand Parisians' livelihoods were turned upside down, and millions of resident rats evicted. From across the political spectrum Frenchmen cried bloody murder, marching in the streets, as their forebears had in 1789, 1830, and 1968. Amid accusations of illegal real estate speculation involving Les Halles and other "development" schemes, the Gaullists were defeated at the polls in 1974. Politicians since then have tiptoed around the neighborhood.

In his broadside *L'Assassinat de Paris*, muckraking historian Louis Chevalier wrote at the time of the demolition, "Les Halles were Les Halles but then, and even more so, they were Paris itself."

Many Parisians still remember the scandals, dust, and chaos to this day. Nostalgia for Baltard's Les Halles and hatred of what replaced them remains surprisingly tangible. And memories of the twenty-year mess the construction of the Forum engendered are even more vivid. That's why Mangin's reputation and Delanoë's political future—he's a presidential hopeful—ride on the project's outcome. How to redo Les Halles without undue disturbance, on schedule and within budget? That is the question.

The bland southern suburb of Nogent-sur-Marne may seem an odd place to seek Les Halles's secrets, but the two sites are linked spiritually and by the RER "A" line. It's in Nogent, reassembled on a leafy hillside over the Marne River, that you'll find the only Les Halles pavilion left in France. As I rode the RER to Nogent for a visit, I couldn't help noting the irony. Victor Baltard's handsome, airy 1850s tin-roofed structures, with their slender fluted iron columns, gingerbread trim, and glass-paned sides, were destroyed in part to make way for what thirty-odd years ago was considered an ultramodern commuter rail network. Now I was riding in a ragged, tired old train from the distant 1970s, a train whose underground station at Les Halles was slated for demolition and rebuilding.

Of ten original Baltard pavilions, eight were sold as scrap metal (and fetched a paltry 395,000 francs). The ninth was bought by the city of Yokohama in Japan, but that seemed a bit far for me to travel. The sole surviving pavilion is now a venue for prestigious events such as the International Cat Salon or L'Odissée de l'Accordéon festival—an orgy of squeeze-box music. It's flanked by cast-iron Belle Époque streetlamps, one of those nifty little Wallace fountains (decorated with dancing caryatids, designed in 1871, and donated to the city by a British philanthropist), a section of Eiffel Tower staircase, and a curbside fire-alarm box, each carefully transplanted and deprived of its functions. A pleasant place, Nogent's Belle Époque theme park of architecture is a remarkable example of 1960s–'70s Paris urbanism, an object lesson in what not to do again.

While riding back into town in a packed RER train I reviewed my own checkered experiences at Les Halles and Beaubourg, starting in 1976, when I watched the high-gloss paintwork being applied to the unfinished Pompidou Center. In my ignorance I imagined the behemoth was a refinery. Much of the quarter had been bulldozed to accommodate it. A resident set me straight: until a few years earlier, he said, a tangle of alleys had converged on the so-called Plâteau Beaubourg, a depot for the trucks that hauled fruit, vegetables, and meat to the wholesale market at nearby Les Halles.

My curiosity piqued, I walked west from Beaubourg to where the marketplace had been and through clouds of dust watched construction workers pouring cement into the celebrated *trou*—the great twenty-five-acre, seven-story deep hole of Les Halles. In 1979 and '83 I was in Paris again, and saw half (then a quarter) of the pit still gaping, and felt the ground still shaking from pneumatic drills. It was only when I'd moved fulltime to the city in 1986 that the hole had finally been filled and the Forum shopping center completed (by several teams of rival architects working at cross-purposes). The once seedy, unmistakably Parisian alleys where Billy Wilder's irreverent 1963 cinematic tale of prostitute Irma La Douce was set, the streets that had inspired Hugo, Zola, Balzac, Breton, and a hundred others, had disappeared, "renovated" beyond recognition. Not that I would have recognized and bemoaned anything: a young San Franciscan intoxicated by Paris, thirty-five years ago "nostalgia" wasn't in my vocabulary.

Since my early encounters with Les Halles I've dashed through the complex a few hundred times—usually to change subway trains or buy an otherwise un-findable item at FNAC, the country's biggest and possibly most claustrophobic emporium for books, CDs, and electronics. Sardonic grumpiness isn't something I aspire to, but over the past quarter-century the labyrinthine underground Forum with its mirrored-glass "corolla" buildings springing from the depths has somehow failed to win my affection. If I live long enough, I probably won't miss the current Les Halles when finally it's gutted and rebuilt to let in air and light, and to ease foot traffic.

Like the eight hundred thousand daily commuters and forty million annual Forum shoppers, I watched the mall decline from mere 1970s architectural absurdity into something spooky and sordid. It bottomed in the late '90s and early 2000s.

In fairness, for a place overrun day and night by an average 150,000 shoppers, the Forum is remarkably clean, safe, and orderly. And the neighborhood does have its boosters. Most are philosophical, longtime local residents, as well as business owners, lovers of 1970s kitsch, itinerant masochists, and restless *banlieusards*—those beardless youths from the suburban housing projects the RER was designed to serve. As the proprietor of several chic short-term rental apartments near Les Halles observed one day, "I suppose they can hardly be blamed, as their own living area must be very sterile and boring!"

It was with trepidation that I alighted from my subway car at Les Halles and talked myself into taking a fresh look again, *again.* The long, steep escalators that strike terror into many Parisian hearts raised me from the Dantesque 1970s darkness of the RER platforms into the sunken plaza via a laminate of fluorescent-lit corridors that are begging to be reconfigured. The plaza and its bulging Plexiglas windows look increasingly like outsized vintage Tupperware, which ought to make them endearing. Still Europe's busiest, with around 3,200 employees and 170 commercial spaces, the mall generates nearly $700 million annually for its private leaseholder, Unibail-Rodamco. Might that explain the eagerness of sixties and seventies real estate developers, and the myriad pressures still exerted on city hall to keep doing business as usual, or to add even more boutiques?

I was happy to confirm that FNAC thrives. On one memorable occasion—in 2005—I rappelled into the cavernous emporium to buy a copy of *Le Ventre de Paris*—Zola's *Belly of Paris*—before striking out into the wasteland. But this time around I carried with me a dog-eared copy of *The Human Comedy* instead. With it in hand, an amulet against prejudice, I was delighted to discover the Forum's multilevel "Rue du Cinéma." This new film center and library has five screens, thousands of movies (5,500 of them about Paris), a movie-theme bar, and a long glass front that lets in more light than has been seen since the *trou*. The color scheme of pink, white, and gray seemed a long way from the mall's dreary browns of yesteryear. Wrapping what is obviously a popular package is lighting designer Georges Berne's "luminous ribbon."

The shops on level Minus-3 nearest the RER entrances were also profitably deploying their wares. Other parts of the complex offered tempting vacancy signs, which to some might increase the old-fashioned gloom, but to others suggests the promise of change.

Reassuringly changeless instead was the air, as salubriously caustic as it was in 1986. It's perfumed by French fries and hamburgers, reheated croissants, sausages, cheap perfume, disinfectants, and an eye-stinging scent many innocent shoppers mistakenly attribute to sewage. "The Belly of Paris aches," quip regulars. Some invoke the supernatural: the Places des Innocents cemetery abutted the site, after all. An RATP municipal transit worker once explained to me that the *odeur* comes not from disgruntled, displaced souls, but rather from decomposing limestone, exposed by the *trou*. Long ago, the district was called Champeaux—"water-field"— and its soil had a fine reputation for consuming corpses faster than you can say Jacques Robinson. Whether Champeaux lies at the origin of "shampoo"—which the French spell "shampooing" and pronounce *sham-pwan*—is a matter of speculation. As it awaits re-modeling, the mall gets a thorough wash daily, which accounts for the soapy layer in the air's complex olfactory blend.

The Forum des Halles has two parts, the more recent and less egregious lying to the west. Opened in 1985, it was designed by Paul Chemetov (of the Ministry of Finance building at Bercy). According to the understandably embittered architect, interviewed by *Le Journal de Paris,* it would cost the city of Paris around one hundred million euros just to tear off his Forum's cement ceiling.

Expense and technical challenges are among the reasons so many sandbags have been piled at Mayor Delanoë's feet in the past decade. How much it would cost (and if it's possible) to eliminate the stench of Champeaux is unknown. Shopping in the supermarket Mangin plans to install in reconverted car tunnels beneath Les Halles could be a pungent adventure.

Spend an hour or so, as I did, exploring the "corolla" pavilions and panoramic terraces excogitated by the long-forgotten Jean Willerval, then sit in the tatterdemalion park that stretches between the church of Saint-Eustache and the handsome, round eighteenth-century Bourse de Commerce. Eleven fountains squirt and splash. Children grab the sculpted ear and scale the giant stone hand and head of *L'Écoute*—a sculpture "listening" to the heartbeat of the city. The park is clearly much used. After decades of patient grooming, its ten thousand shrubs and 480 trees—someone has inventoried them—are finally leafing out, just when the gardens are to be relandscaped, three-quarters of the trees felled, and, some fear, *L'Écoute* displaced in the process. But only if Mangin and his sub-architects' plans go ahead. They might very well be modified again (again).

One reason the project has been held up is Saint-Eustache, an endearingly homely barn with marvelous flying buttresses, several unusual bell towers, and a splendid organ. It's a national landmark church, was restored recently, and is dramatically lit at night. A lantern in the proverbial darkness, it's one of Paris's most popular parish churches, especially among immigrants. Colbert is buried here, making Saint-Eustache a pilgrimage site for historians and royalists. More to the point, the gardens of Les Halles fall within its circle of landmark status, and therefore theoretically can't be altered without a court order.

The charms of Saint-Eustache and other premodern relics in the area are many. But unless you're taking happy pills, you may still wind up sharing the *New York Times*'s brutal 2005 assessment that Les Halles is "the worst of late twentieth-century Modernity, with its tabula rasa approach to history and its penchant for sterile, inhuman spaces."

The "worst"? Maybe. To those sensible, boring souls who suggested in the 1960s that Baltard's pavilions be repurposed as Pompidou's contemporary art museum, and adjacent areas groomed into a "Central Park," Pompidou retorted, "It would be invaded instantly by sixty thousand hippies!"

Pompidou's visionaries dreamed up the Pompidou Center instead, and strove to erect colossi considerably more astonishing than what we currently see at Les Halles. They imagined spaghetti-bowl freeways and slug-like skyscrapers rearing their spiky heads, and other projects branded outrageously outlandish even for those swinging times. Today's visionaries seem immune to history's lessons. Jean Nouvel wanted sleek Manhattan high-rises with rooftop gardens. Rem Koolhaas planned vividly colored "Popsicle" towers poking up from below to broadcast the mall's "energy." The Dutch firm of MVRDV preferred stained-glass expanses, which were judged ludicrous and "un-build-able."

By contrast, Mangin's original suggestion to raze the wilted corollas and blaze a treeless esplanade from the Bourse de Commerce to a low, glass-covered subterranean atrium seemed downright reassuring, though it was hard to see why the greenery had to go. Perhaps because of public outcry over the destruction of the park, but more likely because of the mayor's multifarious agenda, the job of actually designing the new mall was taken from Mangin and given to a pair of architects, Patrick Berger and Jacques Anziutti. Their vision is the latest version of the plan—call it Les Halles 2.011—and centers around "La Canopée." If built, this wood-and-steel canopy will billow about fifty feet above the ground and stretch unsupported several acres across, replacing the corollas. It's an audacious merger of a monster manta-ray, a louvred Bedouin tent, and a thatched tropical hut. La Canopée has many advantages, though waterproofing isn't one of them. Wind and rain are expected as part of the new shopping and commuting experience, fitting perhaps for a globally warmed age. The Canopy is considerably lower than Willerval's pavilions, and it's not mirrored, already a vast improvement. Eventually the underground atrium beneath the Canopy will be fitted with slinky elevators that evoke the neck and back of a golden brontosaurus—or the arches of the multinational fast-food chain that happens to have an outlet nearby, facing the Fontaine des Innocents. And, of course, there will be many more shops.

In the end, Parisians can rest assured, no matter how the remodel is done, the shopping mall and RER station will remain.

Though eager to slip away, I coaxed myself into exploring the car-free district around Les Halles one more time. It's not that I despise the area. I simply prefer other parts of town. The glad news was, the litter, fast-food franchises, down-market souvenir and clothing shops, and edgy atmosphere decrease manyfold the farther from the complex you get. At the same time, a feeling of pride and hope is returning to the perimeter of the neighborhood, perhaps inspired by the impending remodel and a rise in real estate prices. For instance, by the time you reach Rue Montorgueil—a lively market street beyond Saint-Eustache—or the church of Saint-Merri near the Pompidou Center, the *banlieusards* from the commuter trains have largely been replaced by trendy bohemian bourgeois *bobos* from the abutting Marais. The harder you look around Les Halles, the more you uncover pleasing architectural details, including the handsome Fontaine des Innocents and scores of centuries-old façades behind which lurk rebuilt apartment complexes. Until a few years ago the strongest reminders here of the pre-Pompidou era were the Irma La Douces. They plied their trade around Rue Saint-Denis from the Middle Ages onward. But they, too, are losing out to the forces of gentrification, and have decamped en masse to lower-rent districts.

Like Baltard's pavilion in Nogent-sur-Marne, some vintage storefronts in the neighborhood admittedly appear to be bleached bones in a wasteland. As the quarter has grown into its 1970s–'80s Frankenstein skin, however, the scars have healed over, and few people have the stomach to tear them open again. I was especially happy to see the eye-catching window displays of the pest-control specialist Julien Aurouze, whose family business at 8 Rue des Halles has been around from the rat-infested days of yore. The dessicated, dangling rodents, some of them captured in 1925, still give frissons to passersby. A handful of cafés also survived the wrecker's ball. Au Père Tranquille and Le Bon Pêcheur, facing each other and Les Halles's mirrored façades, are two of them.

Once upon a time market workers and slumming party-goers would sup night and day on Au Père Tranquille's "fine, pungent onion soup," as Evelyn Waugh noted in early 1929. Cheap and warming, onion soup was the ideal fast food and hangover cure. The café still has the requisite broken-tile floors, (faux) cane chairs, and puffing poseurs—now banished to the smoking terrace—it had in market days, and even the onion soup. From its tiny round outdoor tables I have often observed groups of Les Halles adolescents, and I always wonder how much they know of the site's historical, literary, and political significance. As a matter of fact, they probably know more than any other segment of society: in the second decade of the twenty-first century every French high schooler still studies Zola's work inside out, upside down.

To understand why the neighborhood means so much to so many Parisians, you've got to do as the kids do and crack open Zola and the history books. You discover that this has always been the city's market district—"always" meaning for at least the past nine hundred years. Granted, nowadays it's a challenge to evoke watery Champeaux, the medieval pilgrimage route that ran by on Rue Saint-Martin, or the succession of marketplaces that operated hereabouts, starting with King Louis VI's stalls of 1137. There's no trace, for that matter, of Emperor Philippe Auguste's walled market compound from 1183. Of François the First's Renaissance market arcades (built from 1534 to 1572) only photographs from the nineteenth century remain. That's because, in keeping with the preternaturally Parisian tabula rasa tradition, Emperor Napoléon III toppled them in his seismic Second Empire redesign of the district from 1852 to 1856. Did Parisians protest then? I wonder. Those who did presumably wound up floating in the Seine, or exiled to a penal colony.

The tale of Baltard's much-lamented pavilions, conceived at the behest of Paris Prefect Claude-Philibert Barthelot, Comte de Rambuteau, in 1848, accounts for a little over one-eighth of the market district's nine-hundred-year history. But the structures were—by all accounts, especially Zola's—magnificent not only to look at. Unlike today's Forum the market's energy was electrifying.

Le Ventre de Paris, written by Zola in 1873, is part of the Rougon-Macquart saga, a multiple-volume series. When the bespectacled, shortsighted author first stumbled upon Les Halles one sleepless night in 1869, he found "all the blossoming poetry of Paris's streets on the muddy sidewalk amid Les Halles's edibles." But as clear-eyed Frenchmen and schoolchildren know, *The Belly of Paris* is no facile ode, and its influence on sensitive souls can be profound. No doubt it influenced my dark vision of Les Halles, and to this day I still have difficulty seeing the lighter side.

The novel's ambivalent hero, Florent, mistaken for a revolutionary rioter and incarcerated on Devil's Island during the coup d'état that brought Napoléon III to power in 1851, upon his return in 1856 discovers the then-new Les Halles. Hemmed in by menacing cartloads of carrots, mountains of cabbages, and piles of potatoes, Florent is swept along by the raucous crowd, slipping on grease and discarded artichoke leaves in a horrifying cornucopia right out of Hieronymus Bosch.

Like Zola himself, Florent is fascinated by the architecture and life of Les Halles—"the luminous, polished transparency" of the panes flooded with dawn's light, the "slender herringbone pillars, the elegant curves of the woodwork ceiling, the geometric outlines of the roofs." In the pavilion's vaulted cellars Florent discovers Champeaux's secret waters flowing into giant urns and tanks full of live fish. In the bright, prosperous charcuterie where he works, Florent is mesmerized by the abundance of hams, sausages, salami, lard, and other fatty, greasy, slippery delicacies, becoming increasingly obsessed by the corresponding plumpness and carnivorous contentment of the men and women around him—exemplars of a budding consumerist economy.

The smell of the charcuterie, of Les Halles themselves, becomes intolerable, however. Florent develops chronic indigestion from the stench. The book's "belly" is no mere organ—it's a metaphor for the mouth, stomach, and burgeoning bowels of the Second Empire's nouveaux riches, for bodily functions, for the disquieting alimentary realities of bourgeois existence. As the novel closes the tormented Florent battles nightmare images of "giant vats, the vile rendering cauldrons where the fat of a nation was melted down."

Sit amid scores of contemporary tobacco freaks on a café terrace at Les Halles and you will soon feel you've been smoked like one of Florent's hams. Zola's words seem to ring in the air like the bells of Saint-Eustache. Was it perhaps the kind of unsentimental view Zola expressed that animated Pompidou and his speculator-sanitizers? From the 1940s on, succeeding administrations had threatened to remove the wholesale market, decried as unsanitary, overcrowded, rat-infested, the cause of traffic jams, and a drag on the economy. Some officials openly regretted the fact that central Paris—Les Halles in particular—had not been

destroyed in World War II. The first official eviction notice was issued in 1958. More than a decade later, the lure of potential profits
derived from building the new market at Rungis, the RER, and
the Forum, not to mention the thrill of seeing a bright new Pompidou Center rise from a remade neighborhood, became irresist-
ible. Reread Zola and you might suddenly realize why Baltard's
pavilions had to go, and why Pompidou exiled the one survivor to
a Belle Époque theme park far away. The pavilions were a threat:
had they been preserved on site they might indeed have become a
rallying point for the "rioters," "communists," and "hippies" Pompidou feared.

Luckily, on this bright spring day in the second decade of the
twenty-first century, I opted to skip Au Père Tranquille and have
coffee at the counter of unsung Le Bon Pêcheur across the street.
I also left Zola at home, and riffled instead my talismanic copy of
The Human Comedy. It was a natural leaven, as it had been when
I first read it in sunny California forty years ago. Try as I might,
though, I couldn't make the connection between Saroyan's classic and Les Halles. Why? A confession is in order: I'm even more
shortsighted than Zola was, and I'd meant to bring along an epi-
sode of Honoré de Balzac's *La Comédie humaine,* parts of which
are set in and around Les Halles. But I'd grabbed the wrong book,
an all-American human comedy. Same name, different setting.

As I sipped my coffee at Le Bon Pêcheur a disconcertingly
friendly gentleman of advanced years ran his index finger over
his pencil-thin Clark Gable mustache, tipped back his handsome
felt cap, and asked if I wasn't, perhaps, an export product from the
United States of America. When he heard an affirmative, he thrust
out his hand. He said his name was Marcel, and he thanked my
forebears for sacrificing so many of their "boys," as he put it, on the
beaches of Normandy. Their deaths had allowed him to live free.
He came from Normandy, he added amiably, though he'd been
in Paris for the past fifty years, and was a neighborhood regular. I
wondered aloud if he missed Les Halles of old. Marcel shook his

head. "My philosophy is simple," he declared, "look forward, do not look back. I don't even see those buildings anymore." He waved at the mirrored pavilions. Startling me again, he broke into song—he was an entertainer, he said. I recognized the old standard "C'est Magnifique," from the musical *Can-Can*. "Cole Porter," Marcel quipped. "I first heard it here in 1953. I love American music."

In a state of mild shock, I left Le Bon Pêcheur enchanted, and no longer recoiled at the view of Jean Willerval's corollas, or the piles of garbage from the golden-arched eatery by the Fontaine des Innocents. Trolling slowly home down alleys lined by architectural antiques, I had a reprise of my comforting thought of years past, a thought I often have when leaving Les Halles's neighborhood. It ushered me home to a premodern part of town spared Pompidou's attentions. Based on past performance, I reminded myself, whatever Les Halles's next version is, it could not be much worse than what's there today, and it will be a long time coming. In the meantime, I will be re-reading Zola, and diving into Balzac's many-volume *La Comédie humaine*. I might even watch *Irma La Douce* again—at "Rue du Cinéma" this time around—and eat a gross of popcorn.

Hit the Road Jacques

Id est oppidum parisiorum positum in insula fluminis Se-quanae. (It is a town of the Parisii situated on an island of the river Seine.)

—JULIUS CAESAR, *The Gallic Wars*

One afternoon on the rooftop terrace of the Pompi-dou Center I gazed beyond the Plexiglas tubes and primary-colored pipes at the people beetling along Rue Saint-Martin. It's the straightaway edging the center's sunken plaza. How many of those pedestrians, I wondered with something like an epiphany, realized they were walking on Paris's oldest thoroughfare, the north-south axis the Romans called *cardo-maximus*—as in cardinal points? This particular *cardo* is older even than Rome, archaeologists agree. It lies atop the trade route that in the Bronze Age linked northern Europe via the Celtic settlement of the Parisii tribe to the Mediterranean.

All roads may well lead to Rome but some, including Rue Saint-Martin, are more direct than others. Entering Paris from the north at what is now the suburb of Saint-Denis, this ancestor of the city's roadways runs underneath Rue Philippe de Girard, changes names half a dozen times, and leaves town heading south past the Cité Universitaire campus. Well, it did leave town once upon a time, until president Georges Pompidou had the Boulevard Périphérique built. Now the road dead-ends into the beltway—and metaphorically goes underground, emerging many miles later in the blighted *banlieue*.

Ever practical, the ancient Romans straightened and paved the beaten Bronze Age path. In the Middle Ages pilgrims adopted it, renaming the Left Bank portion in honor of Saint-Jacques-le-Majeur—Saint James the Greater. Starting in the ninth century, his sanctuary in Compostela, near Spain's Atlantic coast, became Christendom's third-most popular pilgrimage destination after Rome and Jerusalem. Thousands of questers for more than a thousand years caressed The Way of Saint James with their clogs or bare feet. It's hard to imagine how many blisters this road has engendered.

A few years after glimpsing the Roman road from the Pompidou's rooftop, I was seized by a fit of inspired madness. Alison and I set out from Paris to cross France on foot following Roman roads and the Way of Saint James, a three-month, 750-mile romp. It wasn't a religious pilgrimage, but rather a maverick journey of self-discovery and physical regeneration (chronicled in the upcoming book, to be called *Hit the Road Jacques*). Before leaving Paris, we broke in our boots on the *cardo-maximus,* a friendly nod to our Roman forebears and Saint James. Happily the Parisian prelude to our journey proved a pleasant, day-long, six-mile saunter down the city's longest memory lane.

Ours started as all good hikes start, with coffee and croissants.

The setting—the Gare de l'Est—was unusual. But this train station sits astride the Roman highway, its rails teasing out the lay-lines of old. North of it there's nothing much to see, ancient or modern. From the station south, however, the cityscape becomes increasingly intriguing.

We made our first stop across the street at 148 Rue du Faubourg-Saint-Martin. In the early 1600s, Queen Marie de Médicis waved her wand and created the Récollets convent here. It was ransacked by the requisite Revolutionaries, and went from barracks to weaving-works, hospice to military hospital before becoming a squatters' stronghold. Part of the cloister disappeared in 1926. Other chunks were swallowed by the expanding Gare de l'Est. Long a moody place we actively avoided, nowadays it houses the Maison de l'architecture, with working spaces and apartments for visiting architects. Beyond the freshly restored colonnaded front, in a quiet courtyard we discovered Café de la Maison. Had we known of it, we would have skipped the station's paper cups and bitter brew.

In 1844 and 1852, when the Grand Boulevards and train stations were being built, road workers unearthed the northern bed of the *cardo,* from the Seine to the Square Saint-Laurent. Like the layer-cake of stratified roads, Paris's churches also commonly sit atop ancient sites—temples to stone-age Earth goddesses, Celtic deities, and of course Roman gods. About fourteen hundred years ago Grégoire de Tours mentioned a Saint-Laurent chapel on the ancient highway, and here, we discovered, it was, much altered.

The Renaissance nave of Saint-Laurent is part of the hodge-podge whose homely façade and neo-Gothic bell tower date to 1862. Candles flickered, a symbolic link, perhaps, to the Merovingian monks buried beneath the church circa AD 550. Their tombs were uncovered in 1680. Lower strata are older—much older, say experts.

In *Conquest of Gaul,* better known as *The Gallic Wars,* Caesar mentions the country's fine roads. That the Gauls had their own highway network is news to most contemporary readers, and was news to me. Rome demanded standardized straightaways. They were precisely 4.5 meters wide—fourteen feet. This allowed chariots to pass side-by-side unimpeded. Roman roads are the ancestors of our dual carriageways and Interstates. Roman engineers improved what they found as they conquered territory and built cities.

It's not surprising then that Rue du Faubourg-Saint-Martin runs straight and true from Square Saint-Laurent through the three-arched Porte Saint-Martin, a Roman-style triumphal gateway built in 1674 to celebrate French victories in Besançon and Limburg. It's said Louis XIV fancied himself the divine-right heir of the emperors. Here, sculpted on the north entablature, he appears in Roman garb. We walked through and stared up: on the south side the Sun King is portrayed as Hercules, wearing little other than a big wig.

As Rue Saint-Martin runs south the concentration of historic sites along its route multiplies. The Arts et Métiers museum, housed in the former Saint-Martin-des-Champs priory, tempted us to investigate. Martin reportedly worked miracles here in AD 385. The handsome, airy library is in a reconverted thirteenth-century refectory designed by the same architect who created the Sainte-Chapelle. We wandered through it and several atmospheric courtyards, but knew we would need hours to absorb the history and enjoy the displays. They range from steam engines and scientific instruments to Foucault's pendulum—the real one.

We ambled out to the church next door, Saint-Nicolas-des-Champs. It lies just south of Rue de Turbigo. This unprepossessing sanctuary surprised us with a spacious deambulatory for Saint-Jacques pilgrims. We deambulated as quietly as we could in our boots, passing behind the altar. A handful of faithful prayed. Clearly, we were the only outsiders.

It's challenging to keep on the *cardo*'s straight and narrow. Nearby streets beckon. For instance, three blocks farther southeast at 51 Rue de Montmorency stands Paris's oldest house, from

1407. It's raked backward from sculpted stone foundations, and has been remodeled too many times to count. Somehow it maintains the endearing quality of things ancient, those ever-rarer time capsules that survive.

In it lived Nicolas and Pernelle Flamel, wealthy booksellers. It's said they were alchemists, able to turn base metals into gold. To cover their diabolical activities, the couple underwrote part of Saint-Jacques-de-la-Boucherie, or so conspiracy theorists claim. Like the Flamels, the church is no longer, though the tower stands. We could see its summit over the roofs half a mile south.

Former French president François Mitterrand obsessed about the east-west "Power Axis," an imaginary line from the Arc de Triomphe to the Louvre. Pompidou, a classical scholar before he entered politics, preferred the Celtic-Roman-Pilgrim's axis we were on. The buildings on Rue Saint-Martin that still front the Pompidou Center are a mere four hundred years old, and Pompidou clearly felt many others nearby were dispensable. He had them demolished, to make way for his temple of contemporary art. If the center lasts another four hundred years, will it no longer house contemporary art as we know it today? When does contemporary become antique or ancient?

These questions accompanied me two blocks south to Saint-Merri. You wouldn't guess it from the exterior, but this church plunges its foundations into late Antiquity. That was when the early popes in Rome upheld the crumbling empire by forcibly converting "Barbarians" into Catholics. Saint-Merri subsumed an older chapel, the resting place of Carolingian miracle-worker Médéric, whose name was later shortened to Merri. Rebuilt three times in its first thousand years, the current church is late-flamboyant Gothic, from 1520 to 1560. Gargoyle spouts stared down at us, commanding us to enter. We listened to an organist practicing in a cloud of incense, then hit the road again.

Rising over Rue de Rivoli and a handsome corner park, the vestigial Tour Saint-Jacques is a blinding shade of white after bottom-up rebuilding that took many years and cost millions. Another marvel of the flamboyant Gothic, built from 1509 to 1523, the freestanding tower lost its church: Saint-Jacques-de-la-Boucherie was quarried during the Revolution.

At 54 meters—nearly 180 feet—the tower's silhouette is still one of Paris's tallest. It's also among my favorites anywhere, for all the wrong reasons.

As part of the groundwork for our hike across France, before setting out on the *cardo* I read everything I could about the Tour Saint-Jacques, its phantom church, and Paris's role in the pilgrimage business. Anyone with a superstitious rib in his body should flee at the sight of the tower. Its history is a chronicle of misfortunes. They should remind us of the fragility of man and stone—limestone.

Caesar's north-south *cardo* and east-west *decumanus* meet where the tower now stands, making the Square Saint-Jacques the ideal spot for Christians to top a Pagan crossroads with a shrine. Nothing is known of the first sanctuary built here, but by 1259 it had grown into Saint-Jacques-de-la-Boucherie—Saint James of the Butcher Shop. Mystery wraps the figure of Nicolas Flamel, its most famous patron. In 1418 he died and was buried under the church. His ghost came back to haunt the tower, it's said, and caused its ruin.

Crowning the tower is an effigy of Saint Jacques three times lifesize, surrounded by phantasmagoric sculptures nearly as tall symbolizing the Evangelists, all of them copies. Strangely, Saint-Jacques does not point south along his pilgrimage road. He looks west, because his relics arrived on Spain's west coast by sea.

In 1797, the church was deconstructed, with the proviso that the tower be spared. A certain Monsieur Dubois bought it, sold the bells to a foundry, and set up a gun-shot factory inside. Under the tower's roof Dubois's cauldrons melted lead. The molten metal was poured through a broad seive and formed pellets. By free-falling about 150 feet into tanks of cold water they formed perfectly round shot. Dubois was the real alchemist—turning lead into hard cash. Maybe that's why Flamel's ghost returned—with a vengeance. The factory caught fire three times, and the tower periodically cracked and threatened to crumble for the next two hundred years.

It was scientist François Arago who persuaded King Louis Philippe to buy back the gutted ruin in the 1830s. Along came Emperor Napoléon III. Unlike his great-uncle he was no enemy of Rome. In 1854, when Napoléon III commanded that Rue de Rivoli and parallel Avenue Victoria be widened and straightened, the Saint-Jacques compound became a park, designed by the emperor's favorite architect, Jean-Charles-Adolphe Alphand. An octagonal base with fourteen steps was built—and numerologists to this day have failed to assign signficance to the number.

For nearly one thousand years, from the convent and tower of Saint-Jacques pilgrims set forth, crossing Pont Notre-Dame to the cathedral, then striding out to Chartres, Orléans, and Spain, following the ancient Roman road. Today's pilgrims generally take a bus. The Celtic merchants of pre-Roman antiquity—dealers primarily in tin—were not so lucky. Around 1000 BC they began crossing the Seine in dugouts, or they waded across the natural fords on the north and south sides of Île de la Cité. Time and again the Celts erected rickety footbridges in the latter days of Lutetia, before Caesar showed up in 52 BC. Rome eventually transformed the footbridges into Paris's first permanent spans. Rebuilt at least a dozen times, the Petit Pont has bridged the same spot from the island to the Left Bank, with variations on the name "little bridge," for more than two thousand years.

We'd only walked a hundred yards up Rue Saint-Jacques when we reached the churches of Saint-Séverin and Saint-Julien-le-Pauvre, on opposite sides. Both have sixth-century pedigrees. Each is worth a patient visit. The less impressive of the two, Saint-Julien-le-Pauvre nonetheless seemed a must: it's home not only to three holy-water fonts shaped like a pilgrim's scallop shell, symbol of Saint-Jacques. Better still, the church's foundations and the wellhead in the forecourt sit atop Roman paving stones. They were lifted from the crossroads of Rue Saint-Jacques and Rue Galande—Paris's other major Roman road, which branched east from here to Lyon, long the capital of Gaul. Up that road came Rome's warriors, but also the language, religion, foods, wine, and rudiments of culture that the later inhabitants of what's now called France so skillfully absorbed, reinterpreted, and renamed *en français.*

Almost as exciting was what we discovered at 21 Rue Saint-Jacques: a sculpted 1500s doorway, pocket-size courtyards, an eighteenth-century house, and two spiraling stairwells guarded by plump cats. In the courtyard of nearby 67 we found another sculpted door and balcony.

The treasure hunt was on. One block west of the intersection of Rue Saint-Jacques and Boulevard Saint-Germain stands the scallop-shell-encrusted former Paris residence of the abbots of Cluny. They were Rome's right arm in France, with the biggest church outside the Vatican, and were even bigger in the pilgrimage business. Cluny's thousand franchise churches were way stations on Saint-Jacques's highway to Spain. Their turreted townhouse is now the museum of the Middle Ages, better known as the Musée de Cluny.

We marched around the museum's medieval garden, searching for the original sculptures from the Tour Saint-Jacques, the ones symbolizing the Evangelists. Three are here, weather-worn beyond recognition. Inside, on the stairway leading to the "Lady with the Unicorn" tapestry, hanging on the wall we found another Saint-Jacques treasure: Nicolas Flamel's cryptic epitaph carved in stone, many times lost before being displayed here. Appropriately for our quest, the foundations and lower floors of the museum are in the ancient Roman baths of Lutetia, where Emperor Julian the Apostate and countless other patricians soaked and steamed when Paris was the capital of the empire.

Rue Saint-Jacques climbs past the Sorbonne and the ungainly Lycée Louis-le-Grand. At the top of the rise we stopped for the view back, trying but failing to envision the ancient city. A few paces away, a plaque at 14 Rue Soufflot marks where the thirteenth-century Jacobin convent once stood. Ironically it lent its name to a university department where, five hundred years later, in 1789, Jacobin revolutionaries met and wreaked havoc on the church of Rome.

For a millennium—from the Merovingians to the Revolution—this area was studded with monasteries, monuments, and private mansions and ringed by walls. The carriage door at 151 bis Rue Saint-Jacques, a Louis XV townhouse restored in 2006, stood open. We helped ourselves. In the courtyard looms an impressive house with a horseshoe-shaped staircase, curving balconies, and sculpted grotesque faces.

The Roman aqueduct from Arcueil to the baths at Cluny flanked the *cardo* for much of its length. Sections were revealed here in the 1890s and again by excavations in 2006. The road narrows briefly to premodern dimensions. At number 172 a plaque recalls the Saint-Jacques gate in the Philippe Auguste walls, demolished in 1684. Curving Rue des Fossés Saint-Jacques marks the path of the moat.

Enchanted, we tracked back and forth across the street, admiring the gilded grillwork at Au Port Salut, a 1700s pilgrims' inn, still in business. Carved on the heavy door of 169 are scallop shells, usually an indication that the property's owner had walked to Compostela and back. Another kind of throwback in this high-rent district is a mechanic's garage in the cavernous courtyard of 179.

The narrowest point in the *cardo* lies between numbers 187 and 216—where writer Blaise Cendrars lived. Emulating Caesar, I measured out six paces and frowned. The road was even narrower than the original Roman highway. That's because from the 1200s on, convents and abbeys colonized off-street lots. Private buildings shouldered in front along the roadside.

The plaque that used to be on number 218 disappeared with the latest replastering, I guessed. I knew from earlier visits that in a long-gone 1200s townhouse that had stood here, Jean de Meung penned the bulk of the medieval bestseller *Roman de la Rose.*

One of Paris's stranger pieces of architecture is the neo-Romanesque, rusticated Institut Océanique at 193, abutting Rue Gay-Lussac. A Roman villa with thermal baths surfaced under it in the mid-1800s, reaching as far as number 240.

Ever curious, we explored courtyards not yet locked by Digicodes. Instead of finding ancient mosaics we enjoyed unadulterated Parisian atmosphere—until several ferocious concierges chased us out.

The trouble with walking the *cardo* is, there's far too much to see in a day. Determined to make it across town before nightfall, we marched on, into the baroque barn of Saint-Jacques-du-Haut-Pas, at 252. Though only from 1630 to 1685, this church evokes the Order of Haut-Pas—Christian knights who in the 1100s protected pilgrimage routes linking France to Rome. Off the echoing nave we spotted a statue of Jacques. His wall-eyes followed us out.

The Paris headquarters of the Commanderie du Haut-Pas were a few yards south at 254. Above the carriage entrance is their insignia, but the building is gone. Many landmarks like it have disappeared, some as recently as the 1990s. The Ferme Saint-Jacques at 262, for instance, was replaced by an exemplary eyesore. Gutted, number 289 became subsized housing. And 328 might just be the most egregious postmodern steel-and-granite bunker in town.

Happily other landmarks have survived. Courtyards, doorways, and dormers—like those at 283 and 284—hint at centuries past. We were glad to see the former Benedictine Couvent des Anglais at 269–269 bis. "Schola Cantorum" is carved over the entrance. Dance, music, and drama students came and went, seemingly unimpressed by the corinthian columns, a sweeping staircase, and an unexpected garden court.

Repaved and equipped with benches, the half-moon plaza facing Val-de-Grâce convent seemed a good place to rest. From it our eyes inspected the convent's ironwork, forecourt flanked by square pavilions, and immense baroque façade. We lucked out, wandering into a wedding ceremony. The initials "A.L." appear everywhere at Val-de-Grâce. They stand for the insitution's founder, Anne of Austria, and her husband Louis XIII. Saint Peter's and the Chiesa del Gesù in Rome inspired the convent's triple-aisle nave, soaring dome, and Bernini-style baldachin. Dazed by an overdose of architectural details, we fled outside.

Rue du Faubourg-Saint-Jacques starts at Boulevard de Port-Royal. Behind a smog-blackened building and the Stalinesque Cochin medical school hides an arcaded cloister from 1625, these days part of the Baudeloque maternity ward. We sat amid clipped yew trees and heard the future of France wail.

The *cardo*'s last miles pack less charm per step, but we were pleased to remark l'Observatoire on our right and, kitty corner, the centuries-old Faculté de Théologie—a grimy, soulful address whose theology courses are in keeping with the road's pilgrim past.

Saint-Jacques is also the name of a leafy boulevard and an early 1900s Métro station, where the Faubourg becomes Rue de la Tombe-Issoire. As we walked toward Parc Montsouris, a landscaped enclave on the edge of town, I remembered the legendary giant Ysorre, the origin of these curious names. In ancient times, outside the city limits Roman tombs lined the road.

Beyond the Cité Universitaire greenbelt, the *cardo*-cum-Way-of-Saint-James becomes a potholed off-ramp from the Boulevard Périphérique. On it cars roared three abreast in both directions. We pondered the snarled colossus Pompidou built, diesel-scented tears in our eyes. Saint James would surely not have approved, but I couldn't help thinking, irreverently, that Julius Caesar would have loved it.

PARIS
PEOPLE

Coco Chanel

Chanel, General de Gaulle, and Picasso are the three most important figures of our time.

—ANDRÉ MALRAUX

Fashion is the handmaiden of false consciousness.

—Attributed to WALTER BENJAMIN

Haute couture has long struck me as residing somewhere on the scale of human endeavor between useless and obnoxious. Yet I've been fascinated for years by the figure of Coco Chanel, an ambivalent figure if ever there was one, and somehow, for me, the incarnation of a peculiar breed of Parisian. I once had the privilege, usually reserved for VIPs and big spenders, of visiting Coco's private hideaway in Rue Cambon in Paris. Ever since, certain Paris places associated with Coco have echoed with a special resonance for me: Rue Cambon, Rue de Rivoli and its unchanging Angelina tearoom, and Place Vendôme with the venerable Hôtel Ritz. She was not just a denizen of this so-called Golden Triangle—the city's ritziest neighborhood—for some sixty years, until her death in 1971. She was its archetype and mistress.

Arbiter of unfeminine yet unmistakably female elegance for half a century, lover of men both rich and famous, Coco cut and shaped her past like a suit of clothes. For instance, she fancied herself born in 1893, the daughter of a well-to-do winegrower from Saumur, in the Loire Valley. The truth is her birthday was ten years earlier than that, and her impoverished and unloving father, a street hawker, sent her to be brought up by nuns in a draughty medieval monastery in the Massif Central. Coco's mother, Jeanne Devolle, died in 1895 of tuberculosis, in utter destitution.

Throughout her long life, Chanel moved between two worlds, one real and the other imaginary. Unloved, she lived for love. Despite her countless conquests, from English noblemen to Russian dukes, she spent years alone, work her only solace. Coco knew little about literature, art, or music. Yet in Paris her pet celebrities were men the likes of Igor Stravinsky, Pablo Picasso, and Jean Cocteau. She never worshipped money but nonetheless made a fortune with her hats, suits, and perfumes. A social outcast from the provinces, she came to rule Paris society and almost single-handedly revolutionized the way women around the world dressed, smelled, and behaved, a feat impossible to contemplate in today's anything-goes world of street fashion and cultural eclecticism. Cocteau described her as at once spiteful, creative, extravagant, loveable, humorous, generous, hateful, and excessive, "a unique character." Uniquely Parisian, I would add.

Despite the work of a dozen biographers, several of whose tomes I've read over the years, Chanel remains an enigma. However, she has left behind her in certain Paris places an unmistakable whiff of stale perfume, a fleeting reflection in a wavy mirror, like the one that fills the wall alongside table eleven at Angelina, the time-capsule tearoom on Rue de Rivoli, facing the Tuileries.

Coco always sat at table eleven and everyone at Angelina knew her. The establishment opened for business in 1903 under the name Rumpelmayer but Coco would've been too poor to go there then. It became her refuge late in life, in the 1950s, when a quiet cup of hot cocoa was a daily ritual. Back then, the faux Louis XVI armchairs in the downstairs salons were covered in green, not brown patent leather as they are today. Otherwise the pleasantly worn décor hasn't changed. Her marble-topped table is still the third from the back in the main room, set against the fifteen-foot mirror. Coco had a thing about looking glasses. She could observe herself in them, certainly, but she could also watch the world in reflection, one step removed. She would sit at table eleven, order her *chocolat africain* and gaze at her wizened reflection, surrounded by the tearoom's sculpted plaster encrustations and faded Belle Époque murals of Mediterranean scenes. Those who knew her well say she was in fact looking into her past, as into a crystal ball that somehow transported her backward in time.

I sat at her table not long ago, a biography in hand, and enjoyed a plump raisin roll and a rich cup of cocoa. The fashion shows, under way in the Tuileries across the street, had not caused an overflow at Angelina. Near me a blue-rinse matron caressed her lapdog. She dug her spoon into a bowl of whipped cream, topped her cocoa, and smiled contentedly at the young men and women nearby, escapees, perhaps, from the pages of Henry James. I squinted and imagined she was Coco, slipping through her looking glass.

For the record, Gabrielle Chanel preferred to forget not only her infancy and childhood but also her early years in Moulins, in southern France, before the First World War, when she was a shop assistant and seamstress by day, a *café-concert* singer by night. From that far-off Belle Époque echoes the nickname given to Gabrielle by the army officers who hung out at Moulin's La Rotonde to hear her sing. She knew only two songs, one of which ran *"Qui qu'a vu Coco dan l'Trocadéro"*—"Who's seen Coco at the Trocadero?" They shouted *"Coco! Coco!"* when calling for encores. Étienne Balsan, a French gentleman infantry officer of considerable means, was among them. He was Coco's first famous lover.

Addicted to horseflesh and racy mademoiselles, Balsan the bon vivant was smitten. He offered to finance her, first during her short-lived stage career (where she learned about theater costumes and makeup) and later as a milliner. The nuns had taught Coco to sew and embroider. From an aunt she had learned to decorate hats. At Royallieu, Étienne Balsan's lavish residence and stud farm near Compiègne, north of Paris, Chanel was installed as official mistress and soon began making hats for society ladies and *irrégulières*—unmarriageable women like her.

A natural sportswoman, Coco rode horses as well as a man could, and adopted the clothes of the English gentleman rider. Her unusual attire, along with her wit and sharp tongue, quickly earned her a reputation as formidable. Balsan's best friend was the star of this horsey set, a rich English polo player named Arthur "Boy" Capel. His infatuation with Coco was matched only by her passion for him.

Edmonde Charles-Roux, Chanel's longtime friend and probably her best hagiographer, once noted that Coco, the model of the modern, independent woman, was "formed, discovered, and invented by men." Balsan raised her out of poverty but it was Boy

Capel who gave her true happiness—for a time. Chanel liked to say that Boy was the man of her life, the only one who understood her passion and thirst for freedom. Capel introduced her to his society friends and helped her expand from a modest shop at 160 Boulevard Malesherbes in Paris to his own lavish digs at number 138 down the street. He also set her up with a workshop in Rue Cambon and a stylish boutique in Deauville, the Parisians' seaside retreat, summer headquarters of Europe's great and good. He made it clear she would remain his friend and lover but would never become his wife.

After Boy's marriage to a proper lady, and his sudden death a few months later in a car accident, Coco took to men, and work, the way some people take to drink. Her unstoppable rise began in the Roaring Twenties, a decade cast in her image. She bought the luxurious Villa Bel Respiro in Paris's suburbs and began entertaining Stravinsky, Cocteau, the poet Pierre Reverdy, Serge Diaghilev of the Ballets Russes, and the pianist and artists' muse Misia Sert, for decades her closest friend. Gone were the social constraints of her youth. Among her artist comrades Coco was no longer an *irrégulière.*

The taste of Angelina chocolate, and the echo of the slender Coco's high heels, followed me the few blocks from Rue de Rivoli's mosaic-paved arcades north. Swann, the long-established British-American pharmacy in Rue de Castiglione, evoked Proust. A block east the rare books illustrated by Joan Miró, Max Ernst, and Jean Cocteau displayed in the windows of Librairie les Arcades brought my mind back to Coco. The traffic on Rue du Faubourg-Saint-Honoré was thick. Still, I was able to smell the perfume wafting out of the historic Chanel boutiques nearby at numbers 27 and 31 Rue Cambon. It was on these hallowed premises, during my fortuitous visit to Coco's upstairs apartment, that I heard the story of how Chanel No. 5 was born. Shortly after World War I, some Russian friends introduced Chanel to Grand Duke Dmitri Pavlovich Romanov, the murderer of Rasputin, exiled even before the Revolution of 1917. In 1920 Coco took as a lover this penniless aristocrat a decade her junior, keeping him in a style to which he had once been accustomed. In return Dmitri taught her about the heady scents of the tsar's court, and introduced her to Ernest Beaux, perfumer extraordinaire. A year later, Beaux brought her five phials containing scents intended to express the quintessence of her sartorial styles. Coco sniffed the first four and shook her head. She might've named the last one, marked number five, the sweet smell of success.

Winding upward one floor from the showroom of the Rue Cambon boutique is the mirrored staircase atop which Coco perched, unseen, to watch models show off her clothes. The private apartment upstairs is off-limits, marked with a sign: MADEMOISELLE—PRIVÉ. The two immaculate, slightly chilling rooms are not so much a museum as a shrine, dedicated to the memory of Coco—to a certain official version of Coco, I should add. An unrepentant frump troubled by Coco's wartime record, I found myself seated on the vast leather couch where she loved to nap wrapped in a mink blanket. Her eyeglasses sat somewhere nearby and I felt they were staring at me archly, the way insiders say Coco stared at unwelcome critics. Her possessions, displayed for the delight of select reverent visitors, include a pair of Chinese Coromandel screens, plus books, sculptures, and *objets d'art,* all of them reflected ad infinitum in the mirrors Coco cherished. Especially egregious are the Venetian Renaissance sculptures of black slaves of which reportedly she felt particularly fond. On a coffee table facing the couch among the gold baubles lie the heraldic arms of Westminster. I remember asking myself why they were there, and finding the answer months later, in a biography.

Coco's Slavic period lasted a few years, with Dmitri eventually marrying an American heiress who had means and a more pliable character. Coco continued to mount the social ladder, nonetheless, by moving into a sumptuous two-story apartment at number 29 Rue du Faubourg-Saint-Honoré, just a few minutes away on foot.

As I strolled toward it through bumper-to-bumper BMWs and Mercedes I reflected on the fact that at Coco's lavish digs Stravinsky and Diaghilev had been regulars. Picasso came to stay while working on stage sets for Cocteau's *Antigone.* It's well known that Picasso was a peerless womanizer but hardly anyone remembers that the man-eating Coco snacked on him here between meals. It was at this felicitous juncture that the poet Pierre Reverdy, like Chanel an ambitious product of the provinces, became her third famous lover.

The apartment they shared is in private hands and I've never managed to get closer to it than the unremarkable downstairs entrance hall. Nothing remains from the time of Chanel except the memories the site summons. Reverdy, deep in spiritual crisis, eventually left her in Paris. But Coco was not lonely for long. In Monte Carlo she had caught the eye of Bend'Or, nickname of the Duke of Westminster, the richest man in England. He swept her away on his yacht, *Flying Cloud,* and before the year was out they were inseparable. Their whirlwind romance was to last for half a decade. Despite what appeared to be a never-ending vacation, in 1926 Coco managed to invent prêt-à-porter fashion with her "little black dress," the revolutionary garment American *Vogue* dubbed "the Ford signed Chanel."

The Duke of Westminster did as dukes do and broke Coco's heart by announcing his engagement to a certain Loelia Mary Ponsonby, whose very name makes anyone without blue blood sneeze. Again, Coco rebounded. In short order Paul Iribe, a flamboyant caricaturist, jewelry designer, and magazine editor, took up the flame. It was under Iribe's guidance that Chanel began creating diamond jewelry, spin-offs of which are still sold today. In the spring of 1934, tired of the housekeeping, perhaps, she moved from the Faubourg-Saint-Honoré to a nest at the Hôtel Ritz overlooking Rue Cambon, where she lived on and off for the rest of her life.

A stroll from the Faubourg to Place Vendôme takes you

through several acres of old and new money. Leading jewelers such as Cartier, Bulgari, and Van Cleef & Arpels wink at you, the Chanel shop set among them. Fashion boutiques, upscale hotels, and Michelin-starred restaurants abound. This was Coco's Paris, the snooty summit, the tip of the tallest peak an impoverished, uneducated provincial climber could reach. Nowadays the Ritz offers clients what's known as the Chanel Suite, though it has little to do with her digs (she lived on the opposite side of the hotel). It's certainly not a shrine: you can rent the 1,549-square-foot apartment for about ten thousand dollars a night. Most mere mortals who ask to see it are directed to ritzparis.com for a virtual tour to the strains of Mozart. However if you ask very politely, dress nicely, and have the good fortune to time your request with a vacancy, you might be able to peek in without paying.

Redone recently under the direction of an art historian and advisor to Karl Lagerfeld, the furniture embraces the styles of Louis XVI, the Directoire and the Empire; in other words, it is gilt and gaudy, presumably the way Chanel liked it. "Sixty craftsmen worked around the clock for two months," says the Ritz, "to complete this work of art, perfect in every detail." The taps in the stone-clad bathroom are gold plated. There are even Coromandel screens like the ones in Coco's Rue Cambon sanctuary. Views from the windows take in the eighteenth-century architectural gems lining Place Vendôme and, of course, the celebrated column with its imitation Imperial Roman low-relief sculptures. Like so many symbols of oppression, it was toppled more than once by riffraff and re-erected by the powers that be.

The one time I talked my way into the suite I couldn't help staring out of the window, contemplating the column—and the fact that in 1934, when she first checked into the Ritz, Coco's enterprises boomed despite the worldwide Depression and the violent workers' riots and strikes in which her own employees took part. Business roared for her throughout the grim thirties, in fact.

But money wasn't everything to Chanel. The premature death

of her beloved Iribe in 1935 seemed to prove yet again that Coco was as unlucky in love as she had been successful in commerce. A few years later, even that changed: the distant thunder of the Second World War was beginning to shake Coco's comfortable universe. In the summer of 1939 she fled Paris. During the Occupation, however, she quietly moved back into the Ritz. And the darkest period of her life began, a decade in which her name was attached to that of the shadowy "von D.," a German intelligence officer. It's this period that makes Chanel's business heirs cringe, and is rarely, if ever, mentioned by anyone remotely associated with the Chanel fashion or perfume houses.

How did Coco Chanel escape the punishment meted out after the Occupation to the women who fraternized with the Nazis? As André Malraux, the celebrated essayist, critic, and first-ever French minister of culture, said, "Chanel, General de Gaulle, and Picasso are the three most important figures of our time." She had friends in high places in France and, as the baubles on her coffee table in Rue Cambon attest, elsewhere among the war's victors.

Chanel's self-imposed exile to Switzerland after the war lasted until 1954, when she made a comeback. She was seventy years old and had not shown a collection since 1939. Christian Dior was all the rage. Undaunted, Coco revived her Rue Cambon shop and set to work. The show, initially panned by the reigning fashion moguls and called a "fiasco" by London's then-influential *Daily Mail,* was hailed in America. The fame of her youth was revived. *Life* magazine credited her with revolutionizing the industry yet again. Asked who she dressed, Coco snapped, "Ask me who don't I dress!" Over the next seventeen years, until her last snip of the scissors in 1971, she lived between her suite at the Ritz and her Rue Cambon apartment and shop. "I was a rebellious child, a rebellious lover, a rebellious *couturière*—a real devil," she once confessed. That's not a bad epitaph for the twentieth century's greatest mind in fashion, a true Parisienne of the Golden Triangle.

Les Bouquinistes

*They buried him, but all through the night of mourning, in
the lighted windows, his books arranged three by three kept
watch like angels with outspread wings and seemed, for him
who was no more, the symbol of his resurrection.*

—MARCEL PROUST, *La Prisonnière*

Coffins. Dilapidated dolls' houses. Treasure chests encrusted with padlocks and bars. The battered green book boxes of the *bouquinistes,* Paris's quayside booksellers, slump evocatively along the Seine, anachronistic curiosities clinging to riverside parapets as they have for the past hundred-odd years.

A higgledy-piggledy wagon train several miles long loaded with something like five hundred thousand secondhand volumes, the boxes also overflow with posters, engravings, knickknacks, paintings, soft porn, leather-bound tomes, dusty paperbacks, statuettes, coins, coasters, and refrigerator magnets—the sublime, offensive, and ridiculous displayed side by side.

A city official once confirmed to me that there are about one thousand book boxes all told, all of them painted the same regulation *vert wagon*—the dark green of old train cars, old buses, old benches, and old railings left over from the Second Empire or the Third Republic. Despite the *règlement,* each box is a subtly different shade and shape, frosted here by lichen, blackened there by smog, rotted by rain and damp, scarred by reckless drivers and the inexorable passing of time, then patched and trussed and slathered with another layer of green paint. In the dark, especially on a wet moonless night, the boxes glistening under nineteenth-century street lamps take on a sinister, sepulchral cast—the objective correlatives of a dead Paris.

Look again on a sunny morning, though, when the booksellers who preside over the boxes make their way down the stone-paved sidewalks to unlock and prop open their treasure chests following a careful ritual, and the metaphors change. The battered *boîtes* morph into wood-and-tin grasshoppers lifting their legs, or gull-winged vessels carrying precious bundles from the reassuring past toward an uncertain future.

Squint, or use a telephoto lens to eliminate the traffic, and you can almost see novelist Anatole France—the most famous patron of late-nineteenth-century *bouquinistes*—picking through the swirling crowds, lifting a heavy volume then dickering over the price. It was in France's heyday in fact, in 1891, that the itinerant booksellers of Paris's quaysides were finally given the right to affix their boxes to the parapets, after about four hundred years of cat-and-mouse with municipal authorities. That game is now left to the unregistered, largely immigrant groups of bangle-hawkers who pack up and run at the approach of a gendarme.

I'm not sure why but I've always been drawn to the *bouquinistes*. To say I've befriended several would be an exaggeration, but as a regular customer I do know them and their wares. Many are great talkers, and a few know a good deal about the history of their trade. Apparently they take their name from the German *buchen* (books) or the Old Dutch *boeckin*—"little books." In French, therefore, a *bouquiniste* is a seller of *bouquins*. A *bouquineur* is a book lover, collector, or reader like me (and most of us have no room for *bouquins* in our tiny apartments, which is why we do book swaps, to keep down the height of the stacks). It's only logical, then, that the verb *bouquiner* means both "to troll the quays searching for books" and, more commonly, "to read up" or "study hard" by poring over textbooks.

Funnily no one I've talked to seems to know when these expressions were coined, though city records show that Paris's first printing press was installed in 1470 at the Sorbonne—fourteen years after Gutenberg printed the first *buch* in Mainz. *Bouquins* began to circulate immediately thereafter among the scholars and priests headquartered in the Left Bank's university neighborhoods. By 1500, the city's earliest permanent bookstores had begun to spring up there, and by around 1530, groups of itinerant booksellers were walking the streets of the Cité and the bridges connecting the island to either side of the Seine.

As is their wont, from the start, the powers that be regarded with a baleful eye these motley *bouquinistes*—suspicious, perhaps subversive indigents selling their wares off ground cloths or from trays hanging from straps around their shoulders. A 1577 police document compares them to "fences and thieves" in part because during the wars of religion, many *bouquinistes* sold Protestant pamphlets or "subversive tracts" printed abroad. Routinely the king's men would round up and jail the *bouquinistes*—or do worse.

In 1606, Paris police authorities decided to regulate the trade, limiting business activity to daylight hours and restricting the sphere of movement to the riverbanks "in the vicinity of the Pont-Neuf." These early booksellers were allowed to display their goods on the parapets and roadsides (there were no sidewalks back then in Paris, except on the Pont-Neuf itself). The number of vendors skyrocketed during the French Revolution, when the collections of countless noble families were confiscated and auctioned, or stolen by angry mobs, as patrician heads tumbled into bloody baskets in what's now Place de la Concorde. Eventually many of the aristocracy's books made their way into the hands of the *bouquinistes,* and in the course of the past two hundred years these valuable volumes have been sold and resold many times on the quays.

Order and symmetry have long been national obsessions among France's administrators, and they are regularly subverted by institutionalized revolution. The dimensions and distribution of the *bouquinistes*'s boxes go back to the Third Republic, when enlightened municipal officials decided to give the families of wounded veterans and war widows the right to leave their *boîtes* clamped to the riverside walls. A few minor reforms were made to the *règlement* in the 1940s (establishing the total length—exactly eight meters—of parapet allotted per *bouquiniste*) and in the 1950s (the uniform application of *vert wagon* as a color). In 1993, the City of Paris began requiring *bouquinistes* to open at least four days a week, limit consecutive days off to six weeks per year, buy a business license, and pay social security and income taxes (usually about thirty percent of declared gross revenues). Licenses now go to individuals from all walks of life, not just to needy families.

Predictably the *règlement* isn't always respected, but it has kept the worst abusers at bay. Of the four regulation green boxes each bookseller may exploit, at least three must now contain only books. In the fourth, the *bouquiniste* can display "souvenirs related to Paris," which explains the proliferation of miniature Eiffel Towers, Notre-Dame gargoyle paperweights, postcards, and faux-Hermès scarves showing the Arc de Triomphe or other monuments.

One day I buttonholed a youngish woman named Laurence Alsina, who turned out to be a fourth-generation *bouquiniste*. Her boxes face number sixty-five on the Left Bank's Quai de la Tournelle kitty-corner to Rue de Bièvre. "I was born on this sidewalk," she told me with understandable pride. "But we can no longer survive selling only books."

With Notre-Dame as a backdrop, Laurence has an ideal location, yet there are days, she noted, when she doesn't sell a single *bouquin*. Carefully wrapped in cellophane, her classics of literature, history, and travel are flanked by the usual selection of postcards and posters—the moneymakers. "In summer, tourists want secondhand classics like *Madame Bovary*," she sighed. "Off season, Parisian collectors, quayside regulars, and journalists buy out-of-print or rare books, but people just don't read as much anymore . . ."

The Internet, CDs and DVDs, videos and computer games have squeezed the *bouquinistes*'s market share. Still, Laurence's family runs three sets of boxes and shows no signs of giving up. Her father, Marcel Baudon, hails from the Quai de Montebello facing Shakespeare and Company. Her sister, Véronique le Goff, is on the Quai Saint-Michel near the RER station entrance, facing number three. Like most *bouquinistes*, the whole family is driven by an obsessive passion for books—quayside lifers call it *la maladie des livres*. It's also what keeps them going despite meager takings: city officials estimate average monthly earnings per licensee at one thousand to two thousand dollars.

For a long time I wondered where the *bouquinistes* got their books. From regulars like me, certainly, but small-time, occasional swap-traders are notoriously unreliable. It turns out that several days a week most *bouquinistes* rise before dawn's fingers start tickling the Seine, and drive to the scruffy suburbs or distant provinces to scour flea markets, attend auctions, or hit village yard sales—the best sources for books. Sometimes middlemen arrive with a truckload jumble rescued from an attic somewhere. Occasionally, burglars try to peddle stolen tomes, but street-smart sellers usually spot hucksters before they get a chance to finish their spiel. Or so it's said.

Competition comes not only from the Web and high-tech, or other secondhand bookstores. Every weekend year-round the Georges-Brassens book market is held under a nineteenth-century glass-and-iron structure at the Parc Georges-Brassens in the far-flung 15th arrondissement. It has become another favorite of serious collectors, though it lacks the charm—and convenience—of the quays.

Of Paris's approximately two hundred forty *bouquinistes,* perhaps two dozen are specialized—in crime novels, music books, military history, fine art, old magazines, incunabula, and so forth. When I'm looking for thrillers or jazz-related books, I go to bearded, affable Jacques Bisceglia, whose boxes face 31 Quai de la Tournelle. He has the biggest jazz-book collection in town, about eight hundred volumes, plus thousands of crime novels and detective stories—his second passion.

Across the Seine from Jacques, facing 48 Quai de l'Hôtel de Ville, a vigorous fellow named Michel Vigouroux, originally from Brittany, sells every book, magazine, or poster imaginable relating to his windswept native region. Down the same quay, Katia Lachnowicz, across from number seventy-two, deals in movie and theater books. Agnès Talec, facing 21 Quai des Grands-Augustins, displays almost every leaf of high-minded literature published by La Pléiade, while Jean-Claude Picon (across from 2 Quai de Gesvres) boasts a nearly complete collection of *Paris Match*—ah, for those weighty words and punchy photos! Some of the finest engravings and rare vintage books in town (and among the most expensive—up to one thousand dollars) are the specialty of Left-Bank institution Michelle Huchet-Nordmann (facing 35 Quai de Conti).

For most other *bouquinistes,* however, variety is the key to survival, so they sell a mixed bag. That means a dedicated *bouquineur* can spend entire days browsing the hundred Right-Bank *emplacements* between the Pont-Marie and Rue de l'Amiral-de-Coligny before crossing the Seine to the remaining hundred-fifty between the Pont Sully and Pont Royal. It's a workout but the views aren't bad and the characters you meet are often salty specimens of *homo parisianus.*

Fiercely independent, sometimes extroverted, sometimes surly, the *bouquinistes* are a caste apart. Solidarity is essential to survival. It takes about forty-five minutes to open or close a stall, for instance, so neighbors usually help each other. They share bottles of wine and stories, passing information along the quayside jungle *téléphone.* They know each other. They know who's selling what and for how much, and refer clients back and forth. Among themselves, they use only first names—"Go see Robert for that," they might tell you, giving an "address" as people once did before the days of street signs, "in front of Le Montebello . . ."

Robert, it turned out, was Paris's oldest working *bouquiniste* when I met him, a big man still at eighty-something, with luxuriant moustaches and a beard. He sells collectors' books and cheap paperbacks too, from a spot facing Le Montebello, a restaurant on the quay of the same name. Another celebrated sidewalk character is Jean-Jacques, whose *emplacement* faces 31 Quai de Conti. His nickname is *le Jacques Prévert des bouquinistes,* apparently because he's an expansive rhetorician. His passions are film, theater, and dance, and he doesn't have much time for uninitiated browsers.

One hundred yards east of Jean-Jacques, facing 55 Quai des Grands-Augustins, an eccentric newcomer to the business is a retired communications consultant named Guy. He sells a wide variety of books, but his true interest lies in exhibiting his own original oil or pastel paintings, which range from the figurative to the abstract. Purists scoff at Guy, seeing in his unconventional "gallery" the narrow edge of a Montmartre-style wedge. But it's hard to label his paintings as any more tasteless than the hundreds of pseudo-Sigmund Freud posters ("What's on a Man's Mind?— A Naked Woman!") on offer at dozens of other stands, and it's unlikely Montmartre's elephant train will ever catch on here.

I once conducted an informal survey, asking *bouquinistes* if they enjoyed their life. Most waxed lyrical about the freedom of being independent, the wonders of the book world, the magic of the quays, and the stimulation of daily encounters with people from around the world. But if pressed they often sighed or confessed. Weather is the *bouquinistes*'s main worry. Rain, especially, makes business difficult. Snow, high wind, cold, or burning sun can keep people off the quays for days at a time. And the elements take their toll on the booksellers themselves. "We're the peasants of Paris," said one wizened oldtimer I queried near Notre-Dame. "We listen to the weather reports like fishermen or farmers, then we come out anyway and get soaked, frozen, or sunburned."

You can account for the surliness of some *bouquinistes* by the combination of weathering and wear. They're stone-washed by the incessant tides of curious tourists who pick up books, unwrap them, put them back in the wrong place, and seem more interested in rummaging than buying. Then there are the city authorities and tax inspectors—always eager to check on strictly cash-in-hand businesses.

Most annoying and dangerous of all, however, is the car, truck, and bus traffic that thunders by, ever faster and thicker and more poisonous as the years go by. In the early 1990s, UNESCO declared the quays of the Seine a World Heritage Site, yet at the same time the city of Paris turned them into *axe rouge* expressways. Every stoplight is the start of a drag race. By afternoon, if there's no breeze, the air can be black with smog. The *bouquinistes* shake their heads at this and mutter words such as "nightmarish," "idiotic," and "incomprehensible." A modicum of relief has come of late in the form of the bike and bus lanes on the Left Bank and, in some places, wider sidewalks, but not all *bouquinistes* have benefited.

Despite the difficulties, the average age of the men and women on the quays has dropped from sixty (in the 1960s) to forty—proof of the profession's stubborn vitality or, perhaps, an indication of a desperate economic situation that drives the young toward marginal businesses. One thing is certain, there's never a shortage of applicants vying for a license or a spot. The waiting list usually stretches about eighty names long. It takes up to four years to get your first *emplacement*—always in a lousy location—and it might take you decades of hopscotch to wind up near Notre-Dame or the Pont-Neuf.

"You start in Purgatory," lifelong *bouquiniste* Laurence, near the cathedral, explained to me. "Purgatory is what we call the bad spots on the extreme ends of the quays—like the one my grandmother got in 1920 and I got twenty years ago. From Purgatory you work your way to a better life." She smiled, pointing to the buttresses of Notre-Dame soaring above the Seine's leafy banks. When the traffic had subsided, for a blissful moment, it did indeed seem like we were in Paradise.

Midnight, Montmartre, and Modigliani

It is a strange gray study in nature, this midnight Montmartre ... Artists with hope before them, poets with the appreciation of some girl only, and side by side with these the hurried anxious faces of unkempt women and tired-eyed men ...

—H. P. Hugh, 1899

C harles *The-Flowers-of-Evil* Baudelaire was nineteenth-century Paris's archetypal *artiste maudit*—the tortured, sensitive, cursed poet of a dead city that had crossed in a single generation from the Middle Ages into the modern age. He lived intensely and died young, his work imbued with a deep melancholy that resonates to this day. In many ways, the Franco-Italian painter and sculptor Amedeo Modigliani picked up in the early 1900s where Baudelaire had left off. It was a dubious honor, perhaps, but Modigliani's soulful artwork, like Baudelaire's poetry, is more coveted than ever, and the story of his tumultuous, debauched, tragically short life in Paris is as moving today as it was a century ago.

A puritanical biographer of our current age might describe Modigliani as macho, womanizing, obsessive, and demonic, a substance-abusing madman too handsome and talented for his own good, at once self-destructive and murderous, a kind of proto–Jim Morrison (of the Doors), a rebel without a cause, the last of the great bohemian Romantics of the Belle Époque.

Like Jim Morrison, Modigliani is buried at Père-Lachaise cemetery, the graveyard of France's great and good. I have often thought of the tragic pair as I stroll among the tombs. So when a few years ago Alison and I set about mapping the places where Modigliani had lived, worked, and died, Père-Lachaise seemed the logical place to start. Division 96, Avenue Transversale number three is Modigliani's address, in theory for perpetuity. It corresponds to a simple limestone tomb in an uninteresting section of the cemetery. Nearly always covered with flowers, the gravestone bears the inscription: "Amedeo Modigliani, born in Leghorn July 12, 1884, died in Paris January 24, 1920. Death snatched him from the brink of glory." Modigliani died a pauper. But, as Alison, an art historian by training, reminded me, he had a hero's funeral, attended by Picasso, Soutine, Léger, Ortiz de Zárate, Lipchitz, Derain, Severini, Foujita, Utrillo, Valadon, Vlaminck, and the poets Max Jacob and André Salmon, as well as dozens of now-forgotten friends and admirers. He'd found glory, certainly in terms of peer recognition, but it came too late.

Farther down Modigliani's tombstone is a second, cryptic epitaph. It was added some years after the first and reads: "Jeanne Hébuterne, born in Paris April 6, 1898, died in Paris January 25, 1920. Devoted companion of Amedeo Modigliani till the moment of extreme sacrifice."

Extreme sacrifice? I wondered who Jeanne Hébuterne had been and why she'd died just a day after the artist. Alison had only a vague recollection, so before setting out to find the places Modigliani knew, we dipped into the art history books and were fascinated and horrified in equal measure by what we found.

Amedeo Modigliani's mother was French, from Marseille, his father Italian. Both descended from solid, middle-class Jewish families. Amedeo grew up on the Tuscan coast and moved to Paris when twenty-one to study art. A freethinker, he abjured the family faith and declared to his fellow students that he wanted "a short but full life." Dashing, charming, witty, and perfectly bilingual, Modigliani got his "full life" off to a galloping start—he drank heavily, smoked hashish, partied and painted round the clock, changing addresses and lovers about as often as his clothes. It's unclear what stage his consumption, a deadly lung disease, had reached before he arrived in Paris. It's irrefutable, though, that Modigliani was obsessed by fears of the congenital insanity that had plagued his family for generations. He dwelled morbidly on his own impending death, and as his physical and mental health declined he began flitting around the cemeteries of Montmartre and Montparnasse reciting lines from Dante's *Inferno* and *Les Chants de Maldoror* by Isidore Ducasse, known as le Comte de Lautréamont, the notorious adept of De Sade. Tellingly, the nickname his fellow artists gave him was Modi—short for Modigliani, of course, but pronounced exactly like *maudit,* meaning damned, accursed, the spiritual heir of Baudelaire.

While the wine and absinthe flowed no one in his bohemian

circle really believed Modi would ensure for himself that "short but full life" by committing suicide. No one, that is, except Jeanne Hébuterne. She was the last of his many lovers, the mother of his daughter Jeanne, and the mother-to-be of his second child. It was with her, some historians think, that Modi swore a death pact. He drank and smoked himself to death and though nine months pregnant, Jeanne Hébuterne threw herself from the fifth-floor window of her parents' apartment the day after Modi died in an unheated garret in Montparnasse.

But we were getting ahead of ourselves. Modigliani may have lived his last years and died in Montparnasse, though you won't find his spirit there today, despite the "Terrasse Modigliani," a dreary parking lot next to the Montparnasse train station, or the "Atelier Modigliani," his garret, marked by a plaque at 8 Rue de la Grande Chaumière. It's when you wander the streets of Montmartre that the tragic artist's presence seems to flit past you down the zigzag staircases and atmospheric alleys of this hallowed hill capped by Sacré-Coeur.

We decided to rewind to 1906, the year Modi arrived from Italy by train and headed straight for what people called back then La Butte. At the time Montmartre's hilly sprawl took in vacant lots; scruffy, unpaved streets lined by crumbling two-story buildings; windmills, vineyards, and orchards on the city's northern edge. Sundown on a drizzly fall weekday seemed like a good time to me to hit the streets of the Butte; when the light begins to fade the tourist crowds thin but the parks, shops, and cafés remain open. We took the Métro to the Anvers station and, swept along by a crowd of Franco-African locals, made our way up narrow Rue Steinkerque, a straight shot to Square Willette at the base of the staircase leading to Sacré-Coeur. A merry-go-round spun to sour-sounding music. Amid the primly dressed children and their minders sat clutches of placid winos. Modi and his painter pal Maurice Utrillo often sat in this square and sketched the city and the passersby while guzzling cheap wine. Then they would hike up the hill on steep, plaited staircases, past the white hulk of Sacré-Coeur basilica, pausing, perhaps, to stare at the skeletal silhouette of the teenage Tour Eiffel before following the dog's-leg alleys to Place du Tertre where Modi lived.

We dodged an elephant train carrying weary tourists and poked around the souvenir stands looking for Modi. Among the Sacré-Coeur snow-shower paperweights, pot metal Eiffel Tower replicas, and Amélie Poulain posters, we spotted several T-shirts emblazoned with the stylized, elongated, sad-eyed women Modi preferred. I reflected on the fact that a hundred years ago, for the current price of a T-shirt—around fifteen dollars—I could have bought several original Modigliani canvasses. He disdained money. The cost of living in his day was only a fraction of what it is now but even that doesn't alter the equation: Modi wanted only enough for daily survival with something left over to buy his artist's materials.

We took a table at La Bohème du Tertre and did some mental burrowing backward, down an imaginary time tunnel, to the days when Modi lived in a cheap furnished room above this venerable café, now a tourist trap. Back then the square was the center of an artists' colony—most of them authentic, serious, academy-trained artists. They chose the Butte because rents were low yet it was within walking distance of central Paris. In those dying days of the Belle Époque there were already tourists a-plenty on the hill. Some were drawn by Sacré-Coeur, others by the cabarets, cafés, and restaurants. As Alison and I sipped our overpriced beers I was torn by conflicting emotions, at once troubled by the tour-bus hordes yet conscious of being part of them, repelled yet fascinated by the Butte's world-class kitsch. Accordions wheezed. Yellow pennants fluttered by as tour group leaders gave directions through bullhorns. I wondered if there were an undiscovered Modi, Picasso, or Foujita among the caricaturists and other self-styled artists, most of them non-French, soliciting in the square. Modi was Italian, after all, Picasso Spanish, and Foujita Japanese. Each had made his fortune on the Butte's scuffed and littered pavements while others had fallen by the wayside.

During the months Modi lodged above the café where we now sat he had been a tired-eyed regular in the square's troughs but especially at the Clarion des Chasseurs (in business since 1790) and La Mère Catherine, where a full meal cost under a franc—the equivalent in purchasing power of a few dollars today. Naturally both spots charge many times that now, and do a lively trade indoors among bric-a-brac and on shaded terraces using their long-dead, famous artist-patrons to create a faux bohemian setting.

Modi ranged over the Butte for three years, camping in at least five different places. The first was a ramshackle studio in a shantytown area called Le Maquis—a reference to the wild and woolly Corsican outback where thieves, murderers, and renegades hid out. An elderly local woman I buttonholed in a street north of Place du Tertre seemed to think she'd heard of Le Maquis. She pointed down Rue Norvins. We explored until we came to the evocatively named Allée des Brouillards—meaning, literally, fog alley—whose pocket-size front yards were overgrown with tangled, twisted shrubs. From it we crossed a small square into a park with another evocative name, Le Hameau des Artistes—the artists' hamlet. A group of neighborhood seniors polished their steel balls and tossed them down the gravel-and-dirt lanes of none other than Le Maquis, which is now a *boulodrome,* the French answer to a lawn-bowling alley. They glanced over but apparently could not be troubled to acknowledge our presence. I understood. The Butte's inhabitants live in parallel to the tourist flows.

The current incarnation of Le Maquis struck me as something the rebellious, left-leaning Modi might have liked (he often wore a red handkerchief around his neck in the style of the Italian revolutionary hero Giuseppe Garibaldi). The artists' studios of old had been razed, but at least no high-rise apartment buildings had taken their place. The *boule* players appeared to be from the working class, and in the corners of the park sat more of the Butte's winos and outcasts.

Behind the walls of what is now 11 Rue Norvins is a garden fronting the centuries-old house in which Modi lived briefly with English journalist Beatrice Hastings. She famously described him as "at once pearl and swine." Like her swinish lover, the man-eating Beatrice was no stranger to the bottle. She and Modi often fought and on one occasion he reportedly heaved her out of the window into the shrubbery. She was too drunk to notice, however, and the affair continued on and off for years, even after Modi moved to Montparnasse.

Another hundred yards away in a sloping residential square called Place Jean-Baptiste Clément, Modi worked in a studio at number seven (it has since been transformed into a handsome residence with an ivy-clad garden wall). In the early 1900s the neighborhood was edgy, so Modi often carried a pistol—at least, that is, when he was dressed. Apparently he enjoyed dancing naked at night in this lopsided square with his demi-monde models, most of them prostitutes whom he somehow managed to transform in his paintings into ethereal, Madonna-like beings.

To indulge the growing sense of yesteryear enfolding us, we decided to walk a few blocks back to Rue Cortot and peek into the Musée de Montmartre before it shut. With old-fashioned streetlights flickering and a sheen on the cobbles, the set of weathered 1600s buildings separated by a garden exuded a crepuscular charm. This was where Renoir lived in the 1870s, followed, in the early 1900s, by the self-taught Utrillo (and his mother Suzanne Valadon, a better painter than he). Modi is sure to have known the museum's mossy yard and creaking wooden floors. I imagined him now on the window sill, taking in the sweeping views, cluttered today by apartment towers. Though scrubbed and refitted to handle mass-market tourism, the museum nonetheless manages to transport visitors back in time. One room replicates the interior of Utrillo and Modi's much-loved Café de l'Abreuvoir, complete with bentwood chairs, wooden tables, and period posters. Staring out from the dusty memorabilia was the treasure I'd been looking for, a 1918 Modigliani portrait of a swan-necked, almond-eyed woman he doubtless loved, if only for a moment.

Up Rue des Saules a block or so is Montmartre's last vineyard, a terraced reminder of the neighborhood's vinous past, and kitty-corner to it spreads the small cemetery among whose toppled tombstones Modi liked to wander at night. But this street corner is best known for Au Lapin Agile, a *café-concert* open only at night. If you're an adept of kitsch, it's a fine place to experience Old Montmartre song-and-dance routines performed in roistering surroundings. The establishment started out as Le Cabaret des Assassins but became known as "Le Lapin à Gill" when in 1880 a painter named André Gill created its now-famous sign showing a rabbit in a red bowtie springing from a copper saucepan. The name eventually morphed to "the agile rabbit." It was already an old standby in Modi's day, famed for its absinthe and anything-goes atmosphere. Modigliani went there once in 1909 with the Italian Futurist painter Gino Severini, who was carrying with him Filippo Tommaso Marinetti's "Futurist Manifesto" calling for the destruction of Venice—the Lagoon City had to be flattened, according to Marinetti, because it was ancient, rotten, and an impediment to progress. Ever cordial, Modi shared a bottle or three with Severini but refused to sign. In his memoirs Severini described the evening, and the walls of Au Lapin Agile, which were covered with paintings, including a Picasso rose-period *Harlequin* self-portrait titled *Au Lapin Agile*. Artists, including Modigliani, routinely paid their bills here with artworks. The owner, Frédéric Gérard, alias Frédé, had a donkey named Lolo and when it was cold outside he'd bring Lolo in and let him wander among the penurious painters and intellectuals, sometimes with a paintbrush attached to his tail. Nowadays the cabaret's historic sign and the street corner itself are outwardly much the same as they were in the Belle Époque but the clientele couldn't be more different.

Relieved that the cabaret was not yet open and thus preserved from temptation, we strolled back down Rue des Saules, found tilting Rue Ravignan and zigzagged into Place Goudeau. A green, cast-iron Wallace fountain from the 1870s splashed the cobbles under horse-chestnut trees so old that Modi surely knew them. On the square's right flank was the display case of the once-infamous Bateau-Lavoir, an artist's residence. A vintage photograph showed a bare-bones turn-of-the-century studio. Inside we were pleasantly surprised to discover a hive of art students, many apparently convinced of their budding genius. Though completely rebuilt as a nondescript dormitory after a fire in 1970, thanks to that period photo it's easy enough to picture in the mind's eye what the Bateau-Lavoir, a converted piano factory clinging to the hillside, must have been like in its heyday, around 1908. That's when Modi got himself a room, a noisy, messy cubbyhole separated by thin panels and hanging fabric from other cubbyholes occupied by the likes of Derain, Juan Gris, and Picasso. Modi disliked Picasso, the inventor of Cubism, and hated Picasso's aggressive angular art. After several violent altercations Modigliani moved across the street to a seedy rooming house (in a building that no longer exists).

Like the crown of Montmartre, the Bateau-Lavoir is tame these days, an enclave of distinctly bourgeois bohemians. Despite widespread gentrification, however, it would be wrong to assume that the Butte's edgy quality has entirely disappeared. The last dive Modi rented was at the base of the hill, an address in Rue André Antoine. At its Pigalle end, when the sun goes down this cobbled road is almost as malodorous and filthy, and populated with marginal fauna, as it was a hundred years ago. To get there we coasted downhill to the packed cafés of Rue des Abbesses, where Modi and his barfly friend Utrillo would drink themselves silly. A staircase with many flights flanks the Café Saint-Jean, still a local hangout with a zinc-topped bar. We tossed back a *ballon* of red then clattered down the slippery, uneven stairs. Several hundred yards along the crooked alley we found ourselves among Pigalle's creatures of the night—Brazilian transvestites, nervy drug dealers and their disconcertingly normal-looking clients. As we reached the neon-lit Boulevard de Clichy I paused for a final glance back at the Butte and couldn't help wondering if, with his capacity to empathize and his painterly talents, Modi would be able to elevate Pigalle's modern-day denizens from gutter to empyrean. It was a vain thought, perhaps, but it buoyed me nonetheless.

The Boat People of the Seine

The rear of the riverboat coughed out black smoke ... the propeller started to spin ... Jules Naud had caught something with his boathook ... it was a man's arm, the whole arm from the shoulder to the hand. Soaking in the water it had acquired a bloodless color and had the consistency of dead fish ...

—GEORGES SIMENON, *Maigret et le corps sans tête,* 1955

One spring night as I sipped a glass of white wine with friends on their houseboat near the Eiffel Tower I watched an old riverboat labor upstream loaded with sand. "What a life," I said to no one in particular. My hosts, successful middle-aged professionals, shrugged their shoulders.

"I wouldn't know," said one of them as he fed the barbecue. "They live in a world apart . . ."

It struck me as strange to share a river in the center of Paris yet know nothing about the people who depend upon your watery home for their livelihood. But it wasn't until several years after this incident that I attempted to find out how the other half—the *bateliers* or freight-boat people of the Seine—live and work.

Upstream a few hundred yards from the Pont d'Austerlitz in the 13th arrondissement laundry fluttered from the riverboats moored to the sun-baked banks. I walked by them slowly, trying to catch someone's eye. Ruddy-cheeked children romped on the iron decks, scrambling among the potted geraniums, bicycles, and coiled rope. What I gathered were the children's parents patiently swabbed or scraped the family *péniche,* a vintage vessel locked in a losing battle against rust. But, as I learned, battle the boat people must: their source of livelihood is also their home, a universe measuring about 120 feet long by 15 feet wide. These craft, most of them Freycinet-class *péniches* from the 1920s and '30s, weren't at all like the luxury houseboats I'd visited near the Eiffel Tower or Notre-Dame, and the people on them proved to be shy, distrustful even. As it turned out, they had reason to be.

Like many children, I once dreamed of lazy days on a riverboat. When I first moved to Paris I would often pause to watch the brightly painted, snub-nosed *péniches* gliding past the Pont des Arts, the tip of the Île Saint-Louis or the Île de la Grande Jatte. To outsiders like me the lifestyle of Paris' *bateliers* looks footloose and fancy-free, a never-ending vacation spent sailing through Impressionist landscapes. When finally I got on board and talked to working boat owners, I discovered the truth: the river wears you down and exposes you daily to the danger of drowning and collision, or being injured by machinery and loads. Earnings are minimal, hardships abundant. Since the best spots on the quays of central Paris are taken these days by luxury houseboats, the mooring points that are left for industrial craft are often in noisy, seedy areas populated by fauna lifted from the pages of Simenon. If ever it was one, the vacation is now over for the nomadic riverboat people of the Seine, transporters of sand, gravel, flour, potatoes, fuel oil, and other unglamorous commodities. As Jean and Élianne, the sixty-something couple I got to know best, told me, they and their antiquated craft are struggling against the flow of history.

In the age of the TGV and container truck, riverboats haul bulk goods at a sea snail's pace. They are not only slow but inflexible, bound by the rivers and canals they ply. Largely because of this, the *bateliers* themselves are an anachronism, a vaguely suspect people—waterborne gypsies in a sedentary world. Traditionally they work in husband-and-wife or tightly knit family teams, rarely receive higher education, and often marry among themselves. Their living quarters, like those of Jean and Élianne, may appear cozy when viewed from the quayside but are in reality cramped and primitively equipped, with whole families crowded into cabins the size of a landlubber's modest living room. In summer the *bateliers* roast; in winter they freeze. Year round they're exposed to the elements, so that by adulthood they often look like ancient mariners.

At the age of six, riverboat children are placed in state-run boarding schools, where they don't mix easily with terrestrial tykes. Once they've done their mandatory schooling, they move home to the boat, some of them eventually taking over from their parents. A flotilla of specialized doctors, lawyers, and priests, strategically established in riverside centers in and around Paris, caters to the needs of these nomads, further isolating them, perhaps without intention, from the general populace. Endlessly cruising the nearly five thousand miles of navigable waterways that vein France, and sometimes sailing on to Belgium, Holland, Switzerland, or Germany, their floating villages band together and break apart.

Until January 1, 2000, several times a week Paris's boat people crowded into the *bourse d'affrétement,* the local freight exchange on the Quai d'Austerlitz, with the hope of being assigned a cargo. By law, all river and canal traffic in the country had to be channeled through government-run freight exchanges. They set tariffs and regulated many of the boat people's day-to-day activities. An administrative relic of the 1930s, the exchange operated on a first-in, first-out basis. As soon as they'd unloaded their corn or coal or gravel, the boat people had to sign the roll and wait to be called. And wait they did. On a typical day back in the 1990s, a hundred empty boats bobbed side-by-side on the rough-and-ready Quai d'Austerlitz with only a handful of shipments slated to go. Most foreign boats that unloaded in Paris sailed home empty. Together with a variety of evolving technological and social factors, this roll-call system almost killed off France's boat people. Their numbers fell from more than five thousand in the 1970s to under three thousand today; only a few hundred currently live and work in and around Paris.

But the *bateliers* are unlikely to disappear and may even make a comeback.

Both of them bespectacled, bent and bronzed, Jean and Élianne invited me one day onto their 350-ton Freycinet riverboat named *Gondole,* a rare honor. Descended from Alsatian boat families whose roots run as deep as the rivers they were born on, the couple lived their halcyon days on the Seine, Moselle, and Rhine in the 1960s, when French river and canal shipping peaked at more than one hundred million tons per year. By the mid-1990s that figure had shrunk dramatically and the distances covered by riverboats had regressed to pre-1930s levels. The reasons for the decline are many. Mining has all but disappeared in France, explained Jean. Coal has been phased out as a fuel. Heavy industry and manufacturing have given way to high technology, and new factories have sprung up near highways, not canals or rivers. Smaller shipments, delivered directly by truck or train, are easier to handle and more economical to stock than bulk loads. To make matters worse, the aging riverside silos and warehouses of yesteryear have rusted and crumbled, and many smaller canals are now encumbered by debris. The cost of restoring waterway infrastructure is high, on the order of several hundreds of millions of dollars.

Though in excellent condition, *Gondole* was slated for demolition, part of the government's restructuring program for the industry, a program that itself was scrapped a few years ago in favor of a kinder, gentler approach. As we sat in the boat's main room, shaded by lace curtains through which I glimpsed eastern Paris's glassy new skyscrapers, Jean told me about the now-defunct plan that had almost sent the *bateliers* to the bottom. Early retirement had been offered to boat owners willing to decommission and destroy their craft. No new Freycinet-type boats could be built, only larger-capacity industrial boats and modern riverboats able theoretically to compete with trains and trucks. All retirees' craft, no matter how worthy, had to be junked. Thousands were in fact destroyed in the 1980s and '90s in what many *bateliers* termed a government-sponsored genocide.

Scrapping their boats proved a heart-rending experience for *bateliers* such as Jean and Élianne. And as several other prospective retirees told me, the government's golden handshake was less than twenty-four-karat. The standard compensation was approximately eighty dollars for every ton of a boat's cargo capacity, worth, all told, about thirty-five thousand dollars for a typical Freycinet. "A lot of boat owners are bitter," said Jean softly. "But we have no regrets. We had a good life, and we were free to go wherever we wanted, whenever we wanted, though it's all over now."

A red-faced boatman probably in his late thirties joined us and voiced his disagreement. "It may be over for you, but I've just bought another boat, and when my son is old enough he's going to take it over."

A clutch of sullen mariners gathered around and began to debate the relative merits of the government's restructuring programs. As one realist put it, only massive intervention by the Ministry of Transportation to revamp infrastructure, and a concerted campaign to convince industry to reintegrate boats and barges into new distribution networks, could reverse the tide.

That is precisely what is currently going on, under the direction of a new agency, the VNF (Voies Navigables de France). Its revised "multiuse" waterway management philosophy, explained a spokesman I met on the quays, is to continue to exploit the country's main canals and rivers for commercial traffic, while slowly repairing a select few secondary waterways. Many have already been converted for pleasure craft or to power small hydroelectric generating plants, however, and it would be uneconomical to convert them back for freight. Younger boatmen are still being encouraged to transform their families' antiquated craft into tour boats, floating restaurants, or container carriers, or to increase their cargo capacity to a potentially competitive one thousand tons or more—an expensive and risky move.

Bad news is always good for someone. As the roads and freeways of France, especially those in Paris, come to a standstill with traffic, and air pollution reaches record peaks, the demand for river-based freight transportation is increasing. The upswing also comes thanks to construction work on long-term projects such as the Austerlitz-Rive Gauche (Left Bank) redevelopment scheme, and to a push by environmental lobbies to revive low-carbon shipping. Whether this is a bubble or a true tidal shift remains to be seen, but long-term prospects appear excellent. At the dawn of the second decade of the twenty-first century tonnage figures are on the rise.

The VNF publishes impressive statistics proving why waterway transport is both economical and environmentally friendly. According to official reports one twelve-thousand-ton push-tug convoy, for example, represents the equivalent of 342 thirty-five-ton trucks, which if strung bumper to bumper would clog and choke about fourteen miles of Paris roadway. Boats consume less fuel, pollute less, and have fewer accidents on average than other forms of transport. And it still costs less per ton per mile to ship cement, landfill, or wheat in an industrial push-tug or thousand-ton riverboat than in a freight train or truck.

That's great, say the boat people I've talked to, but it doesn't ensure smooth sailing ahead. Industrial push-tugs are beyond the reach of most individual owners and represent the antithesis of the traditional boat person's way of life, with its emphasis on freedom of movement. Because of their length and tonnage, push-tugs are able to ply only the deep-water channels of the Seine, Saône, Rhine, and Rhône, a phenomenon known in the trade as being "a prisoner of a river basin." Their routes are fixed. Working hours are regulated. Crews rarely own their craft and almost never live aboard; there is no purpose-built family cabin on such ships. So there are no husband-and-wife or family teams on them, either. Much the same applies to the huge thousand-ton riverboats, which do not fit in standard locks and are unable to use the four thousand miles or so of small waterways open only to the old Freycinet-class *péniche*. Ironically, because of their relative versatility, converted Freycinets may prove to be the way forward.

Having talked to scores of boatmen over a period of weeks, I could not refuse their invitation to take part in the big annual *pardon de la batellerie,* the blessing of the fleet, held each June in a town called Conflans-Sainte-Honorine. Twenty miles downstream from Paris and still in its suburbs, with regular commuter trains, Conflans nonetheless felt a thousand leagues from the Quai d'Austerlitz. Fish were jumping at the wide, murky confluence of the Seine and the Oise rivers where the town is sited. Boys and old men baited their hooks in silence and watched the boats slip by. Lashed to the wharves were row upon row of Freycinets, block-long riverboats, tugs, and push-tugs—just about every kind of inland watercraft I could imagine. Some were half-submerged with their heavy loads of gravel or grain. Others, bearded with moss, had been transformed into the houseboats of retirees.

Conflans, population thirty thousand, is not only the mecca of the boat people of the Seine. It's also an important shipping center for Belgians, Dutchmen, and Germans. Popular cafés boast names like *Le Batelier.* There are floating time-tunnel dance halls festooned with flowers where boat people play accordions and sing folksy songs from decades past. On a hill overlooking the Seine is the Château du Prieuré. It houses the Musée de la Batellerie, the repository of boat-people's history. And rising near the now-defunct freight exchange is a huge winged Statue of Liberty holding high a wreath to commemorate the boat people who fell in the two world wars. Mariners salute her as they pass.

But the town's center of gravity, it turned out, is an old white riverboat named *Je Sers*—I serve. Its captain at the time was the spiritual guide of the boat people's community, an aging priest named Père Arthur. Most French boatmen are practicing Catholics, and the big moments of their lives from cradle to grave are played out in the company of the presiding priest. The blessing of the fleet is the summer season's signal event in both Conflans and nearby Longueil-Annel, a placid backwater upstream on the Oise River. I joined the priest and dozens of boatmen on a garlanded old Freycinet with a makeshift altar and glided into Longueil where hundreds of boat families, their craft streaming with banners, processed to the riverbank to receive their blessing. It was a moving sight, even for a freethinker. But the festive air was tinged with solemnity. Père Arthur would soon move to Lille, and some of the boats present were receiving their last rites. They would become floating clubhouses or cafés, noted the priest as we motored back to Conflans. This was preferable to the fate suffered by others in the bad old days of the 1990s: they were sent to what locals call the "boat cemetery," in reality a scrap yard in a dead branch of the Seine directly opposite Conflans. Though now closed the scrap yard is a constant reminder to *bateliers* of the precariousness of their situation.

As I stared across the river at the boat cemetery a young *batelier* stood next to me and defiantly swore he would survive against the odds. "I'll get a bigger boat if I have to," he said. "I'll work on someone else's boat if I have to. But I'll never leave the river." They were hard words spoken with passionate determination. I would remember them the next time I sat sipping white wine with our friends on their houseboat near the Eiffel Tower.

Meeting Moreau

*He paints dreams . . . sophisticated, complicated, enigmatic
dreams.*

—ÉMILE ZOLA

I once met a dead man in Paris named Gustave Moreau. It
happened one rainy morning in the 1980s when I had nothing particular to do. I was drawn to the Passage Verdeau, a
nineteenth-century, glass-and-ironwork shopping arcade just
north of Boulevard Montmartre in the dowdy 9th arrondissement.
A thin coat of dust hung on old storefronts such as Pascal En-
tremont Chasseur de Pierres, a rock collector's shop; and Photo
Verdeau, with its array of early cameras in worn leather cases. The
doors of some of the Passage Verdeau's establishments seemed to

have rusted shut. Yet there were the clerks and salesmen bent behind their desks, waiting patiently for the rare customer.

At a bookseller and curio shop appropriately called La France Ancienne I was delighted to discover a box of old postcards marked *sculpture, peinture, beaux-arts.* Looking out at me from among the fountains of Rome and the statuary of Versailles was the portrait of a man with a bushy white beard and the eyes of a seer or a maniac. The card was postmarked 1908. In faded black ink the sender had scrawled "A bizarre and disappointing place."

The postcard had come from the Musée Gustave Moreau. It showed a self-portrait of the artist. The name rang a bell. Where had I seen the work of Gustave Moreau? Wasn't he the Symbolist, the enigmatic recluse who'd lived during the heyday of Impressionism?

Intrigued, I bought the postcard. The museum, if it still existed, was only a few blocks north of the Passage Verdeau, beyond the Folies Bergère and the cheap clothes shops and eateries of the unfashionable Rue du Faubourg-Montmartre. Around here and in nearby Rue Notre-Dame-de-Lorette, I recalled, were the brasseries and cafés Émile Zola described in his bleakly evocative novels of nineteenth-century Paris life. This was "the last bright and animated corner of nocturnal Paris" where Zola's notorious lady of the night, Nana, and swarms of others in the trade did their business "as though along the open corridor of a brothel."

Could this be where Gustave Moreau had lived? Though most of the prostitutes had moved out, the neighborhood wasn't that different in feel—rundown, tired, soulful, seedy, a slice of ungentrified inner city. I walked north past the church of Notre-Dame-de-Lorette, remarkable for its gracelessness, then got turned around in Place Saint-Georges. It was more a traffic circle than a proper square but it had character. No one I asked had heard of the Musée Gustave Moreau—try the Marais, suggested one helpful resident. "The Marais is where all the museums are . . ."

I was about to give up when I came across Rue de La Roche-foucauld. That was the address on the postcard. Wedged between the faded, staid apartment buildings of vaguely Second Empire–style was number fourteen, an ungainly neo-Renaissance brick palazzo. On it was a plaque and an old-fashioned brass doorbell. Visitors were to ring and enter.

"A bizarre and disappointing place"—the words came back to me as I climbed the stairs to the ticket desk. I surprised the woman dozing there. No one else was around. At the foot of the worn and poorly lit staircase I spotted a handwritten biographical sketch of the artist. Gustave Moreau was born April 6, 1826, in Paris, the son of a successful architect. He dearly loved his mother, with whom he lived for decades, until her death. He never married. A student at the École Royale des Beaux-Arts, he traveled extensively in Italy and later showed his work in various salons. Finally, in 1883, at the height of his unusual career, he was named Officer of the Legion of Honor.

Moreau died in this house in 1898, where he had lived and worked for nearly fifty years. He willed the house and its contents to the state with the proviso that it be maintained as it was. The museum was created a few years later and remained virtually unchanged for a century. In it are some twelve hundred paintings, watercolors, and cartoons, and five thousand drawings. Moreau threw nothing away. For the record, only Turner and Picasso have left a greater body of work to posterity.

On the first-floor landing of the house hangs a large drawing of a Persian poet riding a unicorn. Beside it is a sketch of an effeminate Oedipus apparently being seduced or raped by a lascivious Sphinx.

But nothing could prepare me for what I found on the second floor. In a huge hall, scores of oil paintings hang floor-to-ceiling on three sides. The fourth wall of large windows illuminates the room in any weather. Here was the Virgin Mary, depicted as a jewel-encrusted pistil protruding from a giant lily. The artist called the work *The Mystical Flower.* In *The Chimerae,* a hundred or more female creatures make love to dragonflies, snakes, and turtles. Behind them rises a fairytale medieval city at the foot of a rocky precipice surmounted by a tiny cross. This overtly misogynistic work the painter described cryptically as "a satanic *Decameron*" (presumably referring to Giovanni Boccaccio's fourteenth-century tales, many of them prurient) and "an island of fantastic dreams enclosing every form of passion, fantasy and caprice of Woman" (the capitalized "W" is the artist's).

I scanned my memory for an explanation. Did it lie, perhaps, in the fact that during Moreau's adult life, which coincided with what we now call the Belle Époque, relations between men and women stood at a critical juncture? The first assault on patriarchal society had been mounted—a kind of proto-Women's Liberation Movement was under way. A favorite theme of many male artists of the time, especially Symbolists such as Moreau, was the tale of Salomé—the devilish temptress—usually shown dancing or lustily holding Saint John the Baptist's head on a platter. I glanced around. There she was, among the unicorns and swans, lilies and acanthus leaves.

Winged horses pranced and swayed with the reinterpreted mythological or biblical figures in *The Return of the Argonauts, The Daughters of Thespius,* and many other larger-than-life-size canvases, some of them only half-finished, all of them stylistically very different. What did this hodgepodge of symbols mean? Was Moreau insane or had he, like many artists of his day, been an opium addict?

I sat in the center of the room feeling dizzy. A lone museum guard paced back and forth in front of the wall of windows where a gray, glary light poured in from the equally gray, unappealing neighborhood beyond. I wondered where the crowds of the Louvre or the Picasso Museum were. A bizarre place this was, as my old postcard suggested, but not disappointing.

Unable to make sense of the paintings, I decided to go back

down to the entrance area and see if there was a catalogue for sale. When I stood the guard approached me. "Aren't you going to look at the third floor?" she asked. How could there possibly be more of this, I asked without thinking. "But you've only started, monsieur," she retorted, pointing to an unusual spiral staircase—a double helix, in fact. "The best is on the third floor!"

I assured her politely that I would return, then dashed down the stairs.

On the way out of the building I bought a catalogue and began to read it as I walked. The bells of Notre-Dame-de-Lorette and La Trinité, another nearby temple of architectural gracelessness, were tolling noon. The streets, though as outwardly drab as before, started to take on a new meaning for me. Here, said the catalogue, in Rue de La Rochefoucauld, Nana had kept a room. Zola himself had lived a few blocks away in Rue Ballu. This was where Charles Dickens had had his disappointing encounter with Frédéric Chopin's celebrated lover George Sand, "the kind of woman in appearance whom you might suppose to be the Queen's monthly nurse." Turgenev and Thackeray and a dozen other writers and painters had lived in the area, within a few hundred yards of Moreau's house. The ateliers and galleries had apparently been as thick here then as they are now on the Left Bank or in the Marais. The streets had been alive. During Moreau's day the neighborhood was known as The New Athens, and even spawned its own architectural style, heavy with Hellenistic, classical references. Moreau in his youth frequented the salons, restaurants, and cafés with his great friend and fellow painter Théodore Chassériau, who was also among the nineteenth-century's most successful artists, at least from the commercial standpoint.

But as I walked by, on Place Saint-Georges there was only one modest café. Cars swerved around the statue of a now-obscure lithographer named Gavarni, also famous in his day. Locals sifted through bric-a-brac at a tumbledown shop that advertised *antiquités et curiosités*—yard-sale castoffs and oddments rescued from attics and cellars. The neighborhood was quiet, with a few small public gardens flanked by tidy, uninteresting streets. The red-light district of Zola's day apparently had split in two, shifting north to Pigalle and south to Les Halles.

I decided to backtrack to Rue du Faubourg-Montmartre and have lunch at Chartier, a workingman's restaurant in business since Moreau's final days. Perhaps the painter had been a habitué, I fantasized. Given the elaborately decorative, eclectic nature of his work, Moreau surely would have liked the décor. Brass racks run over wooden booths. Customers eye each other in mirrored panels. In a single load waiters carry eight plates and three bottles of *vin de pays* (the menu warns that the management declines responsibility for stains caused by reckless servers).

It was here at Chartier, over pepper steak and a carafe of very ordinary red wine, that I read the catalogue cover to cover and began to learn the details of Moreau's life and career. For some mysterious reason—possibly the death of his intimate friend Chassériau—Moreau stopped attending the salons of the Countess Greffulhe (later immortalized by Proust) and the Princess Mathilde, Emperor Napoléon III's cousin. Over the years Moreau became, as the novelist and critic J. K. Huysmans wrote, "the mystic shut away in the center of Paris." He was thought to be homosexual or bisexual. Highly secretive, only a handful of his friends knew of his twenty-five-year liaison with a certain Adélaide-Alexandrine Dureux, a "spiritual companion" whom he maintained in an apartment in Rue Notre-Dame-de-Lorette.

Moreau was uncommunicative. Often he refused to explain the meaning of his hermetic artworks. To one collector who bought a picture and requested a written key to decipher it, Moreau replied that he had simply to "love to dream." Zola, reviewing Moreau's pictures at a salon in the 1880s wrote, "He paints dreams . . . sophisticated, complicated, enigmatic dreams."

Zola also said that Moreau had had no master and would have no disciples. But Zola was wrong. Rouault, Matisse, Marquet, and many others were his pupils at the École Nationale des Beaux-Arts. Odilon Redon, better known nowadays than Moreau himself, was heavily influenced by the mystic's work, as were Picasso, Dalí, and Matta.

With a well-to-do family behind him, a secure job, and regular patrons, Moreau was the antithesis of the starving artist. Only once did he deign to show his work in a commercial gallery. The real motive for his reticence was a morbid fear of criticism. In the last years of his life he worked frantically to give titles to his pictures and to write notes about them so that future critics—and museumgoers—would not misinterpret them.

Several years after my first visit, I returned to the Moreau museum (and have been back many times since). I was not alone this time. The doorbell had been disconnected and the dust removed. Somehow the mystery was gone, and with it much of the magic. As the guard had said, the best pictures were on the third floor—gemlike canvases sparkling with cobalt and gold that Moreau had labored over for months or years.

The hundreds of watercolors and drawings mounted on ingenious wooden stands revealed another Moreau. Here were gentle landscapes and fine sketches with all the mystical power of the oils, but none of the tortured anguish. Here too was the self-portrait I had first seen on that old postcard, which I had lost in the meantime. Moreau had been commissioned to draw it by the Uffizi Gallery in Florence. It was to have hung in the Vasari Corridor, among the self-portraits of history's greatest painters. But Moreau, believing himself unworthy, had never delivered it. He wished to disappear as a man, and live on in his works, at his museum.

At the Montmartre Cemetery later that day I asked a caretaker where I could find Moreau's tomb. No one had ever asked for it before, he sniffed, and he'd never heard of the man. I gave the full name and the year Moreau died. After digging out an enormous leather-bound ledger marked *sépultures des célèbres,* the caretaker huffed and puffed and searched laboriously. He was startled to hit upon the entry, and was clearly disappointed not to send me away with a wag of the finger. The tomb, registered in a meticulous Belle Époque hand, was in section twenty-two, row seven, grave-stone number two, he said. But I was unsure that day whether I'd found it. The headstone had fallen over, and the name engraved below was worn and mossy. It seemed appropriate, a fate of which the Symbolist would have approved. Cleaned and restored since then, like his museum, Moreau's resting place is no longer dark, forgotten, and mysterious. But the enigma of the man remains.

The Perils of Pompidou

Cernimus exemplis oppida posse mori . . . (We learn from
example that cities, too, can die . . .)
— RUTILIUS CLAUDIUS NAMATIANUS,
De Reditu Suo, fifth century

Few cities can claim a tradition of urban vandalism nobler
than that of Paris. Perhaps it's genetic: archaeologists insist
the Gauls burned their Seine-side settlements before going
to battle, thus depriving rivals of the pleasure. Julius Caesar and
his descendants endlessly reconfigured their fledgling city, as did
generation upon generation of kings, French Revolutionaries, and
emperors, who continued vandalizing Paris right into the modern
age. When a ruler wanted something new he merrily tore down
everything in his way.

But Parisians have not been immune to preservationist sentiments. For the past two hundred years or so those in command
have usually prefaced their assaults by citing public safety, sanita-
tion, or, that magic word, "modernity." Many Paris connoisseurs
think Emperor Napoléon III and his prefect Baron Haussmann
were the archetypal modernizers: they flattened thousands of
buildings for a variety of reasons, from bona fide health concerns
to crowd control and rampant greed. Decried as a rape by sensitive
souls such as poet Charles Baudelaire or Victor Hugo, "Haussmannization" was nonetheless carried out by visionary planners
and skilled architects. Whatever they built was built to last.

What is less well publicized is that the vandal heritage, slowed
occasionally by recession or war, has been the driving force behind each of the various French republics that followed the Second Empire. It peaked under the current "Fifth Republic," which
began in 1958. Predictably the orgy of state-sponsored speculation
the new republic ushered in was dressed up as Haussmann-style
modernization. This time it was not an emperor and a baron directing the show but an aging general and a little gray technocrat
named Georges Pompidou.

Pompidou rose to power as De Gaulle's right-hand man, moving in smooth succession from a 1958 advisory position to that of
prime minister, before becoming president in 1969. A statesman,
De Gaulle didn't like cluttering his mind with minor concerns
such as the economy, the environment, or urbanism. So he del-
egated. "Ask Pompidou," he would say with a vague gesture.

Pompidou's reign ended with his sudden death in 1974, meaning that he presided over France and the capital's fortunes for sixteen years (Paris had no mayoral authority from 1871 to 1977).
This was the height of *les trente glorieuses*—thirty glorious years
of bull market.

When I hear someone say "Pompidou" I lift my eyes to Paris's skyline and see the name writ large. Pompidou lives on in
the opaque, sixty-story silhouette of the Tour Montparnasse

and the nervy university complex of Jussieu that's about half as tall. Look west and there's Pompidou again, mastermind of the mock-Manhattan towers of La Défense. Of course, there are the multicolored pipes and Plexiglas tubes of the Pompidou Center at Beaubourg, a prime example of what was formerly (and without irony) called Brutalism, from the French word *brut,* as in raw or unfinished. That meant deconstructed structures with their guts exposed. Lower your eyes and you'll see many minor examples of the Pompidou era, from unremarkable administrative carbuncles and low-income housing to the mirrored squalor of Le Forum des Halles.

But there's more to Pompidou's Paris than most people realize. The Georges Pompidou Expressway snakes along the Seine where leafy river ports once stood. The Boulevard Périphérique, originally the no-man's-land outside the 1848 city walls, was slated to become a greenbelt until Pompidou had it transformed into an eight-lane cement moat that separates Paris from its surroundings. Facing La Défense alongside the Périphérique is the Porte-Maillot hotel, shopping, and convention center so dear to Pompidou. Though only a few decades old, it was judged ugly enough to deserve a multi-million-dollar facelift not long ago, and it's still an eyesore.

The list of Pompidou-inspired marvels goes on. It includes much of the damage done to the Marais and other historic districts (where streets were systematically widened by destroying rows of townhouses). And don't forget the Place d'Italie apartment blocks on Paris's south side, seemingly lifted from outer Moscow, or the Front de Seine high-rise pseudo-Cubist clusters and garish shopping center at Beaugrenelle in the 15th arrondissement, not to mention the "nouvelle" but already crumbling Belleville, and much of what is now the blighted, high-crime suburban ring around Paris.

Actually, the city got off lightly. Many of Pompidou's most outlandish schemes were abandoned because of public outcry, or because the great modernizer died while still in office, and his successor, Valéry Giscard d'Estaing, either refused to carry them out or was in turn thwarted. Here are a handful of examples of what we missed: a spaghetti bowl of expressways with skyscrapers in their midst, extending from Les Halles to the Seine; a freeway atop the Canal Saint-Martin; a Left-Bank expressway from Tolbiac to the Pont Mirabeau; a bridge across the downstream tip of the Île de la Cité that would have obliterated the handsome Square du Vert Galant; the demolition of the entire Marais except for two churches and one townhouse; and, in 1966, Pompidou planned to build "Paris II," a residential city conceived so that what was left of the real Paris could be gutted and refitted.

"It is up to the city to make way for the automobile," Pompidou pronounced midway through his reign, "and not the other way around." He spoke of "surgical themes" and "necessary transformations," promising Parisians a modern metropolis to rival New York and London, made to the measure not of man, but of the machine.

To this day some people actually admire Pompidou's heritage. So let's be fair: He bequeathed the city the RER commuter-train system and lovely La Défense. He created the Nouvelles Villes satellite cities and a network of freeways any sprawling megalopolis would be proud of. He was a man of his mixed-up, paradoxical times, the days of atonal "classical" music, hard rock and "free jazz," free love, Pop Art, Agent Orange, LSD, and the domino theory. Pompidou may have resided on the historic Île Saint-Louis in a luxury townhouse but he earnestly wanted a freeway in front of his picture windows—and almost got one. The automobile was his God.

Small and swarthy, with a perennial, wolfish grin wrapped around a smoldering cigarette, Georges Pompidou was in fact a provincial from the Massif Central. A lifelong overachiever, he graduated summa cum laude in Greek then fought alongside De Gaulle. After the war he proved his quiet brilliance by rising to

CEO of the Banque Rothschild. In the meantime, he'd netted the *chicissime* Claude Jacqueline Cahour, who was later dubbed "the first modern First Lady of France" and the "godmother of French art"—contemporary art, needless to say. Hard to pigeonhole or place on the political spectrum, Pompidou was backed by some of the great French intellectuals. Literary icon André Malraux, the country's first minister of culture, worked cheek-by-jowl with the little gray man whose real personality screamed in primary colors. Incredibly, Malraux's celebrated urban conservation laws helped save the Marais, but he nonetheless signed the permits for many of Pompidou's catastrophes, including the Tour Montparnasse.

"Pompidou said little and wrote nothing while Malraux talked too much and wrote too much," noted historian and Pompidou-confidant Louis Chevalier in his still-controversial exposé *L'Assassinat de Paris,* first published in 1977. A chronicle of how the De Gaulle–Malraux–Pompidou troika massacred the city, the book points out that Pompidou was at heart a banker. The banks owned real estate and were cozy with building contractors. The rest of the riddle is easy.

Another intellectual bigwig of the postwar period who came to despise Pompidou was author Georges Pillement. In *Paris Poubelle* ("Garbage-Can Paris") Pillement asserts that Pompidou was aware of—and possibly the source of—the systematic vandalism occurring in central Paris. The aim of that vandalism, theoretically, was to get neighborhoods declared unsafe so they could be bulldozed. In this scenario, Pompidou's long-term plan was to transform Paris into *the* European business center, studded with Le Corbusier–style high-rises and veined by highways. Pompidou "seduced" Malraux with visions not of banal skyscrapers for businessmen but of neo-medieval towers.

If De Gaulle was king and Pompidou his white knight then Malraux was the court decorator and savant, writes Chevalier in *L'Assassinat de Paris.* In any case, Pompidou was firmly in control, pressing the right buttons: with De Gaulle he spoke of France's renascent glory and with Malraux, who could have thwarted him, he wrapped his visions in the fluff of whimsy. Thirty-some years later the results—now cracking, rusting, and peeling—are plain to see.

A bad Chicago skyscraper set in what used to be an artists' quarter of two-story workshops, the Tour Montparnasse is so brutally banal and clearly out of place that I've become almost protective of it. That familiar brownish hulk is an ever-visible reminder of what not to do in a historic European city. Several years ago rumors began spreading about the tower's possible demolition. It is universally loathed and, worse from the city's standpoint, has not been profitable. With this peril in mind I spent an hour wandering through the could-be-anywhere shopping center at the tower's base, pondering what might replace it. Then I rode an elevator to the top floor.

Inaugurated in 1973, the tower feels like it's about to deconstruct itself. No one appears to have celebrated its thirty-seventh birthday in 2010, but perhaps they're awaiting the big 4–0. Several windows were missing, replaced by plywood panels. The fingerprints of the project's Chicago-based designers were everywhere: this was a piece of 1960s–'70s Americana owned by the French, a typical De Gaulle–Pompidou act of defiance vis-à-vis the postwar period's new global, English-speaking power.

Soon after the Eiffel Tower was built, novelist Guy de Maupassant began lunching in the panoramic restaurant there because, as he put it, it was the only place in town from which you could not see the Eiffel Tower. The same could be said for panoramic Montparnasse: the view is splendid and there's no Montparnasse tower to be seen. Unhappily, amid the centuries-old mix of inner Paris that spreads below, you're treated to a pigeon's-eye view of Pompidou's other creations. There is simply no escaping them. The 1965 Jussieu university complex, for example, almost obscures the handsome tree-lined alleys of the Jardin des Plantes behind it. And unless you're as shortsighted as Pompidou himself, you can't help staring at the paint-box innards of the Pompidou Center, whose construction entailed the demolition of the historic Beaubourg neighborhood.

As I crossed town along "Haussmannized" yet appealing boulevards toward the Pompidou Center I recalled the time I interviewed Renzo Piano, the center's co-architect. "It was a joke," Piano snorted, stroking his bushy beard. "A parody of technology . . . a great, insolent, irreverent provocation."

Were Piano and fellow architect Richard Rogers really thumbing their noses at Pompidou and his technocrats? Maybe. Piano, I reflected, is an affable and clever man. He has had years to develop a convincing patter. His idea, he now says, was to create a place where the arts and other disciplines would mix and match—a culture factory. When people said that his building looked like a refinery Piano was delighted. As to the destruction of historic Beaubourg, Piano pointed out that Pompidou's men had already wiped the slate.

Love it or hate it, the giant culture-refinery of Beaubourg has been a surprise success. Around seven million people visit it annually, loving it to death. French taxpayers like me spent tens of millions of dollars to restore it a few years ago, even though the building was barely into its twenties. Gaining admission to the Pompidou these days is a feat: typically the lines snake for a quarter mile through the sloping "piazza" out front, among the caricature artists, fire-eaters, and mimes. The high culture starts inside.

This time around I skipped the world-class museum displays and the vast library to look again at the building itself. Light streamed in through the thirty-foot windows. People floated by on escalators in Plexiglas tubes. Transparent elevators bobbed up and down. The color-coded pipes and ducts, another mock-industrial provocation, shone bright. For a moment I thought I'd stepped back into the caustic, gutsy, colorful seventies.

Luckily I hadn't. I poked around the trendy, panoramic restaurant called Georges (a reference, perhaps, to Monsieur Pompidou?) but could not afford to sit down. From the viewing terrace, lower than that of Montparnasse, I could see the roofs of old Paris. Pompidou had disdained them and tried, with a large measure of success, to bring them down. Sadly, he never lived to see his namesake center completed: it opened in 1977, three years after his death. As I exited through the lobby I looked up at the round, deconstructed black-and-white Op Art portrait of Pompidou hanging there for all to see. His wolfish grin shifted as I passed.

In retrospect Pompidou's most impressive achievement was not the building of the Tour Montparnasse or the Pompidou Center at Beaubourg; it was the eviction of the messy old general markets from Les Halles. Planners had been trying to get rid of them for decades. Once the market was gone, the area became a slum in short order. Soon thereafter the nineteenth-century glass-and-ironwork Baltard pavilions that had housed the market were flattened. Another decade went by before a seven-story subterranean RER train and Métro station—the world's biggest underground station—and a shopping center with a sunken "forum" filled the "hole of Les Halles."

I thought of Émile Zola as I rode a steeply raked escalator into the Forum's pit. In his 1873 Rougon-Macquart series of novels Zola dubbed the old market *le ventre de Paris*—the guts or stomach of Paris. Apparently the site has permanent indigestion: it emanates an acrid stench. Some say it's the disgruntled spirits of place. Others believe it's the smell of oozing sewage, scented by disinfectants and bubbling fast-food fryers. Experts claim it's the scent of decomposing limestone. In any case, at least the suburban adolescents, the hucksters, and the drug dealers surrounding me among the stained and broken cladding seemed to be enjoying the Forum. It's soon to be rebuilt, after only thirty-some years of service.

I headed as fast as I could out of the area, the words of the governor of Rome Rutilius Claudius Namatianus, written around AD 415 as Rome collapsed, ringing in my ears: "Cities, too, can die."

In the 1970s, critics of Pompidou pronounced Paris dead. But as I sipped a beer in a landmark building that would have been destroyed had Pompidou's plans been carried out, another thought sprang to mind. Like the proverbial phoenix rising from the ashes, cities can also be reborn. Despite Les Halles, Montparnasse, and many a blighted suburb, it seemed to me that Paris was alive and ready to box its way through the twenty-first century. Now, if only the authorities would follow Pompidou's precepts and dynamite his towers and shopping malls, then close the Seine-side expressways and transform the Périphérique into that mythical greenbelt, we'd really be talking modernity.

Keepers of the Craft:
Paris Artisans

Gold is for the mistress—silver for the maid—
Copper for the craftsman cunning at his trade.
"Good!" said the Baron, sitting in his hall,
"But Iron—Cold Iron—is master of them all."

—RUDYARD KIPLING, *Cold Iron*

I walked one day not too long ago down the picturesquely named Rue du Pont aux Choux—the street of the bridge of cabbages—near where I live in the Marais. As if in a dream I stepped through a set of steamed-up doors and witnessed a scene from Dante's *Inferno*: a blazing-hot furnace showered sparks into a dark workshop where leather-gloved men molded sheets of what I came to recognize as molten glass. A few hundred yards from the glassworks, in a seventeenth-century townhouse near Place des Vosges, I paused to watch a craftsman tap-tap-tapping with an old hammer, finishing a tooled-leather box. About half a mile east, still in the Marais, a solitary woman quietly carved antique wooden panels in an Alice-in-Wonderland workshop with sawdust reposing on wounded collectibles, yellowing plaster busts and cupids suspended on rusty wires.

To me, the word *artisan* evokes just such sepia-tinted images of yesteryear, of atmospheric ateliers where master craftsmen and eager apprentices toil into the night to create or restore goods at once useful and beautiful to behold. This is not the throwaway junk we're used to, but the solid, desirable stuff of our forebears. Happily in Paris by some small miracle the craft tradition has survived not only the fall of the Ancien Régime and the advent of industrialization, but also the myriad manifestations of contemporary mass consumerism.

The French language is ambiguous when it comes to defining the term *artisan*. It can identify anyone from a plumber to a baker or a taxi driver. Often it simply means "independent contractor." But when I use it I'm thinking of crafts people who fashion one-of-a-kind items, shunning large-scale production methods, and catering to clients directly in their workshops.

Over the past several decades I have been lucky enough to meet many skilled artisans in Paris: glassworkers, silver- and coppersmiths, bronze founders, ceramists, enamelers, painters of miniatures, cabinetmakers, leather workers, bookbinders, makers of stained-glass windows, hatters, fan-makers, engravers, gilders, ivory sculptors, violin- and lute-makers, saddle-makers, jewelers, goldsmiths, printers, and others still.

Several thousand artisans work today in central Paris, living proof of the superiority in many fields of man over machine.

One reason the craft tradition remains encouragingly resilient is apprenticeship. It continues in many workshops, though not in the nineteenth-century sense of indentured servitude. Parisian youngsters wouldn't buy that. Almost anyone can learn at any age to be an adequate artisan. The key word is "adequate." For many crafts—inlay and cabinetmaking, for example—the experts are unanimous in saying that budding craftsmen really must begin when very young in order to develop the muscles and reactions needed to mature into a master. So, in this digitalized, laser-guided world of ours, apprenticeship is still the most vital means for training young talents and passing craft secrets down the generations.

Apprenticeship is what the Compagnons du Devoir du Tour de France is all about. This four-hundred-year-old association has long intrigued me, in part because of its quirky window displays of roof beams, stones, or furniture at its headquarters behind the church of Saint-Gervais, a hundred yards east of city hall. Mostly, I've been drawn to the Compagnons because they resemble a medieval crafts guild. Only adepts, and I use the word intentionally, aged fifteen to twenty-five, may join. They must agree to spend up to ten years traveling around France learning their chosen trade from masters—bakers, tapestry makers, carriage builders, stone masons, locksmiths, roofers, carpenters, saddle-makers, plasterers, and so forth. Reportedly, there is no such thing as an unemployed Compagnon. After their tour of duty, once they have set up shop, they must agree to train other Compagnons.

There's another reason the craft tradition survives in France, and especially in Paris: the handful of world-class technical institutions scattered around the country, with four in the capital alone. The most famous is l'École Boulle, named after Louis

XIV's court cabinetmaker André-Charles Boulle (1642–1732). The school was founded in 1886 to train cabinetmakers and workers in related trades. Today Boulle graduates might work in cabinetry or inlay, or venture into the fine arts, jewelry, or industrial design. One graduate I met works for Cartier, another was a member of the TGV high-speed train design team.

Other Paris crafts schools include the 140-year-old EPSAA (graphic arts and architecture); the even older École Duperré (fashion, textile design or printing, interior decoration, tapestry, ceramics); and the equally venerable École Supérieure Estienne (engraving, bookbinding and gilding, printing, illustration and graphic arts). Both Duperré and Estienne offer adult education courses, and if I weren't so hopelessly incapable of working with my hands I would be tempted to retrain and recycle myself through one of them, perhaps as a bookbinder, or something equally out of step with the times.

Of course luxury goods are yet another reason—perhaps the main reason—French artisans continue to thrive. They work for companies such as Hermès, Cartier, or Louis Vuitton. Fashion designers, too, though a pernicious breed in my book, do their part to keep alive a variety of unlikely specialties such as *plumassiers* (feather decoration makers), leather workers, silk dyers, hat-makers and, yes, fan-makers.

There is usually a flip side to a happy story and in this case it is one of numbers: a mere twenty years ago there were almost twenty thousand crafts workers in Paris' two main crafts districts alone, the Marais (comprising the 3rd and 4th arrondissements) and abutting Faubourg Saint-Antoine east of the Bastille (the 11th arrondissement). If several thousand remain, where have the others gone?

To find out, I decided to talk to a spokesperson at the government-funded SEMA (Société d'Encouragement aux Métiers d'Art), which is putatively in charge of developing local assistance programs for artisans all over France. "Where have they gone?" the startled bureaucrat repeated my question rhetorically—he was startled because I'd uncovered the official statistics. "To the suburbs, the provinces, or out of business!" SEMA confirmed that only a handful of Paris artisans actually create new, original goods, mostly for luxury manufacturers or fashion houses. Everyone else now earns his living by making replicas of antiques or doing restoration work for individual clients or the French government.

A few examples followed. Paris spends millions of dollars annually to restore the roofs and wooden structures of the city's churches, it seems, and further millions remodeling townhouses like the Hôtel de Saint-Aignan in the Marais. It houses the Musée d'art et d'histoire du Judaïsme or MAHJ, the Jewish Art and History Museum. Additionally the city commonly spends about half a million dollars annually restoring works of art, furniture, books, woodwork, and so on, mainly in municipal museums and warehouses, those dusty repositories of micro-history rarely visited and most often unloved. The Museum of the History of Hospitals isn't exactly the Musée d'Orsay, but it and others like it keep dozens of crafts workers busy.

From the historical perspective, the number of artisans plummeted early in the twentieth century, the spokesperson explained to me, and again after World War II because of industrialization and standardization. Handmade or custom goods couldn't compete or simply went out of fashion. The French crafts industry seems to have bottomed out in the 1990s. Supply and demand are now more or less in balance.

Despite the loss of thousands of ateliers, the Marais and Faubourg Saint-Antoine are still Paris's main crafts districts, though you might not think so upon casual inspection. Both have undergone profound changes in recent decades. That's a polite way of saying they've been gentrified to the brink of extinction. Redevelopment, real estate speculation, and the restoration of landmark properties in the Marais led from the 1970s onward to the destruction or conversion of scores of workshops that in the nineteenth or early twentieth century had been dropped into palatial courtyards, or added between wings of *hôtels particuliers* (townhouses). Ever poetic, local architects and building authorities call these drop-in structures "pustules." The add-ons go instead by the name "parasites." By shedding their pustules, parasites, and—unfortunately—the artisans who worked in them, many townhouses have come full circle, reclaiming their pre-Revolutionary architectural beauty while losing their souls.

The story is somewhat different I discovered in the Faubourg Saint-Antoine, still the city's woodworking and furniture district. Redevelopment over the past twenty years has led to the demolition of entire city blocks, where many a workshop lurked in a dingy back courtyard. Take a walk from the Bastille north along Rue de la Roquette then down Rue du Basfroi and you'll get a glimpse of how much has been reconfigured.

Even in neighborhoods spared by developers the usual combination of rising rents, stricter anti-pollution laws, and lack of parking and warehouse space began squeezing out crafts workers in the 1980s. Most of them migrated east, to places such as Vincennes, Saint-Mandé, Saint-Maur, and Montreuil. Many moved even farther into the suburbs, so far out that it's unfair to count them as Parisians.

In the too-little, too-late department, government officials have tried various means to stem the flow or lure some crafts workers back. Particularly desirable are sculptors, cabinetmakers, and decorators, whose activities are judged less "polluting." That means they're less noisy or dangerous than other crafts in a crowded inner-city context. About twenty-five years ago Paris began re-housing its beleaguered artisans in new, light-industrial buildings, most of them sited in the 11th arrondissement. A handful of other complexes were tossed up in the 13th arrondissement (the Vincent-Auriol and Tolbiac quarters) and the 20th arrondissement.

As you might expect these modern workshops lack the charm

of yesteryear, and some nostalgic artisans I have spoken with lambaste the city for having created sterile environments while allowing speculators to destroy historical properties. Others point out that these new ateliers are better lit, warmer, and safer than many of the funky, vintage sites they replaced, and that, generally speaking, the artisans lucky enough to have found a place in them are satisfied.

Why not judge for yourself, I often ask friends who inquire about Paris's craftsmen. You can get an idea of what these new complexes are like by visiting the Cité Artisanale de l'Allée Verte, built in the 1980s. My wife used to get her banged-up old cameras fixed there—until digital photography came along. One day while she talked shutters and flash cords I wandered around and met a fifth-generation engraver named Gérard Desquand.

One moment Desquand was stooped over his cluttered workbench like Albrecht Dürer, magnifying lens and antique engraver's point in hand. The next he was designing a family crest on his computer. He smiled and shrugged in one telling gesture, unused to talking about himself. His workshop is called G4 Gravure. He set it up in 1986 with three partners. Like his father before him, Desquand won the Meilleur Ouvrier de France award, the country's highest craft recognition. He might miss the cozy old family workshop but he did not say so to me. His clients have included fashion houses like Yves Saint Laurent and Dior; and famous Paris stationers or genealogists such as Stern, Agry, or Benneton Graveur. Private clients, he said, making sure I took note, need only provide drawings or a description to commission an engraving from him. Many aristocratic families rely on Desquand, for he specializes in heraldry and, he boasted, once engraved the royal devices of the Comte de Paris, the now deceased pretender to the throne of France. Yes, there is a throne of France, he assured me. It lodges in the minds of passionate Royalists, of whom there are several hundred thousand. Detractors consider them a royal pain in the Republic.

Since then Desquand has moved into his own workshop a few blocks away in Rue d'Oberkampf, but Paris officials have continued to re-house other artisans like him in similar, purpose-built complexes in the neighborhood.

It's clear, however, that the enthusiasm of the pen-pusher-and-bulldozer set lies elsewhere. Specifically, it abides in a visibly impressive and publicly accessible urban project that was initiated in 1987: the Viaduc des Arts. It took ten years to reconvert the arches of the mid-nineteenth-century former railroad viaduct on Avenue Daumesnil east of the Bastille into a showcase for the city's upscale arts and crafts. The official inauguration took place in October 1998. The Viaduc des Arts stretches about half a mile with perhaps sixty shops tucked under its arches. This being Paris, several cafés and restaurants are at hand to slake shoppers' thirst. This being France, there is also a good deal of government money being spent by organizations that hide behind acronyms, including VIA (Valorisation de l'Innovation dans Ameublement), which promotes contemporary furniture and design.

The eye-catching activities of the artisans, and the attractively landscaped Promenade Plantée linear garden that runs on top of the viaduct, have turned the Avenue Daumesnil into a favorite walking, biking, and window-shopping area. You could, I suppose, spend several days visiting the workshops and boutiques here, though most passersby simply pause and peer into the tall plate-glass windows. Behind them ceramists paint plates, puppet makers make puppets, glass blowers blow baubles, and so forth, all of them doing their tricks in public view. The artisans double as performers. Luckily some of them obviously enjoy hamming it up and the others manage to forget they're the monkeys at the zoo.

Here's a curious fact to consider: while the Viaduc des Arts has had an enthusiastic reception by Parisians, and appears to be a commercial success, most of the artisans working there came from the provinces, not from Paris workshops. I once chatted with the only family of artisans from town that I could find, the affable Michel Fey et al., a clan of tooled-leather workers whose great grandfather André created Maison Fey in 1900. Until the late 1990s, said Michel as he stretched a hide, the family workshop occupied two dank, cluttered ground-floor spaces in the Faubourg Saint-Antoine a few blocks away. Michel added that though he and his son Christophe continue to use century-old tools to craft or restore leather desks or tabletops and blotting pads, the family is thoroughly delighted to have moved into their light, airy, modern space. As they toil, not only can they see trees and passersby. They also have easy parking and freight loading areas, and three times as much space as before. They pay more rent but that's offset by higher turnover because of increased visibility. So everyone is delighted.

Fey confirmed that he is among the few craftsmen who moved from the 11th arrondissement to the Viaduc. I asked him why other Parisians hadn't followed. "Because," he whispered, "most Paris artisans are secretive, conservative, traditional, ornery, and obsessively independent." As if that weren't enough, he added, many old-timers simply couldn't afford the move, or were discouraged from making it by the commission responsible for allotting space. As the project's name suggests, the emphasis at the Viaduc des Arts is *l'artisanat d'art,* meaning arty things that are pretty, quiet, clean, and good for the city's image.

I was pleased for Fey, just as I was for the artisans of the modern, soulless complexes I'd visited earlier. Still, it was as gratifying as it was saddening for me to revisit three of the city's premier artisans in the atmospheric Marais workshops I'd seen when I first moved to the neighborhood in the mid-1980s. Two were still active, while the third was heading into retirement and selling up. That's where I started my artisan hunt, chez Patrick Desserme, the glass-molder on Rue du Pont aux Choux.

When the Bastille was stormed and dismantled in 1789 some of the stones were used to build the glassworks where, until recently, Desserme, a third-generation *bombeur de verre,* molded magnificent globes, camber-windows, clock crystals, and lantern panes. Wearing T-shirts even in winter, the feisty Desserme and his assistant were working in the infernal heat of half a dozen furnaces (including one wood-burner from the eighteenth century).

Wiping away sweat, Desserme growled that he was among a handful of European glass-molders still using artisan techniques. With more than five thousand new and antique molds strewn and stacked around his workshop, he boasted that he could replace glass elements of everything from Louis XV lanterns to postmodern furniture. His grandfather worked with Lalique, he said, his father with Max Ingrand. He himself teamed up with contemporary design gurus the likes of Philippe Starck, Andrée Putman, Jean-Michel Wilmotte, or Garouste and Bonetti. Whether his son and successor Hugues would do the same he did not know.

The reclusive Desserme was a rarity among glass-molders in that he also created pieces for collectors, one-of-a-kind glass consoles, for instance, or tables and objets d'art, though he never advertised this fact, and indeed preferred to be left alone. Because of the dangerous nature of glass molding, the fate of the family workshop in Paris was writ large. Luxurious private apartments have recently taken its place. But Desserme's son Hugues did decide to carry on the family craft, independently, in Rouen, far from Paris.

A five-minute walk from Desserme's furnaces is Gilbert Rotival's cupboard-sized atelier. Like his father and grandfather before him, Rotival, a tooled-leather craftsman and case-maker, was named Meilleur Ouvrier de France. Though beyond retirement age, he carries on the tradition in an utterly impractical but magical workshop wedged into the ground floor of a 1637 townhouse. Rotival's buttery-soft wallets are worth more than the money in them, unless you're carrying very large bills. His jewelry cases are as precious as the stones they hold—more precious, if you ask me. Quiet, kind, and shy, Rotival showed me again the vintage tools and century-old sewing machine he uses to transform dyed and gilded leather into attaché cases, handbags and steamer trunks for the lucky few, or for companies like Cartier and Morabito. I asked him what his most memorable job had been. He thought then spoke quietly. "An elaborate leather-covered treasure chest for Saudi King Fahd's collection of priceless gold objects," he said at last. "It took me and five assistants more than two hundred man-hours to make."

I reflected on that number: two hundred man-hours for a treasure chest. I wondered if King Fahd had appreciated it. By the time I'd thought that through, and considered its geopolitical ramifications, I'd walked up Rue des Francs-Bourgeois and turned north on a side street, Rue Elzévir. Here, about sixty years ago, a wood sculptor named Jean Renouvel began his working life as a humble apprentice. He carved his way to the top. About thirty years ago Renouvel began training a young, timid apprentice named Anne-Marie Nicolle. In the early 1990s when I first met them, Renouvel and Nicolle were working together to recreate wood panels for Marie-Antoinette's boudoir at the Petit Trianon in Versailles. Nicolle, as shy as ever, eventually took over the workshop. But nothing in or about it has changed. Antique sculpted wood and plaster casts—used as models—hang from the ceiling above cupids and Corinthian capitals, festoons and friezes. When I met Renouvel for the first time he told me he absolutely refused to use new chisels and gouges for the simple reason that they were no better, and were usually considerably less good, than the heavy, cumbersome tools he'd inherited in the 1950s. Nicolle, now a middle-aged woman and herself a crafts master, has inherited Renouvel's twelve hundred antique tools and is quietly following his example.

Dear Dead Vincent van Gogh

Some day or other, I believe I will find a way to have my own exhibition in a café.

—VINCENT VAN GOGH to his brother Theo,
June 10, 1890

The commuter train from Paris's Gare du Nord took about an hour and a quarter to cover the twenty miles to Auvers-sur-Oise via a bedroom community called Saint-Ouen-l'Aumône. "That's a quarter of an hour more than it took Vincent back in 1890," scoffed the man at the café facing Auvers's vintage train station. He sipped his coffee and spread his arms. "When Vincent came out here from Montmartre the train was direct and we were in the countryside—farms, the Oise River, thatched houses, it was beautiful, beautiful . . ."

Traffic on the road outside was heavy. Suburban housing projects hedged in the south side of town. Auvers is now part of Greater Paris, a city Vincent van Gogh hated and loved in equal measure, as do many of its residents.

Two essential things emerged from what this loquacious local had told me. First, he called Van Gogh "Vincent," as if he knew him. Second, he was obviously suffering from acute nostalgia for a period he couldn't possibly have known. I judged him to be around fifty years old. Van Gogh came to Auvers on May 21, 1890. He died here at the Auberge Ravoux, at the time a cheap lodging house, seventy days later, on July 29, having shot himself in the chest during a fit of the intermittent insanity that came over him throughout his tumultuous thirty-seven-year life. It might have been a form of epilepsy or possibly porphyria, a hereditary nervous disorder. Theo van Gogh is thought to have succumbed to it, too: he died six months after his brother, aged thirty-four.

Vincent and Theo van Gogh were buried in Auvers's otherwise unremarkable cemetery. Since then the village's fame has increased manyfold. It draws about half a million Van Gogh pilgrims yearly. After living in the capital for decades I thought it high time I join them. Most beeline to the graveyard, the Auberge Ravoux and the locales Van Gogh painted. I decided to do the same.

Boosters call Auvers the "cradle of Impressionism." Before Van Gogh arrived, painters the likes of Pissarro, Guillaumin, Monet, Daubigny (of the Barbizon school), and Cézanne lived or worked here from the mid-1800s onward. Vincent remains the star of the show, however, because of his tragic end and the notoriety (and astronomical prices for his paintings) that followed.

Having finished our coffees and said good-bye to the chatty man in the café facing the train station, Alison and I marched a few hundred yards north to the village church. It's easy to spot.

Notre-Dame-d'Auvers started life at about the time the Normans conquered England, that is, in 1066 (and all that). But the Romanesque tower and buttressed backside that Vincent loved were built in 1170. Or so said the friendly woman volunteer at the table inside the church. She was eager to show us around, though there wasn't much to see. Apparently we were the only visitors so far on this winter weekday, early in the morning. The cold, musty, echoing sanctuary instilled in us poignant thoughts propitious for Van Gogh–hunting.

It was Alison who noticed the panel outside the church, flanking the road to the cemetery. The panel showed a full-color reproduction of Van Gogh's painting *L'Église d'Auvers*. As we stood bemused before it, a group of tourists trudged up the hill from their bus and paused. Several framed the panel and the church on the screens of their digital cameras. *Bzzz, bzzz, bzzz* went the cameras. There was a good deal of jostling. Everyone gave suggestions on how to reproduce the mad genius's framing while also including the panel.

A raw-boned white horse roamed freely in a field between the church and the cemetery, which sits on an elevated plateau. This part of Auvers hasn't been developed and looks pretty much the way it did in 1890, to judge from period photographs. The horse led us toward another panel. It showed Van Gogh's summertime painting of a wheat field with crows and curling unpaved roads. The crows and muddy roads were still there. *Caw, caw, caw* croaked the crows as we tramped in the icy mud.

In Vincent's day, the view from up here reportedly took in the Oise River, endless farmland, and thatched houses (though they were disappearing already in 1890, noted the artist). Now you can't help noticing the inevitable spread of apartment buildings, small industry, and commerce.

Somehow we managed to miss the maps indicating the whereabouts in the cemetery of the Van Gogh brothers' tomb. A smiling local showed us to it. He turned out to be the gravedigger and was disarmingly friendly, like the woman in the church and the man in the café by the station. Chilly Paris, rising just across the fields, seemed distant.

We hurried over to have a look at the grave before the busload of fellow visitors arrived. To me it evoked old-fashioned twin beds, except that here the headboards were lichen-frosted stone knotted with ivy. The gravedigger removed a few decomposed offerings left by Vincent's admirers, said farewell to us, and disappeared.

I couldn't help feeling queasy. Here we were, two unwitting pilgrims sighing and looking forlorn, already calling Van Gogh by his first name. Vincent.

We failed to find the resting place of Dr. Gachet (the art collector–doctor who ministered to Van Gogh is in fact buried at Père-Lachaise cemetery in eastern Paris). We could not find a single historic personage whose name we recognized, and soon squelched back across the plateau to the wheat-field panel. On it was a quote from one of Vincent's many letters to Theo: "Immense expanses of wheat under troubled skies, and I don't mind trying to convey the sadness, the extreme solitude . . ."

Apparently it was a few hundred yards from this spot, behind the Auvers château, that Vincent shot himself. I couldn't help wondering how many visitors to Auvers overlook the fact that something about this place drove the mad Dutchman to commit suicide.

The muddy road led us from the plateau down to the edge of another part of town. Long and narrow, Auvers straggles along for about three miles, wrapping around the plateau. Soon we stumbled upon the workshop of landscape painter Charles-François Daubigny (1817–78). Stumbled? Well, not really: there were several signs pointing to it. In fact there are signs on just about every street corner in Auvers pointing to one attraction or another. You can't get lost for long.

Daubigny was an illustrious member of the Barbizon school of painters who worked primarily around Fontainebleau. Nonetheless he spent much of his life in and near Auvers. Thirty years before Van Gogh arrived, Daubigny was here to welcome the aged master Camille Corot, sometimes called a "pre-Impressionist," and the young Claude Monet.

Although Daubigny's atelier wasn't supposed to be open in winter we weren't aware of that and boorishly rang the bell. Instead of snarling, the owner smiled winningly and let us in. He turned out to be Daubigny's great-great-grandson. A small, soft-spoken man in his sixties or seventies, Daniel Raskin Daubigny sported worn leather slippers and a woodsman's shirt open at the collar. His wife shook our hands then returned to the kitchen where she was cooking something that smelled delicious.

Delicious was the word that kept dancing in my mind as Monsieur Raskin Daubigny showed us from room to room. It was a humble family house and workshop, built in 1861 and decorated by Corot, Daumier, Oudinot, Daubigny *père,* and his son Charles (alias Karl). The plank floors creaked. The heady smells of beeswax, dust and age-blotched paper mixed with those of Madame's slow-simmering stew. Wintry light slanted in through high windows. On the walls hung lovely landscapes and seascapes and light, joyful representations of bundled wheat, roosters, and the four seasons.

As we shuffled along, Monsieur Raskin Daubigny told us how he'd spent years and a small fortune restoring the place then decided to open it to the public in 1990. The convoluted tale of the inheritance and the travails of his relatives seemed straight out of Balzac or Zola. To top it all, once he'd fixed the atelier and thrown open its doors, the French tax inspectors tripled his taxes, or so he claimed with disgust. But he was a cheerful man nonetheless and proud of his heritage.

"Oh yes, this was my room, too," he announced, showing us the children's room, called "*la Chambre de Cécile.*" "I was terribly afraid of the big bad wolf," he added. In 1863 Daubigny, his daughter Cécile, and son Charles had painted the walls with fanciful scenes from the tales and fables of Perrault, Grimm, and La Fontaine. Little Red Riding Hood was there, and the wolf. I, too, would've been afraid of him, staring out at my crib, licking his chops.

The best was yet to come. The atelier, furnished like a living room, has a cathedral ceiling and a wall of windows. Enormous landscape canvases showing Italy's lake district, herons, and French country scenes cover the other three walls. "Corot conceived them," said our host. "Daubigny father and son painted them, with Oudinot. Some parts may have been done by Corot himself..."

Whoever painted them, after more than a century they remain perfect for the site, a true, unself-conscious work of installation art. We stared at the landscapes long and rapturously as Monsieur Raskin Daubigny told us in fascinating detail about his great-great-grandfather's friendship with Corot and Monet. And about how an unscrupulous art dealer tried in the 1980s to buy the whole house and atelier from him planning to dismantle and ship it to America. "I don't care about money," he said, eyes twinkling. "I care about this." Happily the atelier is a registered landmark and no one can touch it.

By the time we'd studied the clutter of Daubigny souvenirs in a glass case (medals from painting salons, a daguerreotype, plaster casts) and stepped into the garden, it was nearly lunchtime. Monsieur and Madame showed us a last oddity: the floating painting workshop that Monet used. It was a small riverboat with a studio-cabin for painting, cooking, and sleeping. "Actually this is a replica Monet built of the boat my great-great-grandfather used when he drifted down the Oise to the Seine, painting as he went, all the way to Normandy and the sea..."

It was this delicious image that accompanied us as we followed the signs back to Auvers's church and a lunch spot recommended by Monsieur Raskin Daubigny. Though the interior was studiously twee, it was a good choice: the ham and cheese omelets were the size of Frisbees, and the homemade pear-and-chocolate pie alone was worth the trip from Paris to Auvers. Visitors like us talked in hushed voices of "poor, sad Vincent." A table of locals, instead, noisily applauded a freshly coiffed white poodle that yapped and sneezed on command. "Is he called Vincent?" I asked. "Vincent? No, his name is Event," answered his owner. "Because he was such an important event in my life . . ."

The official Daubigny Museum—not the atelier—and the Museum of Absinthe were both closed. But the inevitable signs pointed to Dr. Gachet's house. We recognized it immediately from the full-color panel near the front gate showing Van Gogh's *Portrait du Docteur Gachet.* A soulful little man with a crinkly white hat and blue coat, Gachet clutched in his hand a spray of foxglove, also known as medicinal digitalis.

Some of the same trees Van Gogh shows in another Auvers picture, *Dans le Jardin du Docteur Gachet,* appeared to be still alive well over a century after he painted them. The tall white house (also painted by Cézanne, another of Gachet's artist friends) once held many priceless paintings. Closed for decades, to locals it became a haunted house whose reopening as a "Place of Memory" only partly dissipated the ghoulish feel. The red window frames are no longer peeling as they once were, and the green shutters that flapped in the wind like the gills of a dying fish have been restored. The Maison du Dr. Gachet is ostensibly a house-museum, but as I wandered around its echoing, somber rooms I felt a chill. There isn't a lot to see—some vintage photos, a reproduction of Vincent's only eau-forte etching showing Dr. Gachet. I have never been fond of shrines, especially when they're associated with commercial enterprises, and a commercial shrine is precisely what the house seemed to be. It's managed by the same people who own the Auberge Ravoux, the hallowed place where Vincent drew his last breath.

At Auvers's seventeenth- to eighteenth-century château we discovered one of the town's most popular family attractions, a multimedia extravaganza called "Voyage to the Time of the Impressionists." We hesitated. It sounded like high kitsch. But the weather was foul and we soon tired of sloshing around in the château's muddy grounds, unable because of the rain to see from the panoramic terrace.

Inside the château we were issued with outsized headphones and pointed at the first room, the Portrait Gallery. There were the usual suspects: Renoir, Monet, Pissarro, Caillebotte, Sisley, Boudin, and the sole woman Impressionist, Berthe Morisot.

Suddenly we were whisked by voices and images into the dark, dank Paris of the 1860s, among the riffraff of Rue de la Tuerie ("Slaughter Street") and other charming addresses wiped out by Baron Georges-Eugène Haussmann in his colossal Second Empire remake of the city. Period photos showed Haussmann's destruction of medieval Paris—about twenty-five thousand buildings razed—and the birth of the modern capital the Impressionists painted.

As we walked from room to room in the château the tableaux and voices changed automatically with eerie ease, activated by motion sensors. Here were Haussmann's comfortable new buildings aligned on wide boulevards, with new train stations, grand cafés, legally registered whorehouses, iron bridges, bourgeois families out for a stroll. Here, too, were dozens of wonderful political cartoons hanging on the walls or projected on a screen. All referred to the works of the Impressionists. In one a disgruntled viewer comments: *These paintings need to be seen from afar!* Another retorts: *I know, that's why I'm leaving.* Other rooms faithfully reproduced historic Paris interiors where nineteenth-century music-hall songs played, the period's charm and seediness evoked side by side.

By the time we'd learned in a replica Impressionist Café-Théâtre about the irresistibility of absinthe (the LSD of the nineteenth century); waited in a mock-1870s Paris train station; then "ridden" the steam train out through beautiful projected countryside to Auvers, the way the Impressionists did, we were both thoroughly taken in. Having already eaten our giant omelets ear-lier, we resisted the temptation to lunch at the château's Impres-sionist *guinguette*—a popular eatery as depicted in the paintings of Renoir et al.

This may be Auvers's answer to Disneyland Paris, I thought, but it's cleverly and intelligently done, the best evocation of the City of Light in its heyday I have yet to encounter. Even the silly, computer-modified image of Monet's self-portrait blinking its eyes at you is contagiously funny.

There was just enough time to get to the Auberge Ravoux before it closed. We raced a mile or so back through town and squeezed in. The auberge dates back to 1855. It faces the town hall on one side, a cobbled courtyard on the other. In Vincent's day its owners sold wine and wood, served meals, and rented out three rooms upstairs. Authur Gustave Ravoux took it over not long before Van Gogh arrived. For 3.50 francs a day the Dutch-man got a tiny room and three squares: meat and vegetables, salad, and bread.

Theo Van Gogh had probably hoped that his ailing brother could stay at Dr. Gachet's house and get treatment there, but that proved impossible. So he arranged for another young Dutch painter named Anton Hirschig to move into the room next door to Vincent's at the auberge and keep an eye on him. No one really knows precisely where or with what kind of gun Vincent shot himself. He managed to get back to the auberge, drag himself upstairs, and hang onto life for a painful day and a half. After he died, no one wanted to sleep in the room of an insane suicide victim, so it was used for storage and somehow escaped alteration.

Having paid the entrance fee we climbed up to the room via a well-stocked, luxurious bookstore-boutique on the second floor. The Auberge Ravoux is no longer a quaint little inn: shortly after Van Gogh's paintings became the most valuable in the world, in 1987, a businessman named Dominique-Charles Janssens bought the place, created the Institut Van Gogh, restored the building to its original configuration, and in the early 1990s reopened it as the Maison Van Gogh, a tourist attraction. Janssens did a consummate job.

From the bookshop we opened a shabby old door and hiked up the final flight of steps. Anton Hirschig's room had been restored to its 1890s simplicity: period wallpaper, a single box-spring bed, a washbasin and chest of drawers. Vincent's even smaller room next door was barren, without furniture or wallpaper. You could taste the raw plaster in the air. On one side of the room was an empty plate-glass display case with an extract from a June 10, 1890, letter Vincent wrote his brother Theo: "Some day or other, I believe I will find a way to have my own exhibition in a café."

Starting in the mid-1990s Janssens's institute began lobbying France's museum bureaucracy for permission to decorate the room with *Landscape of Auvers After the Rain* (at the Pushkin Museum, in Moscow), but decades have now gone by. The empty bullet-proof display case conceived for it clashed somewhat with the garret's spartan walls and somber mood, which generated the same shrine-like quality as the Maison du Dr. Gachet. Janssens's desire to exhibit a real Van Gogh seemed perfectly understandable. The restored auberge draws about seventy thousand paying pilgrims a year. With a multi-million-dollar original in Vincent's room that number would soar.

In the third upstairs room we watched a twelve-minute video about Vincent's seventy days in Auvers. Skillfully made, with music by Richard Strauss, it pressed all the right buttons. I blew my nose and dried my cheeks as we walked downstairs and dropped thirty dollars for a thin book on Vincent's life in Paris and Auvers. I resisted the temptation to buy the Van Gogh–inspired cookbook.

Our last stop was the ground-floor restaurant, an authentic recreation of something a bourgeois traveler could have experienced hereabouts a century ago, with wooden tables, period settings, and carafes and glasses designed to look like those in the Van Gogh painting *L'Absinthe*. The restaurant quickly became a favorite among Paris's glitterati. Hanging on a wall was a sketch by the celebrated French political cartoonist Sempé. In it a throng is trying to get into the Grand Palais for a Van Gogh exhibition. The caption says, "This is the guy who wanted to have a show in a café . . ."

Beaumarchais's Marais

Je me presse de rire de tout, de peur d'être obligé d'en pleurer. (I make myself laugh at everything, for fear of having to weep.)

—Pierre-Augustin Caron de Beaumarchais,
The Barber of Seville

You can walk across the Marais in half an hour or, like me, spend a lifetime exploring the leafy squares, alleys, and mossy courtyards of one of Paris's more atmospheric neighborhoods. They're woven along imperfectly traced arteries between the Bastille and Beaubourg, the Seine and Temple, in the 3rd and 4th arrondissements. Nowadays *le shopping* may well be what draws most visitors to this self-consciously chic theme park for what Parisians call *bobos*—bohemian bourgeois. Boutiques, art galleries, and faux-bistros are shoehorned wall-to-wall between museums and administrative offices in landmark Louis-something townhouses.

But behind the restored façades and under the cobbles lurk layers of history. Since the mid-1980s I've lived near Place des Vosges, the neighborhood's centerpiece, and when it comes to understanding and appreciating the Marais I've barely scraped the icing off the layer-cake.

Despite its inauspicious name—*marais* is old French for swamp or marsh—and equally murky proto-historical days as a floodplain, the neighborhood has long lured an impressive roster of humanity. Some contemporary admirers like to hark back thousands of years, but in my wanderings I've never heard the rumble of chariots on Rue Saint-Antoine (the neighborhood's ancient Roman backbone) or the clatter of medieval knights en route to their fortresses at the Bastille or Temple. But echoes from the Marais's past, especially those from the seventeenth and eighteenth centuries' Golden Age, continue to resonate above the white noise of cell phones and street-corner ensembles. One voice in particular often calls out to me, the voice of Pierre-Augustin Caron, better known as Beaumarchais. "I make myself laugh at everything," Beaumarchais's Figaro famously quipped, "for fear of having to weep."

Clockmaker, musician, playwright, pamphleteer, arms dealer, and spy, Beaumarchais was born in 1732 on Rue Saint-Denis, a few blocks west of the Marais, and later lived in a Rue Vieille-du-Temple mansion in what's now the Marais's gay district. He died in 1799, having made and lost several fortunes, in an extravagant palace he'd built on Boulevard Beaumarchais, abutting Place de la Bastille and Boulevard Richard Lenoir. Beaumarchais certainly loved the Marais. Would he love it today?

A bronze statue on Rue Saint-Antoine in a small square on the corner of Rue des Tournelles shows a handsome, vigorous Beaumarchais. His walking stick is bent: for the last hundred-odd years people have been hanging bouquets from its tip, during the protest marches that start at Place de la Bastille and, traditionally, move up Rue Saint-Antoine to city hall or along Boulevard Beaumarchais to Place de la République. A hotel just off Rue de Rivoli, and plaques on walls scattered here and there, bear Beaumarchais's name. They remind the Marais's window-shoppers that Beaumarchais was the author of the plays *The Barber of Seville* and *The Marriage of Figaro.*

Like the neighborhood's façades and cobbled recesses, these physical testimonials open the doors of speculative fancy. To my mind what really makes Beaumarchais ever present amid the Marais's bumper-to-bumper trendies is his eerily contemporary, disconcertingly ambiguous character. It merged in a single person the brutal contradictions and wild paradoxes of an age more like our own than many might think. If such a thing as "spirit of place" exists then Beaumarchais's might very well have been—and still be—the spirit of the Marais and that of many of its residents: ambitious, litigious, subversive, licentious, arrogant, nostalgic, progressive, enlightened, opportunistic, self-important, at once aristocratic and thoroughly parvenu. Sound like the designers, architects, statesmen, fashion models, and starlets who call the Marais home today?

If he were alive the contrarian Beaumarchais would probably be director of the Opéra de la Bastille, receiving a salary plus subsidies (as a librettist, musician, and playwright) from the Ministry of Culture while simultaneously trying to dismantle the old-boy bureaucracy sustaining him. Since Boulevard Beaumarchais is traffic-clogged and undistinguished nowadays, he might choose instead to live in, say, the quietly posh Place des Vosges, perhaps in the same restored townhouse as former Socialist minister Jack Lang. Or maybe he'd gut and reconvert a historic property in Rue des Francs-Bourgeois, like celebrity architect Jean Nouvel, whose bald pate and flashy black designer-wear are a neighborhood curiosity.

More likely, Beaumarchais would knock down a landmark mansion or two and build something new, vast, and provocative—after all, he was a passionate innovator, and he did help bring down the sclerotic Ancien Régime despite his closeness to Louis XVI and Marie-Antoinette. Doubtless a modern Beaumarchais would dine regularly at such Michelin-starred Marais perennials as L'Ambroisie or Benôit, breaking bread with politicos from left and right, needling and wheedling both, soliciting and dispensing kickbacks, making and breaking allies and enemies alike. Perhaps he would lobby the Greens to turn the Marais into a car-free zone, as some misguided inhabitants are currently trying to do, while ensuring that he could still drive his SUV or Ferrari to his sumptuous digs (and those of his many mistresses).

"Drinking when we're not thirsty and making love year round, Madame, that's all that distinguishes us from other animals," sang Figaro. And, as Beaumarchais's biographers agree, Figaro and his creator were one and the same.

It was among the clocks, jewels, and musical instruments with which his father was entrusted that Beaumarchais, barely out of his teens, invented a spring mechanism that made watches run more accurately. And it was in defending his invention from Jean-André Lepaute, the royal watchmaker who stole his idea, that Beaumarchais demonstrated his preternatural talents as writer and orator. He won his case before the Academy of Sciences and soon replaced Lepaute at Louis XV's Versailles court, quickly becoming, among other things, harp instructor to the king's daughters, the associate of the kingdom's biggest arms dealer, and protégé of the king's official mistress, Madame de Pompadour.

The young Beaumarchais craved respectability, and while the city's best addresses at the end of Louis XV's reign were being built in the Left Bank's Saint-Germain neighborhood, the Marais was still a fashionable enclave, just as it is now, for blue-bloods and professionals at the top of their career. Only after years of social climbing, court intrigue, spying on the king's behalf, gunrunning, and two marriages (the first to a rich widow with a property named "Beaumarchais," whence his title) did the watchmaker-become-nobleman manage to move from Versailles via London to a Marais townhouse. That townhouse was the luxurious Hôtel Amelot de Bisseuil, often called the Hôtel des Ambassadeurs de Hollande, in Rue Vieille-du-Temple.

If you stroll up this café-lined street from Rue de Rivoli you'll see immediately on your right the three-star Hôtel Caron de Beaumarchais. It liberally derives its name and theme décor—a 1792 Erard pianoforte in the lobby and cozily faux–Ancien Régime–style rooms—from the proximity of Beaumarchais's residence, two blocks north. Hidden among the bookshops and the fashion accessory and specialty food boutiques, the mansion stands at number forty-seven. Its exterior is grimy, its heavy carriage doors elaborately carved with writhing Medusa heads.

Rebuilt in the 1650s atop medieval foundations, and repeatedly remodeled by the time Beaumarchais rented it in 1776, the townhouse was more than merely the budding playwright's dream residence. It was here, in the gilded, frescoed salons frequented by emissaries and artists, that Beaumarchais headquartered Rodrigue, Hortalez et Cie, a cover worthy of a modern spy novel. The company was at the heart of an intricate clandestine operation to supply American revolutionaries with ships, arms, and gunpowder. With one adroit hand Beaumarchais brought Figaro to life in this townhouse, while with the other he spent more than six million *livres* of French and Spanish gold to help the Insurgents beat the British. Without Beaumarchais, historians say, the decisive Battle of Saratoga could not have been won and America might never have gained its independence. Without Figaro, add others, the Bastille might never have fallen.

It shouldn't detract from his achievements that Beaumarchais undertook both his arms dealing and playwriting to turn a profit—his motto ran, roughly, "Do the public good while lining your own pockets." He was prototypically modern, with eyes firmly on the bottom line. That explains why, in the salons of this mansion in the heat of July 1777, he also created the Société des Auteurs Dramatiques, paving the way for the first laws on intellectual property and royalty payments. It was here too that Beaumarchais became publisher of Voltaire's collected works. This ruinous venture heightened suspicions among hereditary divine-right Ancien Régime aristocrats and plutocrats terrified by Beaumarchais's subversive atheism and beliefs in meritocracy. "You made the effort to be born," says Figaro to Count Almaviva, "but nothing more than that."

Ring the bell marked "Concierge" on the right of the carriage door and push past the carved medusas into the mansion's outer courtyard. The custodian will intercept you; this is still private property. By a series of flukes the building has changed little since Beaumarchais's day. Even the low-relief sculptures surrounding the court have survived (they show Romulus and Remus nursed by the She-wolf; and allegories of Strength, Truth, Peace, and War; plus the goddesses Ceres and Flora). You can only peer through the vaulted passageway at the tantalizing main courtyard, freshly restored, with more sculptures, masks, and garlands. If you're lucky, you might glimpse through parted drapes the dazzling ceilings the playwright-spy knew so well.

Imagine Beaumarchais's gold-encrusted carriage rattling down Rue des Francs-Bourgeois, past the sumptuous Hôtel Carnavalet, now the History of Paris Museum, across Place des Vosges, to the wide boulevard that today bears his name. For several hundred yards along the boulevard's east side stretch the landscaped grounds of the estate Beaumarchais and his third wife have been building since the late 1780s for the phenomenal sum of 1.6 million *livres*. Inheritances and settlements, plus real estate speculation and a controlling interest in Paris' first-ever water utility, have made Beaumarchais fabulously rich. Known as the "Mansion of the Two Hundred Windows," Beaumarchais's estate is a parvenu's paradise, with a semicircular colonnade, temples to Bacchus and

Voltaire, a Chinese humpback bridge, and a waterfall. The Bastille rises to the south, its towers and bastions an ominous theatrical backdrop. The main house is not yet finished when, in April 1789, Beaumarchais and a party of aristocratic friends, including the future King Louis-Philippe, watch with horror as rioters ransack a nearby mansion then assault royal guards, with a loss of some two hundred lives. Have Figaro's spiritual heirs gone mad? Beaumarchais can't help wondering. A few months later, on July fourteenth, Beaumarchais again watches from his terrace as rioters from the blue-collar Faubourg Saint-Antoine neighborhood storm the Bastille. And the rest is history.

"If we were to allow that play to be performed," remarked the otherwise unperceptive Louis XVI in 1784 about *The Marriage of Figaro,* "we would have to demolish the Bastille." Fittingly, when the demolition began on July 15, 1789, Beaumarchais, as president of the Marais's Blancs-Manteaux district, was sent with other dignitaries to supervise. With his typical pragmatism and aplomb he bought—or requisitioned—some of the Bastille's stones and sent them trundling to the worksite of his personal theater under construction at 11 Rue de Sévigné, between Saint-Paul and the Carnavalet—the heart of the Marais.

Demolished in the mid-1800s, there's nothing left but the façade of the Théâtre Beaumarchais (sometimes referred to as the Théâtre du Marais). In 1791–92 the chameleon citizen-playwright staged here the third of his Figaro series, the little-known *La Mère Coupable.* More recently, starting in about 1960, for forty years a Hungarian delicatessen ensconced in what was the theater's foyer sold some of the best salami in Paris. An elegant, could-be-anywhere boutique has now replaced it. Like dozens of unglamorous shoe repair, grocery, and hardware shops, the deli was one of those Marais touchstones from the blue-collar age that have given way to gentrification. When I look up at the former theater's pilasters, my mind's eye sees a slice of the Marais layer-cake. First there was a swamp, then came Philippe-Auguste's medieval city wall, followed by part of La Force prison, then a theater built with the stones of the Bastille, next a Hungarian deli, and now a trendy boutique.

Rewind to Beaumarchais's speeding carriage—by now a nondescript vehicle sans glittering gold, in keeping with Revolutionary etiquette. Who knows how many times it rumbled from the theater to the Mansion of Two Hundred Windows, racing past carts loaded with prisoners on the way to the guillotine? Ironically, the Committee of Public Safety together with Robespierre almost managed to execute the subversive author of Figaro. True to character, he had reinvented himself as gunrunner for France's new revolutionary despots. Only by luck, chance, and intrigue did Beaumarchais, declared a "counterrevolutionary" and exiled, keep his head on his shoulders. During his absence, troops stormed his Marais estate expecting to uncover weapons. All they found were thousands of unsold volumes of Voltaire's collected works.

There's nothing left of the Mansion of Two Hundred Windows and its grounds, where Citizen Beaumarchais spent the final years of his life, still rich and full of fire but no longer a hero. He died in the last year of the eighteenth century, on the cusp of the modern age, and was buried in his garden near Voltaire's temple, on the edge of the Marais. The final irony, a postscript to this extraordinary life, is that, before the estate was demolished to make way for the Canal Saint-Martin and Boulevard Richard Lenoir, King Louis XVIII's men dug up the freethinking playwright's bones, in 1822, and moved them to Père-Lachaise, a cemetery named for a Jesuit priest. Even in death the itinerant iconoclast knew no rest. Over the rumble of traffic on his boulevard I sometimes hear Beaumarchais chuckling, reminding me that if you don't laugh you're destined to cry.

Madame X's
Seduction School

Frenchmen aren't seducers the way they were . . .

—MADAME X

A small black sheepdog darts over the lawns of Paris's fashionable Bois de Boulogne parklands, among coiffed pooches and Catherine Deneuve lookalikes. The middle-aged man at the other end of the retractable leash eases over to a chic Parisienne with a poodle. "Ah, you must be Madame Fifi," he splutters, taking cues from another woman standing nearby. "Perhaps you could advise me on how to help my dog adapt to Paris life—I've just moved here you see and . . ."

Cut to the outdoor terrace of a crowded Paris café. Another

man, this one a frump in his mid-thirties, has been eyeing the young woman at the next table but hasn't screwed up the courage to talk to her. On cue from a half-hidden figure seated at the table behind him, the man clears his throat, leans toward the object of his desire, and smiles winningly. "*Pardonez-moi,* I know this is going to sound strange, and I don't usually do such things, but I have to say there's something really interesting on the back page of your newspaper. Could I take a look at it?"

At an upscale boutique in Rue Saint-Honoré, a cute saleswoman shows a pair of expensive shoes to a fortyish man dressed like someone from Federico Fellini's *La Dolce Vita.* The man is exquisitely polite and charming, though he's obviously shy, and after paying for his shoes returns a few minutes later with a single white rose. "Your eyes are so beautiful I just wanted to thank you," he says. The saleswoman—used to dealing with gruff or blasé types—is speechless. He hands her his card. "Next time I'm in Paris may I take you to lunch?"

"But my boyfriend . . ." the woman begins to object.

"It's just lunch, I assure you, your boyfriend has nothing to fear, but there's something about you, your eyes . . ."

What do these corny pickup scenes have in common?

A shadowy puppeteer I'll call Madame X, the feisty founder of Paris's first École de Séduction—a school where you learn the fine art of seduction. Madame X and her crack team of Latin Lover "seduction coaches" accompany advanced students into the field for hands-on sessions. Dogs in parks, newspapers in cafés, and roses in boutiques are just a few of the tricks Madame X uses to push her tongue-tied French males to take the plunge, to make the move and try to pick up the femme fatale of their dreams.

A seduction school in Paris—land of adultery and philandering, the fountainhead of De Sade and Casanova? Yes indeed. The operation got started in the mid-1990s and was such an immediate success that other Seduction Schools popped up (and disappeared overnight). One may be coming soon to a town near you, possibly even in what the French still regard as puritanical middle America. Madame X featured heavily in the French press for a time—she made more than three hundred TV appearances and was written up in about a hundred articles. Then several American TV stations interviewed her, and she was set for stardom. Over a decade and a half later, she's still at it, and still a regular feature on French talk shows. Why?

The answer is straightforward: it's difficult for anyone to believe that Parisian men need to be taught how to pick up women. What has happened to the Jean-Paul Belmondos, the Jean Gabins, the Alain Delons of the country? Most people consider France to be a paradise of the senses—fabulous food, an excess of culture, and sex a-go-go.

"Frenchmen aren't seducers the way they were up to the mid-1980s," Madame X told me in rapid-fire French, flinging her arms around for emphasis. "The relationship between men and women began to go downhill starting then. The reason is fifty years of feminist revolution. At a certain point it had to backfire for women. We've become victims of the war we've waged."

A tall, muscular forty- or perhaps fifty-something, Madame X is an ex–Club Med staff member, a former sales team manager and business consultant, matchmaking agency director, and dancer. She has the imposing presence of a permanently bronzed Alpha Female, with large mobile features, big brown eyes, serious hair, lavish gestures, and canon-shot exclamations. Her body language shouts out conflicting words—randy, bossy, tough, pushy, single-minded, saucy, outspoken, physical. To hear her speak of French women as "victims" of feminism struck me as comical.

In my three decades in Paris I have encountered French women like her, though none wearing, as she was, a loose white shift paired with red basketball shoes, her hair crowned by a pair of sunglasses (despite the fact that we were inside an office building). Most of the

Parisian Alpha Females I have known sport smart Chanel suits and flirt dangerously with the executives come to cut deals with them.

High-strung, impatient, guarded, Madame X moved around her small office in Paris's Opéra neighborhood like a caged lioness—or a Puerto Rican dancer in *West Side Story*. She plucked the sunglasses off her Medusa curls, twirled them, dropped them on her cluttered desk by her shrilling cellular phone, replaced them, scratched her stress-martyred hands, then answered the mobile with a sigh.

If previously I had doubts about her qualifications as a seductress—she certainly had not conquered me—this telephone conversation dispelled them. Her face and voice altered as she purred into the cellular phone, cajoling the woman at the other end in several languages. If nothing else, I sensed, Madame X was a good actress.

"Seventy percent of my clients are men," she confirmed once off the phone, "thirty percent women." Almost all her women clients, it turned out, come not to learn how to seduce men. Some want to master more effective business communications techniques. But, in a country with a thirty-three-percent divorce rate, where bed-hopping is the national pastime, most of them simply want to learn how to keep the men they have.

"Between you and me," she said, getting colloquial and chummy, "we French women are spoiled. We've got full rights, we can have an abortion, we can take the Pill, we can cheat on our husband—no one busts your ass anymore if you commit adultery and it sure wasn't like that once upon a time. We work, we're independent—I just don't understand why we complain. My grandmother always told me, 'You're so damn lucky!' I've got to say, I'm very happy to have been born and to live now."

The main problem with Frenchmen, it seems, and therefore the raison d'être for Madame X's school, is the result of the power of French women today—women who don't have time for men, families, love, or courtship.

Madame X's men—most of them engineers, computer programmers, professionals, or business executives aged thirty to fifty—don't know how to behave with these superwomen, have difficulty communicating with them, and have come to fear them. Madame X's school is the last resort, the Last Chance Saloon for many who've already been to shrinks, matchmakers, and a variety of singles clubs. So her clients spend several thousand dollars and two to nine months learning how to overcome their fears—of rejection, ridicule, or psychic castration.

"For a while there, I wasn't exactly cuddly with men myself," she said, fixing me with a razor-sharp gaze. "I was one of those *castratrices*. Yes, a ball-cutter. Yes, we are ball-cutters, but Frenchmen have become pretty wimpy, too, pretty weak. It's like, 'We were victims, now the men are victims—everyone gets his turn.' But that's not going to fix anyone's problems."

A similar set of problems, related to post-feminist psychic castration, arose at about the same time in Italy, long believed to be the heartland of the Latin Lover. I mentioned this to Madame X and told her how I attended and reported on a school similar to hers run by a certain Giuseppe Cirillo, alias the Prince of Seduction or Doctor Seduction. In real life, Cirillo is a Neapolitan lawyer-turned-psychologist-sexual-therapist. He directed the 2009 movie *Impotenti esistenziali*—about "existential impotence." With increasing social mobility and waning family values in Italy as in France, starting in the 1980s Italian men were suddenly finding themselves washed by their careers onto the shores of strange cities, surrounded by unfamiliar and demanding women. Liberated Italian feminists of the day dreamed up the slogan "Bread but also roses," a baffling refrain to many Italian men and one which spawned countless then unheard-of lonely-hearts clubs, as well as Cirillo's seduction school.

The colorful Cirillo Method, as I experienced it, involved individual and group activities that ranged from the banal—matching facial expressions with Cirillo's so-called "seventy-five primary

emotions," gauging "gait and body language," using "voice modu-
lation, eye and hand techniques"—to the outlandish. Not only
did we engage in thigh-to-thigh role-playing (in one session I
had to explain my way out of being caught sleeping with my girl-
friend's best friend, in another I had to try to sell seminude ballerina figurines to the Salesian Brothers' Oratory). We were also
introduced to Cirillo's secret weapon, the *tavola delle esclusioni,*
a painted wood silhouette of a woman, with strategically placed
slots at head, shoulder, and waist level. Out went the lights. In
came a female presence. After sliding the silhouette's panels back
and forth, allowing us to see the mystery woman's eyes, lips, cleav-
age, or waistline, Cirillo ordered us to step up and knead and
stroke her. This was one of the most extravagantly embarrassing
episodes of my adult life, but my fellow students, some of whom
hadn't touched a flesh-and-blood woman in years, were delighted.

Being French, and a woman, Madame X did not offer her clients anything remotely like Dr. Cirillo's silhouette contraption.
When I finished telling her about it she became pyrotechnic. "He
must have a bunch of basket cases as clients, guys in death throes,
morbidly shy guys," she said, referring to Cirillo and his men. "I
don't have morbidly shy types, I have normal guys." As proof she
showed me a few photographs. Her clients did look normal. The
first thing she does, she said, when she meets a potential client, is
interview him, then send him to a clinical psychologist she works
with. After he's been profiled, she and the psychologist consult
with the client and set up a strictly personal course of instruction.
It can include everything from role-playing to field trips (pickup
practice in clubs, cafés, parks), to dance classes or visits to a sexual
therapist. "Some of my clients are virgins," she admitted, "others
say they don't know how to put on a condom."

Often the beginning of a typically Parisian course with Madame X involves the sartorial and hygienic remake of a client. She
showed me a series of photos demonstrating how she and her crew
have transformed one client from a hopeless slob—mismatched tie

and shirt, baggy outdoorsy pants and rain gear, unkempt hair—to a snazzy hunk. In the photos the remade man wears a gray suit and dark turtleneck and his hair is raked back like a rake with a license to seduce. This makeover technique is called *re-lookage,* a wonderful example of the Franglais Madame X favors. "I often use Alain Delon as an example of how to dress," she said deadpan, adding that she believes clothes do indeed make the man. "He's a successful role model. You might or might not like him, but he's not your run-of-the-mill actor, and he did it himself, so it means you *can* transform a man. When you work at it, when you have the will to change yourself, you can."

Dr. Cirillo may have his silhouette, but Madame X has two secret weapons of her own. The first is the small black Belgian sheepdog that snorted and padded around the office as we spoke. Parisians are dog obsessive; Madame X lends her pet to her clients so they can easily pick up dog-owning females anywhere.

The second weapon comes in the form of field trips to one of Dr. Cirillo's stomping grounds: Rome. She met her husband there, an Italian who picked her up in a café. This explains why Madame X is convinced that Cirillo's clients are total basket cases.

"I take a bunch of Parisian men, we fly to Rome, go the center of town, and I and my women helpers are the bait," she explained. "We sit at a café and demonstrate how Roman men pick us up. We get all dolled up, we sit down, with our clients nearby, and then we wait. And I assure you we don't wait long. Go sit at a Paris café and unless you're wearing a miniskirt pulled up to your panties you can wait two hours before a guy will even talk to you."

So, I asked, despite Cirillo's basket cases, the secret of being a great lover is to be Italian? I could just imagine the Bill Gates lookalikes at Madame X's future American campuses exchanging their pen-protectors for *Dolce Vita* suits, worn boldly to help them shark in on single gals slurping twenty-ounce lattes at the local Starbucks.

"I'm not going to teach American men to pick women up like

Roman men," she protested. "The essential thing is to be likeable instantly in the first seconds when approaching someone."

I soon understood why Madame X was hoping to open a school in America, specifically in California, a Mother Lode of dot.com nerds, luckless bohemian bourgeois *bobos,* and geeks surrounded by post-feminist *castratrices* with sharp sheers, fat wallets, and dating contracts (*You shall not touch me until I specifically request you to do so . . .*).

One question remained in my mind, however: was she qualified? Madame X has traveled to, but never lived in, America. She speaks fluent though flawed English and demonstrates a deep understanding of American culture. "My impression," she confided, "is Americans don't know how to flirt. There isn't a single American who knows how to flirt, and I mean the mating dance, the seduction dance, they don't know how to do it. They don't have good table manners either. I'm not saying all Americans are like that—some aren't of course but . . . The guys in Silicon Valley, in front of their computers all day, they barely know how to hold a fork. American guys can be jokesters, bon vivants, and suddenly they reach out and grab your ass and say *I want to fuck you* or whatever. They're capable of behaving like real hicks. Whereas the bourgeois American guy is calmer, more puritanical."

Once I had left her office I formulated in my mind the "Madame X Method" in three easy steps. One: if you're a man, have Roman gene–implant therapy. Two: if you're a woman, fly to Rome and drink your latte there (despite the fact that no grown Italian drinks latte, which simply means "milk"). Three: if the first two methods don't work, buy a dog. In any case, do not bother coming to Paris in search of romance. Apparently the women nowadays are viragos, the men wimps.

PARIS PHENOMENA

In the Spring

When good Americans die they go to Paris.
— OSCAR WILDE, *A Woman of No Importance* (1893)

Il fait beau, c'est le printemps, ran the lusciously enunciated, taped dialogue at the Pompidou Center's language laboratory. "The weather is beautiful, spring is here," I repeated, joining my own to a dozen eager voices as snow fell beyond the windows. Wherever I went that first April in Paris—now three decades ago—through sleet, rain, wind, and snow, I would cheerfully say my *bonjours* in grade-school French, adding with a wink, *c'est le printemps.* As if in answer the cloudy sky would blow for a few minutes into a blue expanse shot through with light, brightening the wet tin-and-tile mansard roofs time and again, like pebbles on a beach.

Cynics will remind you that the tune "April in Paris" got its

name because the lyricist needed a two-syllable word for his refrain, and "May" or "June" wouldn't do. So what if the "thrill" of
a wintry Paris April rhymes with "chill?" Springtime in Paris is a
celebration, a chant, a hope—a modest dream that keeps millions
going. Even people who have only visited the city in their imagin-
ings know about it. They have sniffed and tasted a Paris spring in
books, movies, and paintings, and felt it warming their skin from
Moscow to Manhattan. To Romantics and adepts of Shakespeare
a Paris spring means sweet lovers loving on the Seine. To foodies
it's the arrival of the year's new Michelin *Guide France* to hotels
and restaurants. To footloose walk-aholics like Alison and me,
spring stands for flower-spangled gardens and sunny hikes. Of
course, to those who view life through jade-colored lenses, and see
horizontal pollution where cobbles glisten, it means rain, wind,
and the first crowds of noxious tourists.

I actually like spring rain: when it stops and the puddles
grow still, you see two cities at a glance, one reflected—and
often framed serendipitously. I like to think of post-Impressionist
painter Gustave Caillebotte's *Paris Street; Rainy Day,* the umbrellas of the passersby held high like the masts of ships navigating
the gleaming boulevards, with buildings, carriages, and people
mirrored in them, plus much more of a commentary on bourgeois
life than meets the eye at first glance.

W. Somerset Maugham's hero in *The Razor's Edge* reveled in
the "light, transitory pleasure, sensual without grossness" of a Paris
spring that filled him with the glow of youth. Émile Zola wrote of
"the charm of awakening desire, the thrill of hope and expecta-
tion." So just this once, leave the pseudo-sophisticates to fret about
clichés, and don't let them spoil your enjoyment. The season will
always have a special significance to me: every year the magic of
those first months I spent in Paris, months full of adventure and
promise, returns fleetingly, flowering like the city's horse-chestnut
trees, the quintessential symbol of springtime in Paris.

Though the city is a year-round destination nowadays, the

number of visitors still spikes at Easter and midsummer, the beginning and end of spring. In January, when April, May, and June seem a lifetime away, I start receiving postcards and, these days, e-mails, announcing friends' spring itineraries. Will it be cold, they ask? They forget that Paris exists geographically (and not simply in their dreams) and is north of Saint John's, Newfoundland, north of Montreal, Boston, Vienna, and Budapest. To be even-handed when I write back, I copy out statistics from encyclopedias and guidebooks. "The average temperature in March," I say, "is 50.4 Fahrenheit, April 60.3 and May 61.9, while June hits 74." And I leave it up to them to judge whether that's warm or not. I often wonder whether these friends imagine, from where they write in sunny Rome or Los Angeles, the effect their messages have. In the dead of a leaden Paris winter, the mention of "spring" steels residents against the unremitting gray. In the mind's eye the Champs-Elysées bursts into elapsed-time leaf, rowboats in the Bois de Boulogne nose along lazy lakes, and ten thousand sun umbrellas sprout like kaleidoscopic mushrooms at street-corner cafés.

Anticipation, the weathering of that seemingly interminable Paris fall and winter, is what makes the spring so special here. It's as much a question of your state of mind as of meteorological phenomena. After a few false starts in February and early March, when picnickers are snatched off benches by icy claws, a sudden change occurs. The roasted-chestnut sellers stow their steel drums and shopping carts, reappearing with fresh-cut mimosa in hand. Lap dogs appear sans doggie jackets. Tulips and forget-me-nots pop up in the Luxembourg Gardens. Bright little sailboats skim across pools in the Tuileries. The bellwether youths of the Latin Quarter dress even more cavalierly than usual—a shirt and a loose-knit sweater, or a thin blazer with a scarf tossed defiantly around a ruddy neck. No-nonsense northern and eastern Europeans pour out of the tour buses behind Notre-Dame wearing warm, practical clothes, which they quickly shed when they find they are no longer in Helsinki, Warsaw, or other places with weather much harsher than Paris's. They rush, camera in hand, from the flying buttresses behind the cathedral to the Seine-side garden to be photographed in front of the cherry blossoms. The Italians, hidden in fur and shearling coats, shiver happily no matter how hot it gets.

On either bank of the Seine, the first things to sprout are not crocuses and daffodils but sidewalk tables and faux-cane chairs. Locals eye them cautiously, hesitating because no one recognizably French has yet dared to sit outside. Clever café-keepers—notably on the Île Saint-Louis, in Place des Vosges, and around Saint-Germain-des-Prés—beat the elements early by investing in Plexiglas windscreens and glowing outdoor gas heaters. These are a surprisingly effective cross between a Second Empire lamppost and a Coleman stove, and they have caught on all over town. No wonder: "The café," states my surprisingly up-to-date, 1912 Ward, Lock & Co. *Paris Guide,* "is the pre-eminently French institution. . . . Verlaine, the great French poet, never wrote a poem anywhere else!"

Indeed, the café still doubles as office and cozy living room in cold months, turning into a lively garden party the rest of the year. No true Parisian will be kept from his great spring communion for long. Once a fearless few have begun to brave the elements by sitting out of doors, the *terrasses* soon overflow. Waiters in their old-fashioned black-and-white penguin uniforms dash to and fro bearing beer, espressos, and steaming hot chocolate.

Another bellwether of spring is the city's outdoor markets. If you arrive early enough you'll see the greengrocers arranging their fruit and vegetables into color-coded pyramids, domes, or Cartesian rows. Flanking last winter's cabbages and mud-spattered cauliflowers nestle tiny zucchini swaddled in protective wrappers and crisp sweet peas from the hothouses of Provence. New potatoes with skins as pale as a Parisian's cry out to be eaten unpeeled in a single bite. Flanking the mounds of cold apples and still-hard pears are baskets of berries, anemic cherries and the first ruinously expensive melons coaxed from the fields of Cavaillon more than 350 miles to the south. So gorgeous is the display that you hesitate before buying, unwilling to deconstruct these succulent still lifes. *Bon melon!* shouts the grocer as you pass by, promising the first taste of honeyed sweetness, nectar, and joy. Seduced by his spiel, you buy an unripe melon, fully aware that you'll be disappointed, but happy to be taken in, as you are each year.

Once spring is in the air, the plein-air painters appear in numbers: glimpsed through trees about to bud, monuments materialize on their easels. I find it difficult to visit museums or galleries in spring unless the works on show are divorced from nature. Instead I choose a vantage point on the edge of town, or an open spot within it, and settle in to watch the greatest exhibition of all—the spring sky and changing cityscape. There are no waiting lines and the show is free. The Pont Saint-Michel, or the Champs-de-Mars, the overlook at Père-Lachaise cemetery, the panoramic park at Belleville or even meretricious old Montmartre are my favorite spots. The shifting light seems to parade the masterpieces of the Louvre and d'Orsay across the heavens. There are swirling, puffy Tiepolo cloudscapes over the Italianate Institut de France and the lacey Pont des Arts. Billowing Renoirs clothe the ridiculous cupolas of Sacré-Coeur. Giddy Pissarros and Signacs float over the Grands Boulevards, the Seine, and the Tuileries. At dusk the mauve Monets and the flaming blues, pinks, and reds of Fauvists like Derain clamp down on this old gray city that is itself an artwork in progress.

The Lac Daumesnil in the Bois de Vincennes on the second, third, or fourth Sunday in April, depending on the calendar year, offers one of the oddest spring double-headers I know: the traditional Foire du Trône funfair, and the Buddhist New Year's celebrations held next door at a municipal temple. At the funfair, bumper-cars bang and merry-go-rounds spin to the nostalgic wheezing of accordions, with the smell of French fries hanging thick enough to slice. Under the Pointillist clouds of horse-chestnut trees lovebirds peck, kids run wild clutching cotton candy, and anglers fish for muddy *goujon* they will never eat. Here are the celebrated rowboats of Paris, each with a name, and here, too, are the swans and ducks and sculpted flowerbeds splashed with primrose, narcissus, and daffodils. A few hundred yards down the lake the gongs and chants of Buddhists fill the air. The atmosphere is scented with spices, frying spring rolls, and roasting meats. The peaceful coexistence of these two fundamentally different festivities, the complete absence of fear or anxiety among the picnickers and pedestrians of every imaginable color and age, makes me think of e.e. cummings's celebration of Paris as a spiritual place "continuously expressing the humanness of humanity."

Sure, Paris is no paradise, though you might be excused for thinking so now and again, especially in the spring. The joyous, homespun rites of *le printemps* possess none of the primordial horror of Stravinsky's music, which seems to suit so many modern megalopolises to a tee. Take, for example, the Parisian version of April first. Each year I receive an urgent telephone call offering me a lucrative book contract, a free trip to a nudist colony in Malta, or something similar, and I invariably fall for the gag. When I go down into the Marais street where we live, not far from the Lycée Charlemagne, a big high school, I inevitably wind up with a large paper fish plastered to my back, cleverly out of view. *Poisson d'Avril!* shout the mischievous but harmless teenagers. April Fool's Day! Then I realize that the book contract and the titillating trip to Malta are bogus, and I console myself with an April Fool's Day treat. The bakers of Paris vie with each other to make the most mouthwatering pastries, cakes, and breads in the shape of fish, and the day becomes yet another excuse to celebrate life and stuff yourself with food. This April Fool's Day I might just spread the word that I'll be running in the Paris Marathon, to work off the cakes, cookies, and winter fat, but somehow I don't think anyone will believe me.

Perhaps the best spring fête of all is May Day. The museums and public buildings close in honor of the workingman and -woman, and not even the most skillful misanthrope or puritanical workaholic can avoid the day's festivities. *Muguet* hawkers appear on every corner, their ingeniously packaged lilies-of-the-valley arrayed in water-filled phials, moss-stuffed pots, or elaborate baskets. Come rain or shine, several hundred thousand merrymakers, most of them leaning to the political left, converge on Place de la Bastille with their bullhorns, wearing sprigs of lovers' *muguet* in their lapels. *Il fait beau,* chant the schoolteachers and students, the factory workers, bus drivers, grocers, and nostalgic socialists with their banners of fallen idols. *C'est le printemps.*

La Ville Lumière:
Paris, City of Light

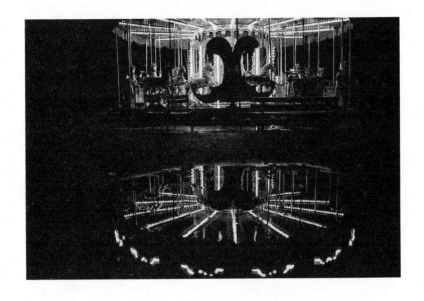

Museum cities are like old cocottes—*only fit to be seen in a soft light.*

—ROBERT DOISNEAU, 1989

Webster's defines "cliché" as a "trite expression" and "trite" as "worn out by constant use." Happily, the title Ville Lumière or City of Light is neither a cliché nor trite. Though it is constantly used in reference to Paris, it has become a nickname, a sobriquet, an endearment.

For me, the images it evokes are rooted in history yet very much alive. Say "Ville Lumière" and some will see old-fashioned street lamps spilling pools of light along the Seine where lovers stroll hand in hand. Others will think of the Champs-Elysées and Eiffel Tower ablaze. Still others will envision night-lit monuments perched on hills—the Panthéon, Sacré-Coeur, Trocadéro—and a cityscape bathed in an otherworldly glow.

Personally I've often imagined the expression had more to do with the welcoming lights of the city's cafés, its bookshops, museums, and universities, where minds meet and tongues wag into the night.

Professors and philosophers like to say that the appellation Ville Lumière isn't about physical sources of light at all. Rather it's a metaphor for political, spiritual, cultural, and intellectual energy. Louis XIV, an enlightened despot, was known as the Sun King (though he abandoned luminous Paris for swampy Versailles). The eighteenth century's Enlightenment found fertile ground here for its philosophical, social and political ideals: empiricism, skepticism, tolerance, and social responsibility. Voltaire, Diderot, Jean-Jacques Rousseau, and other proponents were called *les lumières*.

In his writings on the French Revolution, historian Jules Michelet (1798–1874) was probably the first to call Paris *la Lumière du Monde*—Light of the World, a beacon for humanity. During Michelet's lifetime, Paris underwent radical change: its population more than doubled. By the second half of the nineteenth century (starting with the Second Empire in 1852), Paris had indeed become the most stimulating, the most modern and best-loved of European cities.

In some ways it was an ideal city, a military man's Utopia conceived by Emperor Napoléon III and engineered by his prefect Baron Haussmann. It was anything but ideal, though, for nostalgics or romantics. In *Les Fleurs du Mal* and other works, Charles Baudelaire scented death and urban anguish in Haussmannization—the radical modernization that resulted in the demolition of the medieval city. "Old Paris is gone," Baudelaire wrote in *The Swan*. "No human heart changes half as fast as a city's face."

Haussmann's was an ideal cosmopolis for those who believed in order, uniformity, and the hygienic properties of open air and sunlight. At Napoléon III's behest, the prefect brought down some twenty-five thousand buildings in fewer than twenty years. Broad cannon-shot boulevards and regular street alignments with uniform façades rose where a tangle of dark alleys had once been.

With few exceptions the Impressionists and early photographers who documented this remade world were fascinated by its novel cityscapes and seemingly endless perspectives. They sought above all to capture the effects of a new kind of light that was at once physical and spiritual. It was the light that sifted through the trees planted on the new boulevards. Or the light cast by the hundreds of *réverbère* gas lamps installed in the 1860s on the sidewalks of those boulevards. Light streamed into the tall French windows of modern buildings. Lights burned around the clock in the new cafés, theaters, and train stations that sprang up around town. By association, *la lumière* was also the enlightened attitude of the inhabitants of this marvelous new world.

The late nineteenth century's Universal Expositions, in particular that of 1889, which marked the centennial of the Revolution and the building of the Eiffel Tower, seemed at the time to herald a new age of technical progress and scientific reason in parallel to the artistic flowering of the Belle Époque. We may marvel today at their ingenuousness, but most of the spectators of all classes and walks of life who crowded around to watch the Tour Eiffel's inauguration in 1889 were astonished, transfixed, and delighted. The world's tallest structure at the time, it was lit by ten thousand gas lamps. Fireworks and blazing illuminations drew the spectator's eye to various levels. A pair of powerful electric searchlights—among the earliest of their kind—raked the city's monuments from the summit at a height of 986 feet. Some say it was this signal event that engendered the name Ville Lumière. If so, no one bothered to write it down.

Admittedly not everyone was bowled over by the tower, its lighting display, or what it stood for. Caricatures and political cartoons of the period show strollers shading their eyes at night, blinded by Paris's newfound modernity. One cartoon's caption noted that from then on, people would need to use seeing-eye dogs to go out for an evening stroll. By the 1890s, most of the city's gas lamps had already been replaced by even brighter electric lighting (though the last gas *réverbère* in central Paris was removed only in 1952, and at the dawn of the twenty-first century one still existed just outside the city limits).

It's no surprise then that at the Belle Epoque's zenith, which coincided with the Universal Exposition of 1900 and its further technical wonders, a novelist named Camille Mauclair wrote a book titled *La Ville Lumière*—"The City of Light." This is the earliest documented use of the term as applied to Paris. The book was published in 1904 and has been out of print for decades. No one seems to remember precisely what it was about. Georges Frechet, *conservateur* at the Bibliothèque Historique de la Ville de Paris, has suggested that the novel probably drew inspiration for its title and content from both the 1900 Universal Exposition (one of the exhibits, La Fée Electricité, was a celebration of the miracle of electricity) and the intellectual ferment generated by the period's artists, performers, and writers, Stéphane Mallarmé foremost among them.

But what of the actual lighting of Paris? Though it has been "modernized" repeatedly, Paris *intra-muros*—meaning the city within the Boulevard Périphérique beltway—retains many Second Empire features. Other than minor damage in 1870–71 caused by the Franco-Prussian War and Commune uprising, it was never bombed or burned. Real estate speculation has caused the greatest damage.

This apparent changelessness goes beyond the physical. Jean-

Paul Sartre described Baudelaire as a man who "chose to advance backwards with his face turned toward the past." In many ways the same can be said of Paris and the people who reside in it. Photographer Robert Doisneau once called Paris a "museum city," though "amusement park" might have been more accurate, at least as regards the attitude of many visitors. The weight of history, institutions, and culture forces natives and other inhabitants to glance back while moving forward.

Sartre's and Doisneau's observations seem particularly apt when applied to the nuts and bolts of lighting the Ville Lumière and to the philosophy, if one can call it that, underlying the myriad of light-related technical and bureaucratic constraints at work. For a down-to-earth example, consider the many light fixtures on Paris streets that were installed before or during the Second Empire. Haussmann-style lamps are still manufactured today. There are also Art Nouveau fixtures and others added in the 1930s. Are they obsolete? Of course. But no one would dream of removing them. Why? Atmosphere. The atmosphere Paris's old-fashioned lamps create is warm, welcoming, and infused with nostalgia. Nostalgia is both a state of mind and a cultural ID card. No other city goes to such lengths or spends as much money—about three hundred thousand dollars a day—to create a retro "light-identity," an ambience that immediately declares, "You're in Paris, the City of Light." In many places you could be walking alongside Baudelaire or Brassaï or Sartre through a crepuscular time tunnel.

This is something most residents and visitors alike take for granted. But behind the scenes, a score of *éclairagistes* and *concepteurs-lumières* (lighting designers)—plus architects, engineers, and some four hundred technicians—are hard at work around the clock creating Paris's evening magic.

Raise your eyes from just about anywhere in town and you'll see how lighting designer Pierre Bideau has illuminated the Eiffel Tower with hundreds of small sodium lamps. The tower's golden lacework glows from within, recalling the gas lighting of 1889. A twenty-first-century novelty, like clockwork it sparkles and bursts into a glittering dance every hour, as a searchlight rakes across town, another reminder of 1889.

Louis Clair's delicate lighting of the Rotonde de la Villette underscores the curves and colonnades of architect Claude-Nicolas Ledoux's fanciful eighteenth-century canal-side customs house. Clair's luminous transformation of the church of Saint-Eustache from inhospitable hulk into glowing beacon traces the flying buttresses and lets light leak outward through the stained-glass windows.

Roger Narboni and Italo Rota—two other bright stars in the French lighting firmament—have worked together or separately to capture with lights the physical and spiritual essence of Notre-Dame cathedral, the Louvre, a handful of bridges over the Seine, and famous avenues such as the Champs-Elysées. Architect Thierry Van de Wyngaert managed to transform the banal 1970s skyscraper at the notoriously unappealing Jussieu university campus into an intriguing, multicolored lighthouse. But there are dozens of other equally impressive nighttime scenes: Place Vendôme and its storied façades look to me like a stage set; the fountains of Place de la Concorde or Boulevard Richard-Lenoir splash both water and light.

What these projects share, their planners assure, is the goal of bringing forth the history and symbolism of each site. Flamboyant, experimental, or garish lighting displays that might seem marvelous elsewhere don't work here on anything more than a temporary basis—and sometimes they provoke an immediate outcry. For instance, a few years ago Paris's lighting engineers were playing around at Sacré-Coeur atop Montmartre and turned the basilica mauve, precipitating a kerfuffle with the priest in charge.

True, avant-garde French light-sculptors like Yann Kersalé do create works in Paris for special occasions (July fourteenth extravaganzas, bicentennials, and so forth). And many French lighting designers rightly consider themselves artists or *créateurs*.

But for them to succeed, their talents must be solidly anchored to the city's multilayered historical reality. To transpose Sartre's celebrated description of Baudelaire—moving forward with his eyes on history—they must light the future by illuminating the past.

"If you don't know exactly where you're going, at least you can look back to the past and form some ideas," said François Jousse, musing about the Parisian worldview in general and how it applies to lighting in particular. For decades Jousse was the chief engineer of Paris's municipal lighting and street maintenance department, a title that described only a few of his functions. He's the man who turned Montmartre purple for a fleeting instant. Not long before he retired, I met him at his office in a remarkably nondescript, ill-lit building near Paris's beltway.

Modest yet contagiously jovial, the bushy-bearded Jousse is famous among French lighting professionals for his expertise on everything from the performance of electric bulbs to the philosophy of monument illumination or the history of lighting since Antiquity. Indeed if any one person is responsible for setting the city's nocturnal mood, it's Jousse.

Individual monuments, buildings, and bridges may take on a beautiful sculptural quality at night, Jousse readily admitted to me, but what most intrigues him is the night-lit city as a physical, metaphysical, and emotional whole—the grand display case of Paris and its lifestyles. "Drive into town at night from the suburbs and you feel the difference immediately," he told me, his eyes twinkling. "From the linear, traffic-oriented lights leading you through and out of the suburbs you enter the floating blanket of Paris light—a destination, a place, the arrival point." He stroked his beard and leaned back into his unfashionable office chair, readying himself for a stroll through centuries past.

As far back as the Middle Ages, lanterns or candles marked the city limits and the three most strategic points in town, Jousse explained. They were above all symbolic: the Louvre's Royal Palace; the Tour de Nesle (a watchtower that once stood on the Seine);

and the cemetery of the Saints Innocents, a favorite meeting place near Les Halles for thugs and lovers. Over the years, oil lamps were added around town. But it was the Sun King who lived up to his title and in 1669 inaugurated the first systematic public lighting scheme (he even had a commemorative lantern medal minted to celebrate it). By the 1780s, a pulley system had been devised to hang new, elegant lamps over the streets. And then came *le déluge* of 1789. "The refrain in the Revolutionaries' song *Ah! ça ira* is all about hoisting aristocrats from the lampposts," Jousse laughed. "And those new pulleys came in very handy."

Paris's nighttime identity as we know it today was largely defined with the advent of modern outdoor lighting in the mid-nineteenth century. Ever since, the city's streetlamps have been erected at the same heights: six, nine, or twelve meters—about twenty, thirty, and forty feet (the Champs-Elysées's fixtures, designed by Jean-Michel Wilmotte, are exceptions at 11.5 meters). Lampposts are staggered along the sidewalks on both sides of the street to create overlapping, gentle pools of light. The light laps at the buildings and hints at the roofline above the tops of the posts. The overall effect is to give Paris a human dimension, making it an inviting yet safe place to enjoy after the sun goes down.

"It's the little things I like most," said Jousse, echoing the sentiments of many Parisians. "For example, there's a nineteenth-century wall fountain on Rue de Turenne not far from Place des Vosges that no one notices during the day. Even at night, drivers don't see it. But when it's lit with two small spots, it's a wonderful discovery for strollers."

Beyond the poetry and aesthetics, skillful lighting is one way to diminish vandalism in rough neighborhoods. Jousse is still proud that ever since his technicians illuminated a contemporary sculpture in the 18th arrondissement's long-notorious Goutte d'Or quarter near Barbès, the locals have adopted it as their own. At Porte de Clignancourt, under the sinister spaghetti bowl of freeways where the city's main flea market is held, Jousse and his lighting technicians lit a wall that was erected as a safety measure, to divide a wide sidewalk. Now, instead of being viewed as an ugly obstacle, the wall is a noctambulist's landmark, a kind of luminous welcome mat on the city's edge.

Half a dozen other cities probably have more and brighter lights than Paris. New York is a forest of flaming skyscrapers and throbbing, colored bands. Parts of Tokyo and Berlin look like immense, garish outdoor advertisements, the objective correlatives of our consumerist age. These forward-looking cities also sparkle as among the world's great artistic, intellectual, and economic centers. Yet no one would dream of calling any of the three the City of Light, and not only because Paris claimed the title a century ago. There's another, intangible reason. Something about the city's quality of life, the skeptical outlook of so many residents, and the sparkling yet sardonic essence of Paris, makes the name Ville Lumière ring true. So even if it sounds like a cliché to some, others—including me—will go on using it for as long as the city shines.

Of Cobbles, Bikes, and Bobos

Sous les pavés, la plage. (Under the paving stones lies a beach.)

— Slogan of Paris student rioters in 1968

What city's streets are paved with dreams and peacock-tail mosaics—thousands of them? No prize if you guessed. The classic Paris cobble is an eight- or ten-centimeter granite cube, a *pavé mosaïque,* laid down in patterns road builders call *queues de paon.* Many of the capital's 5,993 streets—totaling more than 1,000 miles—are cobbled, and cover a quarter of Paris's surface area. That translates to millions of cobbles, often unseen under the asphalt, and always unsung.

Cobblestones are as much a part of Paris's identity as the Eiffel Tower. Read a classic from Anatole France to Émile Zola, find a riot or revolution, and cobbles will star in the show. The pavements rose in righteous wrath in 1789, 1830, 1848, 1870–71, and again in 1944, when the Nazis decamped. There's nothing better than cobbles for barricade-building or shot-putting. *Aux barricades, camarades!* And there lies the irony. Cobbles did not disappear when Paris streets were widened, paved, and modernized. Modernization—"Haussmannization"—aimed to rid Paris of medieval alleys, where rioters could ambush troops. The cobbles merely went underground—under the asphalt.

Sound like ancient history? Click forward to times recent enough for hoary fifty-somethings like me to remember. Behind the cobblestone barricades of 1968, rioters shouted not only *aux barricades* but also *sous les pavés la plage*—under the paving stones lies a beach. The cryptic chant egged on students to tear up stones as their forebears had, but also hinted at a different world, a beach in the big city, symbolic of a better, more carefree life.

In reality that "beach" was the sandy layer the cobbles are embedded in—or were. Nowadays sand is mixed with mortar, and joints between cobbles are grouted. Rioters would be hard pressed to pry them out. That's telling of our times. So, too, is the current positive value attached to the humble cobblestone, at least for those with green credentials, meaning green politics or a swelling wallet full of greenbacks.

The sometimes idealistic *soixante-huitards* of 1968 are as dead today as the barricade builders of Rue Royale in 1848. Everyone but commuters, it seems, is embracing cobbles and their petrified relatives as heralds of low-carbon prosperity. Wherever the peacock's tail is laid down anew or exposed by *débitumation*—the stripping of bitumen, meaning asphalt—real estate values soar. Neighborhoods are revolutionized not by rioters tearing up cobbles, but by cobble-prone developers, new-paradigm moguls, Greens, and *bobos*—Paris's celebrated bohemian bourgeois.

"Cobble-ification" is an integral part of pedestrianization and means that streets or neighborhoods are car-free or benefit from restricted traffic flow. In Paris, these areas go by the designations *zone piétonnière, aire piétonne, quartier vert* and, most recently, Réseau Vert—a specific pedestrian-cyclist roadway network.

Like other attempts at social engineering through urban planning, Europe's first and biggest pedestrian zone was created in the 1960s. The Strøget area turned historic Copenhagen into a giant mall, complete with fast-food joints, roughneck street fauna, men dressed as Vikings, and what boosters called "street entertainers"—musicians, performers, artists, jugglers, and fire-swallowers. They've become a permanent feature of pedestrian zones worldwide, and a powerful argument against building more of them.

Given the motor-mania of the 1960s, Paris was slow to follow Denmark's lead. The City of Light's first and still its largest pedestrianized area was begun in the mid-1970s. It spread around the former wholesale markets at Les Halles, and the Pompidou Center at Place Beaubourg. The idea was to redesign European cities such as Paris for cars, creating safe havens for tourists, especially shoppers, in traffic-clogged historic neighborhoods. After the Les Halles–Beaubourg experiment came the Saint-Séverin–Saint-Michel precinct and its wall-to-wall couscous joints and Greek tavernas, an object lesson in how not to masterplan a city.

Mall-ification continued under pro-automobile mayor Jacques Chirac, and the policy only began to morph during the reign of his successor Jean Tiberi. But with traffic, noise, and air pollution untenable, instead of beginning the process of limiting cars throughout town, Tiberi initiated more refuges. These weren't the malls of the 1970s and 1980s, but they maintained the fiction that Paris and cars could live together. The Les Halles–Beaubourg enclave grew, and more were planned and built.

Throughout the late 1980s and 1990s near Rue Montorgueil northwest of Les Halles, the barricades against traffic went up, creating a fortified city-within-the-city, this time with cobbled streets in white Carrara marble. On the periphery, pneumatically activated telescopic piston-bollards—called *bornes téléscopiques*—do today what drawbridges did in the past. They're linked via audio and video to a remote police squad in a centralized *poste de contrôle* security HQ, with a 24/7 maintenance crew. Only residents, delivery trucks, and emergency vehicles are allowed into the citadel.

In recent years, the Montorgueil zone has spread to Rue Saint-Denis and abutting streets, extending as far as Rue Montmartre. Running across it is the first section of Réseau Vert, an experimental linear network of semi-pedestrianized, partly cobbled streets with limited car access. To slow traffic, cobbles also mark intersections and pedestrian crossings elsewhere. For now, Réseau Vert runs from Châtelet to Canal Saint-Martin. It may well prove the twenty-first-century answer to twentieth-century citadel-pedestrianization.

Though invented by Green Party planners nearly twenty years ago, Réseau Vert is a weapon in Socialist mayor Bertrand Delanoë's anti-vehicular arsenal. The days of denial are over. The mayor's "de-Haussmannization" campaign to keep cars out of town means pain to drivers will increase until they switch to public transportation, bicycles, and walking.

Aptly, a few hundred yards west of the Les Halles–Beaubourg–Montorgueil–Saint-Denis pedestrian zone–cum–Réseau Vert, in Rue du Louvre, is Paris's Direction de la Voirie et des Déplacements. The roadworks department is on the front line in the war against automotive oppression. Here I met architect Yann Le Toumelin, in charge of the Réseau Vert. Mild-mannered, Le Toumelin is too young to remember Les Halles before the wholesale market became a mall. For Parisians under fifty, Les Halles and the Saint-Séverin–Saint-Michel pedestrian zone "have always been there."

Longevity isn't always a measure of success. The mistakes of past pedestrianization—lack of access, increased street noise from cafés and musicians, radical demographic shifts, aggravated congestion on perimeter streets—are being studied from the ground up. "Starting with the cobbles," said Le Toumelin mildly. "Nothing makes a pedestrian area look and feel more seedy than broken or missing paving stones."

Some stones crack under the weight of a single delivery truck, he explained, adjusting his frameless designer glasses. While sketching on an A3 sheet, he described the various cobbles and flagstones found in Paris. There are the classic *pavés mosaïques* in peacock-tail patterns. The best are granite; other stones wear too fast. Second-most popular is the *pavé échantillon,* shaped like a bread loaf in a variety—a Whitman's Sampler—of colors. They're rectangular, measuring twenty by fourteen by fourteen centimeters, and laid out side by side. The *dalle* is a flat, rectangular flagstone and varies widely in size. Usually gray, heavy and expensive, *dalles* are used not only on streets but also on sidewalks, such as those of Rue de Rivoli or the Île Saint-Louis. A novelty is the *dallette,* a smaller flagstone measuring twenty by thirteen by fifteen centimeters. "They're tricky to keep in place," Le Toumelin admitted, citing recent problems in the Marais's main street, Rue Saint-Antoine, fronting the celebrated baroque church of Saint-Paul.

I left the affable architect's office having learned a new vocabulary, from *débitumer* and *dépoteletisation* to *axes civilisés, ralentisseur, dos d'ânes,* and *gendarme endormie.* Whether stripping bitumen off cobbles and removing poles from sidewalks, trying to teach civility to Parisian drivers, or installing cobbled speed bumps (aka "sleeping policemen"), Le Toumelin and his department have their work cut out. They can design a pedestrian-friendly world with low sidewalks, handsome paving, ingenious one-ways and deadends, plus limited, snail's-pace traffic, but the city of Paris lacks police authority to enforce driving and parking regulations. That's the job of the Préfecture de Police, which controls the Police d'État, which is often at odds with the mayor. Paris is the only city in France without its own police force.

The oddity of the situation continues: a major source of

revenue for the French government is the tax on gasoline. It varies with petroleum prices and exchange rates, but generally yields about a euro per liter, meaning four to six dollars per gallon. So how much does the government really want to reduce car use? Bankruptcy would probably follow if green policies were ever adopted. On the other hand, the city of Paris depends on revenues from parking and driving violations, and they increase as it becomes harder to drive in the city, so the anti-car war the mayor is waging is not only virtuous, it's profitable.

Curiouser still, city planners have yet to commission studies to determine whether residents in pedestrianized areas are satisfied, and whether, as anecdotal evidence clearly suggests, cobbles lead to gentrification—meaning higher real estate prices, and radical shifts in resident profiles, street-level business, and noise problems. Once a policy has been adopted on high, the man in the street either adapts or moves out. Why are there no statistics showing how the demographics of cobbled neighborhoods shift? It's hard to get eye-witness reports before and after cobbling, for a simple reason: locals of pre-cobble days disappear.

At the top of Rue Montorgueil near the Sentier Métro station, the date 1991 is spelled out in cobbles. I remember watching the roadworkers laying them down, and wondering what Carrara marble had to do with Paris. Back then Alison and I used a ragtag gym in a tumbledown building off this street. Reportedly it was the oldest gym in Paris. We wagered ourselves how long it would be before the *bobos* showed up. We've lived in Paris for decades, in the Marais for more than twenty-five years, and have witnessed the changes cobbles bring.

As I strolled down Rue Montorgueil on a recent visit, heading toward Les Halles, I couldn't help being impressed by the chain-store bakeries and cafés, designer boutiques and trendy restaurants, not to mention the offices of Web consultants, artists' studios, and real estate agencies, most on side streets. Never mind that the Carrara marble pavements wouldn't stick, and have been replaced by classic cobbles.

It was reassuring to find a handful of traditional places—among them the landmark pastry shop at 51 Rue Montorgueil, with a nineteenth-century storefront and painted ceilings, Stohrer. They invented the Baba au Rhum and Puits d'Amour. I always bought sweets here after a workout; the gym was next door. The gym is no longer. A luxury apartment complex has replaced it.

The landmark oyster eatery from the mid-1800s, Au Rocher de Cancale (at number seventy-eight), still has its wonderful murals of birds and boozers, and carved wooden oyster decorations out-side. Lounging on sidewalk tables, thirty-somethings half-hidden by cigarette smoke pecked at their laptops, hooked up via WiFi. Indoors a couple of codgers rustled newspapers and looked dis-tinctly out of place.

The totally un-PC façade of Au Beau Noir (number fifty-nine) is still around, and new neighborhood regulars I buttonholed find the establishment's dry-cleaning services handy. Farther down the road, historic restaurant L'Escargot Montorgueil appears little changed, with its private dining rooms and cozy décor, though most of the snails are imported from eastern Europe nowadays, and the longtime clientele is gone.

For better or worse, the feel of the neighborhood has changed, utterly. As one curmudgeonly butcher told me, Montorgueil has gone from a rough-and-ready "authentic" market street, to a certified *bobo* playground, preferred, it's claimed, by the *gauche caviar*—the caviar-eating Left, what we would call "latte liber-als." It's a fact that the Socialist party's local HQ is on the corner of rues Montorgueil and Léopold Bellan, but, ironically, given the rents, you have to wonder how much longer the Parti Socialiste will be able to afford it. Real estate sells for about $1,000 per square foot in the Montorgueil citadel, up tenfold since pre-cobble days, and $1,400 a month to rent a closet-size studio is typical, among

Paris's highest. There's no question of chicken or egg. As with Les Halles–Beaubourg–Saint-Denis, the cobbles came first.

Closer to home, I toured the Marais's newest pocket-size pedestrianized areas, my eyes on the peacocks' tails and Whitman's Samplers of cobblestones, not to mention the dalles and *dallettes*. Most of the Marais was gentrified in the 1980s and '90s without the help of cobble-ification—exception made for streets and squares like Place du Marché Sainte-Catherine. But it took the recent repaving and semi-pedestrianization of the old Jewish neighborhood on and around Rue des Rosiers, and on Rue Saint-Antoine, to complete the process. The boutiques stand cheek by jowl and real estate prices have spiraled up, apparently unaffected by the Great Recession of 2008–'10. So far, some longtime residents have held on, anchored by religion, family, and culture. More walkers and bikers than ever crowd in, yet complaints about increased noise are few: the street was always chaotic.

After months of jackhammering and snarled traffic, another semi-pedestrianized zone was born in 2008 on Rue Saint-Antoine, fronting Saint-Paul. If architect Yann Le Toumelin is right, rues des Rosiers and Saint-Antoine are the way of the future. They're part of Réseau Vert. Instead of a citadel with piston-bollards—which often malfunction, damaging vehicles—other means will be used. They include easy and cheap traffic signals, 15-kph signage, cobbles, and traffic cops to bar the unauthorized. Sidewalks have been widened and lowered, and the poles that keep cars at bay—but hinder strolling—have been removed. No parking is allowed—in theory. Civic sense is key and plainly doesn't always work. The Saint-Paul experiment and the Réseau Vert in general often feel like war zones, with frustrated drivers facing outraged bikers and pedestrians. Perhaps war is part of the process.

New-generation cobbled areas can only work in tandem with car-hostile roads flanking them, and bikes are essential. The Vélib' rental scheme—in which riders pick up and drop off bikes at dozens of parking areas—is astonishingly popular, peaking at more than a hundred thousand users a day. With armies of walkers and bikers, drivers will have to yield—or so the theory goes. War? *Aux barricades, camarades!*

Cobbled, semi-pedestrianized areas continue to crop up around town, from Rue Cler in the 7th arrondissment to Rue de la Forge-Royale in the 11th and Rue Cavallotti in the 18th. If—a big "if"—it is fully implemented, the Réseau Vert roadway network will link these green islands. Much depends on who sits in the mayor's office. Another irony is, were the whole of Paris to be de-Haussmannized as Mayor Delanoë plans, the first generation of pedestrian citadels might morph back toward normality. They would be absorbed into a saner, gentler, less car-clogged cityscape. No one expects real estate prices to go down within them, or *bobos* to move out. Once the oldtimers have left, they do not return. Meanwhile, investors are watching to see where the cobbles—and bike lanes—are headed next.

Philosophy au Lait

Yesterday it was Jurassic Park; tomorrow will it be Homo-Sapiens Park?

> —Budding philosopher at the Café des Phares

"I think, therefore I drink," quipped my studious-looking neighbor at the Café des Phares, the so-called Philosophy Café, whose terrace spills onto Place de la Bastille. "One *petit crème* for the *petit* Descartes," chuckled a nearby jokester as the waiter turned to me.

"Monsieur?"

I wrung my memory for a clever *mot*—from Plato perhaps—with which to order my late-Sunday-morning coffee. "An *express* to raise me out of the Cave of Illusions," I said, blushing. The waiter moved off without batting an eye. As always, the café's small round tables were elbow-to-elbow, a blue fog of cigarette smoke hovering over the terrace. The day's newspapers hung from sticks. Mirrors quivered with humanity. It was the archetypal Paris café scene, of the kind abhorred by those who wish the city and its residents would stop living with one foot in a sepia photograph. I glanced outside and couldn't help smiling at the beehive formation of latecomers thronging the sidewalk, trying to get in.

The Café des Phares's name means "lighthouse" or "beacon" and the symbolism of its storming-of-the-Bastille location is lost on few. It is the mothership that spawned dozens of *philocafés* in Paris, the provinces, and abroad (in Europe, Japan, and America).

The concept—an open-mike, improvised public debate on philosophical quandaries—was the brainchild of the late Marc Sautet, a would-be professor alienated by the French university system. His goal was to make philosophy accessible to everyone, highlight its cathartic and therapeutic value, and earn a living. Predictably when the perma-tanned, blue-eyed Philosopher King took the Bastille by storm he was savaged by the press, and by mainstream philosophers ("nonsense propagated by a sophist . . ."), few of whom could be troubled to participate in his eleven-a.m. Sunday salons. Undaunted, Sautet published the book *Un café pour Socrate* and, perhaps inspired by Lucy and Snoopy, hung his shingle on a *Cabinet de Philosophie* at a chic Marais address. Soon dozens of philo-moderators, some with impressive academic credentials, were leading enthusiastic if motley groups of apprentice philosophers across the country.

Sautet's apotheosis came in 1996 when he and best-selling philosophy writers Jean-Luc Marion, André Comte-Sponville, and Luc Ferry were guests on culture arbiter Bernard Pivot's then-popular TV show *Bouillon de Culture*. Philosophy is a perennial favorite in France: high school students study it and their *Bac* graduation exam questions make front-page news. Radical-chic, telegenic Nouveaux Philosophes such as Bernard-Hénri Levy— BHL for short—have even made "philo-films" (BHL's credits include *Le Jour et la Nuit,* widely considered one of cinema history's all-time dogs).

To academe, though, *philocafés* remain suspect, a plebian Collège de France (where distinguished professors lecture, free, to the rapt and reverent, most of them retirees). Instead of welcoming the maverick Sautet and his adepts, France's legions of savants began lacerating themselves over the *succès de scandal* of the *phénomène philocafé.* Was it, they asked earnestly, because the Age of Ideology died in 1989 with the fall of the Berlin Wall? Or could it be a manifestation of "collective despair" linked to globalization, waning family values, and chronically high unemployment? Perhaps it signaled a fin-de-siècle crisis of the spirit, the conjugation of lost piety and the advent of the Second Millennium, or a revolution against "Anglo-Saxon values" embodied in commercial TV, the movies, and the Internet?

Strangely, few French intellectuals asked themselves whether the popularity of philosophy cafés could be put down to the simple fact that they offer good, ribald fun, in keeping with the best Parisian café tradition. That is precisely what you sense on a Sunday morning at the Café des Phares, still the city's liveliest *philocafé* after two decades of tongue wagging. The ritual pecking of cheeks and passing of cigarette packs starts at ten a.m., when several dozen regulars show up to make sure they'll find a spot inside, near the bar. That's where the action is. A hundred or more casual participants ebb and flow between the bar and the sidewalk terrace, where they hear the debate through loudspeakers. Cellular telephones and other handheld devices disappear as budding philosophers brandish their notepads and reference books—everything from Plato's *Republic* to Heidegger's *Sein und Zeit,* Sartre, Foucault, Camus, Baudrillard, the Larousse dictionary, even the Bible.

At the appointed hour a philo-moderator rises to his feet, tests the mike and, in consultation with a roundtable of regulars, sets about finding the theme of the day. It's like a college-town literature workshop and a Quaker meeting rolled into one, with a pinch of karaoke and a splash of pop-psych.

"Yesterday it was Jurassic Park," suggested the first speaker, "tomorrow will it be Homo-Sapiens Park?" The theme was met by baffled groans.

"Nothing is to be hoped for, everything is to be experienced," offered another speaker. More grumbling from the peanut gallery.

"Could it be that unemployment isn't a problem, but rather a solution?" asked a provocative old hippie. This quandary, too, was discarded. Political.

Meanwhile coffee and beer were floating by on trays, and a *philocafé* regular had begun squeezing among the tables, hawking a stack of *Philos,* a monthly newsletter justly celebrated for its turgid, impenetrable prose. "All roads lead to Rome," warbled the moderator's disembodied voice through the mike. "How about considering the real meaning of this ancient saying?"

The question seemed genial enough so was accepted as the theme of the day.

"Because of the Paris marathon," began an eager woman, "it took me two hours to get here this morning, and I thought to myself, traveling toward an objective is sometimes difficult, so perhaps the hidden meaning in 'all roads lead to Rome' is that if you try hard enough you can reach your goal. . . ."

"Rome meaning the seat of all power?" asked someone.

"The Vatican? The church? A symbol of oppression?" questioned a second.

"The incarnation of totalitarian moralism, the first manifestation of religious globalism . . ."

"This evokes the schism of the popes in Avignon, and is anti-papal . . ."

"Nonsense! The quote is much older, it refers to Imperial Rome!"

Soon the debate was rolling along, the mike passing from hand to hand. Sitting on the terrace a pipe-smoking professor with wrinkled trousers had his say, then a bird-boned sophisticate wearing an Hermès scarf. "All roads lead to infinity," quipped a youngster hidden by the cigarette and pipe smoke, "Rome is finite, therefore the saying isn't valid!"

The permutations of this millennial cliché turned out to be manifold. Roads are experience and all experience is valid. Roads are the ways of the Lord, and they're unknowable. Rome is shorthand for beauty, love, art, and death, and all roads lead to death, preferably via sex. The road to knowledge passes through sin, Rome is sin, therefore. . . . A bookish man quoted sixteenth-century chronicler Montaigne ("By different means we arrive at the same end") while an irreverent wit paraphrased Jorge Luis Borges ("If you put a monkey at a typewriter for eternity sooner or later he'll write Shakespeare's entire oeuvre"). Things were beginning to spin out of control. Someone I couldn't see started a convoluted philosophical argument but lost his train of thought, stuttering and spluttering like a motorcycle out of gas. Amid cruel mocking the mike passed to the next apprentice philosopher.

"All roads lead to sex," said a Rabelaisian man in his thirties, picking up the libidinous subtext abandoned earlier.

"All roads, or just sex-tions of them?" teased a voice. "Errantry or Eros?"

"In the dark, all women are beautiful!"

"And all men are desirable!"

A handsome young fellow in a tweed jacket made eyes at the soulful-looking young woman across from him. She rewarded him with a coy smile and a riffle of her notepad. Several other potential couples chatted away, oblivious to the debate. Eventually the moderator's voice of reason intervened to put things back on track. My neighbor leaned over and remarked, "Isn't this silly and pretentious?" Before I could answer a gaunt intellectual leaned over me from the other side and sniffed, "It lacks rigor, it isn't philosophy at all." Just then a middle-aged woman with a blonde bouffant pushed by, loaded with groceries from the Boulevard Richard

Lenoir outdoor market whose stands I could see across the square. The smell of ripe cheese wafted up as she reached for the mike. "She's been haggling over chickens and eggs," quipped my jocular neighbor, suppressing hilarity. Suddenly a roller-skating teenager slalomed past, crashing into a table before being rescued by her philo-mom.

Finally an authoritative voice with a distinctly Italian accent began thundering through the microphone like an opera singer. "So far the lesson," he sang, "seems to be that any sentence can lead us all anywhere!" A collective guffaw went up, and by the time I managed to flag a waiter, several couples had been formed, strangers had laughed, argued, triumphed, and failed together, and lots of drinks had been sold. At their worst *philocafés* are innocuous, I decided. Posturing or spouting pretentious philo-babble never hurt anyone, after all. At their best they can be stimulating and fun. In any case they're money-spinners. "*Ça tourne rond*," beamed my waiter as I paid for two distinctly upscale espressos. The babble is good for business.

Sidewalk Sundae: What Makes Paris Paris

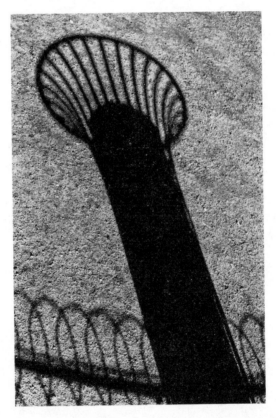

Give Parisians water, fresh air, and shade!
—CLAUDE BARTHELOT, Comte de Rambuteau,
Prefect of Paris, 1830

[For the "collective,"] glossy enameled shop signs are a wall decoration as good as, if not better than, an oil painting in a bourgeois's drawing room; walls with their "Post No Bills"

*are its writing desk, newspaper stands its libraries, mailboxes
its busts, benches its bedroom furniture, and the café terrace
is the balcony from which it looks down on its household.*
                                            —WALTER BENJAMIN, 1934

S ay "Paris" and with the predictability of Pavlov's dog millions
the world round will bark "Eiffel Tower," "Musée d'Orsay,"
or "Louvre." For many people, monuments and museums
define what the French capital is all about. For me monuments
are navigational tools in a cityscape whose character manifests
itself in humble, vernacular realities: the alignment of façades,
trees, and lampposts, and the placement on sidewalks and streets
of signs, bus shelters, trash cans, toilettes, phone booths, benches,
and bollards. Yes, bollards.

An open-air collection of cultural ID cards, it's the sidewalks
of the city and their unsung "furniture" that help make Paris,
Paris. Stand on just about any corner in town and you'll know
instinctively that you're not in Lyon or Lille, let alone London or
Lisbon. Like minor artworks only a curator can love, each piece
of Paris's urban décor reflects the spirit and needs of its day and
provides insight into the city's past, present, and future.

Take the bollards, for instance, those unsightly lumps of stone
or cement that the French lovingly call *bornes*. Unfamiliar to most
nations, like the proverbial pearls before swine *bornes* tell more
about Parisians and their culture than do the contents of most
museums. For one thing, *bornes* and their phallic brothers *les
poteaux*—alias *les bittes,* those serried ranks of spindly brown posts
bristling on pavements—are the only effective means of keeping
cars from invading the territory of pedestrians. Left to their own
devices Parisian drivers would mount *les trottoirs* and park everywhere and anywhere, including on your toes. *Bornes* have been
around for centuries: the first daguerreotype, from 1838, shows
rows of them on Boulevard du Temple near what's now Place de

la République. *Bornes* gave rise to that quintessentially French expression, *dépasser les bornes*—meaning beyond restraint, beyond reason, beyond the control of the bureaucrats whose job it is to enforce *liberté, égalité,* and *fraternité*. The argot meaning of *bitte* is obvious enough. Real and metaphorical, blocky *bornes* and phallic *bittes* are only one element of a complex system of barriers and signage whose purpose is to restrain, thwart, and redirect unruly natives.

In 1910 the poet Guillaume Apollinaire, bemused by the rapidity of technological progress in street lighting, only half-jokingly proposed that the City of Light create a museum of lampposts and related equipment. Apollinaire saw perhaps a dozen models of lamp on the city's streets, from ancient oil lanterns mounted on pulleys to pressurized-gas burners on elegant ironwork posts and, of later manufacture, a variety of electric types, including Hector Guimard's praying mantis–like illuminated 1900 Métro entrances. Since Apollinaire's death in 1918 at least another dozen generations of lighting fixtures have been added to the mix. More surprising than this continuing tech evolution is the cultural tendency to adapt the new to the old, to convert a cast-iron gas lamp of the 1850s again and again, for instance, thereby demonstrating an attachment to the past only in part ascribable to economics.

My personal sidewalk epiphany occurred while I was researching the origins of the nickname Ville Lumière—City of Light. A bulb flickered on in my brain, highlighting those proverbial pearls scattered before my snout. I began to take notice of Paris's peculiar décor and realized that, just as the City of Light has a luminous identity created by engineers and designers, so too it has dozens of architects, planners, and administrators in an array of interlocking government departments whose life's work is the creation, placement, and upkeep of street furniture that declares "You're in Paris," nowhere else. Now, whenever I step beyond the *bornes* separating my building's courtyard from the public realm, I think about the crucifixion of Saint Andrew as represented in the city's metal crossbars that protect sidewalks from traffic on the streets (they show a capital X on their sides and are found at nearly every intersection). I ponder the age-old symbolism of the red (passion, danger), yellow (caution), and green (hope, safety) of stoplights, first used here in 1923. I delight in the double-sided 1850s-style benches draped with young lovers or with garrulous geezers. I weigh the relative merits of granite or asphalt underfoot as I side-step horizontal pollution, and wonder what Paris was like before it had sidewalks, a relatively recent invention. With a curse I blink at the luminous, revolving, flashing outdoor advertising on a thousand panels, poles, and columns, and marvel at the hideousness of the so-called *sanisette* toilets encased in concrete bunkers.

The ad panels and toilets (plus many other contemporary sidewalk items) were designed for and are operated by JC Decaux, the world's biggest street furniture supplier and Europe's top outdoor advertising agency. In concert with a municipal committee, they hired prize-winning British architect Norman Foster to come up with his glassy bus shelters, international design star Philippe Starck to excogitate faux-Gallic canoe paddles (with potted histories of Paris sites), and Jean-Michel Wilmotte to replace the benches, lighting, and signals on the upper end of the Champs-Elysées. Foster bus shelters, intentionally unobtrusive, are now in many cities worldwide. Wilmotte's furniture is nice enough but could be anywhere. And the best that can be said of the Starck paddles is, they supply useful information.

I'm not predisposed to reactionary sentiments and have nothing against current design gurus. But when it comes to the objects on Paris's sidewalks, generally speaking the older they are the better. Whether or not you side with Victor Hugo and despise Baron Georges-Eugène Haussmann for the way he destroyed medieval Paris during the Second Empire, sooner or later you'll have to admit that Napoléon III's zealous prefect did an impressive job equipping the city from 1853 to 1870 with site-specific, only-in-Paris fountains, benches, kiosks, and newsstands set up under freshly planted trees, on novel sidewalks, and in squares or parks, for the delectation of all social classes.

It was Haussmann's head engineer Jean-Charles-Adolph Alphand and architect Jean-Antoine-Gabriel Davioud who masterminded the transformation of public areas into "flower-filled salons" where beleaguered Parisians and their horses could quench their thirst, relieve themselves, breathe fresh air, rest in the shade of more than one hundred thousand trees, and, if they had time to spare, watch the world go by. Davioud may not be a household name, but city planners everywhere hail him as the unwitting father of "street furniture" (the binomial was coined by Frenchman Jean-Claude Decaux in the 1960s). To his mind, Davioud was merely "decorating" the capital. At a distance of more than a century since Davioud's death, if Paris can still be said to have its own unmistakable street-level look and feel, that achievement is largely attributable to him.

Despite his lengthy name and Prix de Rome pedigree, Davioud was self-effacing, rarely signing his work. After furnishing Paris's sidewalks, he dashed off blueprints for twenty-four parks and garden squares, detailing everything from the paths, gates, and grilles to the tree-corsets, water fountains, and amusement stands—an onion dome here, a playful mask there, and plenty of foliage faux and real. Then he turned his hand to the twin theaters at Châtelet, and the fountains of Place Saint-Michel, l'Observatoire, and Daumesnil. Dozens of the old green pavilions, rotundas, and shelters in Paris are of his conception. So all-encompassing and lasting is Davioud's influence that it's tough to imagine a Paris street before him. But his designs didn't come from nowhere. They were rooted in European history, drawing on the Italian Renaissance and the English reinterpretation of it that followed the eighteenth-century Grand Tour.

Rewind to the preindustrial Paris of the Ancien Régime, a city of under half a million, with layout and building styles still marked by the Gallo-Roman Lutetia, with medieval and Renaissance overlays. On the spider's web of alleys spreading outward from Notre-Dame there are few signs and no sidewalks. Gutters in the center of dirt roads run black with sewage. Garbage is piled high against the half-timbered buildings. The air reeks of boiled cabbage and the burning rapeseed oil that fuels the lanterns hung from scabrous façades. In the shadowy rankness, carriages thunder by scattering pedestrians whose only refuges are rows of stone bollards, posts, and mounting blocks. There are no benches or trees outside the sealed royal enclave of the Tuileries or the private gardens of the rich. Public fountains are besieged: indoor plumbing hasn't been invented. Most wells are contaminated. Water-bearers serve neighborhoods that have no drinking water. On the edge of this squalor, the sole neighborhood conceived for pedestrians and pleasure-seekers is Boulevard du Temple, a chaotic esplanade built atop former bastions, where five rows of sycamores from the late 1600s shade theaters and café terraces.

Fast forward from the mid-1700s into the early industrial age, when hundreds of thousands of French provincials driven off the land begin moving to Paris to work in factories. Suddenly, the great unwashed are swarming onto the streets. The number of traffic accidents skyrockets. An anonymous writer in *L'Espion des boulevards* notes that, "The pedestrian lacking agility is a dead man!" Cholera spreads through overcrowded tenements, killing thousands. Old Paris has become a hellhole of disease and famine, wracked by riots culminating in the Glorious Revolution of July 1830.

Enter Claude Barthelot, Comte de Rambuteau, prefect of Paris as of 1830. Upon taking office a mere 146 drinking fountains supply a population nearing one million. Only three streets have sidewalks. Rambuteau's slogan is "Give Parisians water, fresh air, and shade!" A chronicler of the day quips that the count "would rather have his own teeth pulled than uproot trees he's planted." It is Rambuteau who begins the process of "sanitizing" medieval Paris: the road that bears his name, driven through Beaubourg in 1838, destroys six streets of the eleventh and twelfth centuries and scores of buildings. Under Rambuteau, in 1841, the Faubourg Saint-Martin becomes the first neighborhood to get a complete set of "furniture": sidewalks, lights, benches, trees, drinking fountains and, what is considered a miracle of hygiene, urinals. By the time Napoléon III fires him, Rambuteau can report totals of 1,840 fountains, about 150 miles of sidewalks, hundreds of benches, and thousands of trees.

These are the tumultuous years captured on polished metal plates by pioneering photographer Louis-Jacques-Mandé Daguerre, inventor of the daguerreotype. His studio just happens to be sited high above Boulevard du Temple. Continuity? In Paris the historic present tense reaches far beyond grammar. If you get out a magnifying glass and study the images Daguerre produced in Spring 1838, you'll see *bornes* edging the road just as they do now in many places, iron corsets supporting saplings, and streetlamps with fishbowl globes held aloft by lyre-headed poles identical to ones in use today.

However hard he tried, Rambuteau's efforts failed to cure Paris's growing pains. The city was rocked by unrest again in 1848. The new government was soon subverted from within, and, in 1852, Charles-Louis-Napoléon Bonaparte declared himself emperor. An enlightened despot, Napoléon III was bent on making Paris the world's most modern city. He assigned the task to Baron Haussmann.

The baron's was as much a revolution in social engineering as in urbanism. Since industrial workers' apartments had few conveniences, the empire supplied basic necessities on the sidewalks. For a people who were inclined to build barricades with cobbles piled across narrow crooked alleys, the empire decided to straighten and widen the streets so they could not be easily barricaded and knock down residential labyrinths ideal for guerrilla warfare. Workers needed a modicum of R&R to keep them from rioting? Give them parks and squares where fountains or artificial waterfalls splashed. Military music played from bandstands, reminding citizens who the boss was.

Rioters and road apples were a major preoccupation for Alphand and Davioud. What these architects didn't have to contend with was the subway, electricity, motor vehicles, telephones, and consumerism—five phenomena that brought about a rejiggering of the city and radically changed the behavior of its inhabitants, from about 1900 onward. Gradually virginal Second Empire streets and sidewalks morphed. First came the Métro entrances, grilles, signs, and maps. Then, as streets and buildings were electrified, hundreds of circuit boxes appeared. Cars, trucks, motorcycles, and buses needed wider lanes, parking spaces, signage, stoplights, gas stations, and, later, parking meters. So the sidewalks were narrowed, trees felled, and benches removed. Along came the telephone and, overnight, booths sprang up on every corner. More people swelled the capital's population, meaning more street furniture and urinals for busy gents (the total number of *pissoirs* peaked at twelve hundred in 1930, when a campaign to eliminate them began). The postwar throwaway consumer culture and its daily tonnage of trash forced city officials to fit garbage cans into an ever-more-cluttered puzzle.

By 1975, arguably Paris's modern nadir, the street furniture crisis had become acute. The head of the city's historical library was moved to begin his preface to an exhibition catalogue entitled *Paris, la Rue* with the words, "The traditional Parisian street is dead." He lamented that roads were anonymous people-moving spaces and no longer a lively spectacle unto themselves. Soon after that exhibition I arrived in Paris and stayed in Rue de l'Odéon. Little did I know that in 1781 the street had been the first ever flanked by sidewalks. I do remember the congestion of most Paris streets and the decaying, battered objects on them—police call boxes, phone booths, urinals—so full of character.

Since the mid-1970s the pedestrian's Paris has improved by most measures, despite more cars and motorcycles fouling the air and hogging space. In recent years, sidewalks have been growing wider, with many insulated by bus and bike lanes. The graceful so-called Wallace fountain has made a comeback, as have the slightly older (1868) Morris columns—those comical, onion-domed towers bearing theater posters or, increasingly, JC Decaux advertising. New, free toilets of a Second Empire style are gradually replacing 1980s bunker models. As part of a campaign to green the city, under the tin-eared name *végétalisation,* some eight thousand promised saplings will one day bring the total of Paris trees back to the one-hundred-thousand level of the 1870s. City authorities talk reassuringly about a return to sidewalk "conviviality" with improved hygiene, meaning less dog dirt and redesigned transparent trash cans to replace the current antiterrorism, see-through plastic bags. Step by halting step Paris is rejoining the ranks of the world's great cities for walking. Perhaps, who knows, one day a contagious form of civility might even affect French drivers, and allow city planners to uproot those ageless *bornes* and *bittes* protecting people from vehicles.

Vie de Chien: A Dog's Life

Happy dog owners please take note: your companion is surely not vicious but since we wish to maintain cordial relations with him and to preclude any unpleasant eventualities we advise you to restrain him during our visits.

> —Notice to Parisians from EDF/GDF
> (the French national electricity and gas utility)

Samba! Scirocco! Satan! The trio of Bois de Boulogne dogwalkers called their pets to heel. Alison and I glanced over to see what the commotion was about. The pit-bullish mutt with the spiked collar and shocking name of Satan had tangled pedigreed Samba and Scirocco's precious Hermès leashes. The three animals and their masters struggled briefly and with aplomb to set things right, then disentangled themselves from each other as quickly as they could. The friction was palpable.

When the incident occurred Alison and I were walking along a tree-lined path near a lake on the fancy, Neuilly-sur-Seine side of the park. As Alison pointed out, there was more to this canine leash conundrum than met the eye. In Paris, dog breeds, dog accessories, and dog monikers have tales to tell—about their owners' social, educational, and marital status, even their political leanings.

"*Satan* is such a suburban name," sniffed Samba's matron as we edged our way by on the lakeside path. Scirocco's glamorous owner agreed, using a gloved finger to indicate the unfashionable outskirts on the far side of the park, where Satan and his tattooed female owner, *la patronne,* as she put it, appeared to be heading. "You never know anymore who you might meet at the ends of a leash, not even in *le bois,*" Madame Samba acknowledged. The two aging socialites, who did not seem to have known each other previously, now shared conspiratorial confidences as their pure-bred animals licked and mounted each other.

"Owning a dog," remarked Alison, a Paris native, "is the best way to get to know people here." She was thinking in particular of a pair of American friends of ours whose Paris lives bloomed once they bought their adorable border collie, Randy. We often dog-sat Randy, a bouncy black-and-white boy with long hair and a ready smile. Whenever we did, we seemed to meet and exchange civil discourse with perfect strangers—the countless Mesdames and Messieurs of Paris whose last names are in fact those of their dogs. That's why, whenever we took care of Randy, we became *Monsieur et Madame* Randy—not a bad name to have in a lusty city like Paris.

I'm not necessarily prone to citing statistics, which are massaged by the press, politicians, and the vox populi the world round. But when it comes to Parisians and their dogs, numbers talk. According to recent studies I've read, an estimated 16 million dogs live in France, a country with about 58 million inhabitants. That means on average there's a dog for every three and a half people. Statistics on the number of dogs in Paris vary wildly, from 150,000 to nearly 500,000 (the capital's human population is 2.2 million). That makes Paris not only the City of Light but also the European Capital of Dog Dirt—sixteen to twenty tons per day—and the world mecca of the Canine Obsessed. The dog dirt is a major health hazard, number two after car-related accidents, and has been the object of many, so far unsuccessful, advertising, poster, radio, and television campaigns whose goal is to toilet-train Parisian dog owners.

Randy's owners initially shocked the locals by cleaning up his daily mess. As we've learned, generally speaking, the Parisian love of domestic animals does not extend to humans, so *les crottes* pile up even in fashionable areas, where to deal with the problem the city initially sent out squadrons of motorcycles equipped with dog-dirt vacuum devices, plus extra contingents of street sweepers with green plastic brooms. Nowadays the canine detritus is also theoretically cleaned up by dog owners—if it's cleaned up at all. Some years ago I asked several dog-walkers we became friendly with, and even ventured into several pet shops and salons, but no one could tell me how to say "pooper-scooper" in French, or suggest where I might buy one. Perhaps, I reflected, the Académie Française hadn't yet come up with an official French translation, and the language police had therefore banned the import or manufacture of such suspect implements. Eventually not one but two equivalents were found: *ramasse-crotte* and *toutou-net*. They mean, literally, "turd-picker-upper" and "doggie-clean." Solving the linguistic conundrum has done little to improve the filth underfoot, though it must be said that in the middle of the first decade of the twenty-first century the city of Paris began setting up experimental dog toilets in some park areas. Essentially, they're sandboxes equipped with, for lack of a better term, peeing posts. Some are supplied with plastic bags in suspended dispensers.

Panels instruct dog owners to pull off a bag, pick up the poop, flip the bag inside out, tie it, and drop it in a garbage can—standard practice across the Atlantic.

"There are limits," one dog owner in our building shivered with disgust at the thought of handling horizontal pollution. Her pocket-size terrier has more than once soiled the cobbles of our courtyard, and I mentioned to her the *crotte* bag concept. "You in the New World sometimes go too far," she scowled.

Maybe. Our concierge wound up posting a sign politely inviting dog owners to remove their pets' *excréments*. Soon thereafter several celebrities and politicos were photographed by newshounds wielding bags and publicly declaiming the merits of dog-related civility. The municipal authorities finally broke down and created a dog-dirt brigade, whose fearless police inspectors lurk behind trees (presumably wearing plastic pants) and leap out, ticket-book in hand, if you don't clean up after Fido. Fines start low but increase for repeat offenders, and can reach four digits. Having felt pain in their wallets, it's estimated that nowadays about half of Paris's dog owners do clean up, at least part of the time.

As to Parisians' peculiar canine obsessions, they're another tale. Dogs are the source of pride, prejudice, and big money. Start with the purebred phenomenon. Here as in certain other parts of the world, the first letter in the names of purebred Parisian pooches follows calendar years and the alphabet. That's why at any one time there are so many Alfas and Artistes or Zebras and Zoros, with all the imaginable others in between. When Sambas and Satans abound, Tommy and Tiger pups soon follow. Those Tituses and Tut-Tuts you knew yesterday when fully grown and replicating will produce Ursulas, Unics, and Uranuses, Venises, Virginies, and Violettes. Odettes and Oscars give birth to Peters and Prunes, Quantums and Quatuors. And so on. The obligatory letter explains why, as you travel around Paris, you keep hearing the same dog names again and again, or diabolically similar variations on them.

Why so many dog names are formulated in something resembling English is a mystery no one has adequately explained to me. Perhaps it's a subtle way of getting revenge on *les Anglo-Saxons* for a variety of perceived crimes. But I doubt it: Parisians love their dogs more than anything in the world except possibly their cars. *Les Anglo-Saxons* may have invented hero-dogs such as Rin-Tin-Tin and Lassie—real dogs that looked, behaved, and probably smelled like animals—but at some point last century the French hijacked dog-worship and raised it to a higher realm, a place in which curls, perfume, and manicured paws are the ultimate measure of refinement, civilization, sensuality even. What better toy for an aging Parisian vamp than a coiffed lapdog—infant and tender lover rolled into a single, loyal, furry package? And for a graying womanizer with hormones on the wane, a lively, bouncing big dog—a Golden Lab or Rhodesian Ridgeback—could be the ticket to some canine-inspired philandering.

For an ethnically mixed American mutt like me, brought up with casually, often monosyllabically named human friends and mongrel pets rescued from beaches and parking lots, the complexity of Paris's dog world is baffling. I still do a double take when someone here explains earnestly how Parisian dog owners treat their pets as lovingly as their children—if they have children. The late, great Parisian comedian Coluche once quipped that French families procreate only if they can't afford dogs. An updated corollary might be, if you can't be bothered to invest emotionally in your family—your aging parents, for instance—get them a lapdog. Parisian Little Old Ladies and vintage gentlemen, particularly widows and widowers who live to what busy youngsters might consider an overripe age, rely heavily on dogs for company.

Loneliness is a big part of the equation. The other is control. Those many proper little baby-boomer Parisian *jeunes filles* and *garçons* with names like Louis-Amadéus, Marie-Astrid, Jean-Luc, and Paule-Andrée have grown up and left home; and they just might have families of their own one day, families whose tyrannical only-child offspring's references will not be the choir stall or the centuries-old estate in Burgundy, where vacations must be endured. No. Their references will be the cellular telephone and other hand-held devices, *le texting,* social media, body piercing and tattoos, reality TV, Arabo-French hip-hop and rap, and independent travel to distant places where English is spoken and junk food is considered gourmet fare. But good old coiffed Samba, Uranus, and Vénus will never abandon *maman* and won't listen to French techno music, either. After several thousand dollars' worth of obedience schooling, they will wear their ribbons and collars until the day their little paws no longer make that pitter-patter on the parquet.

What most Parisians do with their *chiens,* I discovered, in part by taking care of lithe-tongued Randy, is precisely what other nations do with children—and husbands, wives, or lovers. Want a romantic stroll? Take your partner but don't forget your dog: the Bois de Boulogne is *the* place to show off your Yorkshire, Westie (West Island Terrier), or accordion-muzzled Tibetan Shih Tzu in his new houndstooth coat. The chihuahua is back—in a big way—but forget Fifi the passé poodle. The above-mentioned quartet of dog breeds is the rage among Parisian pedigree lapdog lovers. Labradors and bulldogs continue to top the purebred Big Bowser list for the central-city bourgeois set, with border collies like Randy down the roster but not entirely unfashionable. Pit bulls and mastiffs are de rigueur for tough guys and gals, particularly those in *la zone*—the dreary ring of suburbs and satellites swirled around the city by visionary 1960s planners.

Here is a further handful of statistics and prices I've come across and found particularly revealing, given the state of the French economy, with its chronically high unemployment, and the country's increasing variety of complex social ills related to mass immigration, urban alienation, globalization, and the ingestion of beef-based fast food in combination with foie gras and goat cheese. France has an estimated three thousand canine beauty salons, hundreds of them in Paris, and they all seem to be prospering. The fishmonger's or dry goods store, not to mention the authentic local bistro we all once loved, are things of the recent past, but the dog salon trade is booming. Most coif shops are modest neighborhood operations. One of them I heard about, however, is famous for organizing runway fashion shows for hoity-toity hounds. It's called Marie Poirier, after its chic owner, and is located on Boulevard des Batignolles in Paris's 17th arrondissement, one of those deeply bourgeois arteries in the vicinity of which well-fed, well-bred dogs abound. At this salon a haircut for Uranus will run you somewhere in the vicinity of 130 dollars—or so I was told when I telephoned to inquire. In addition to doggie fashion items like coats and booties costing many hundreds of dollars, you can also purchase swish four-digit accessories such as gem-studded collars and designer leashes.

Should you need to ride across town with your pet after an intense coif-fashion experience, the cordial woman at the other end of the telephone line added, the salon's management will gladly call you a Taxi Canine, Taxi Animalier, or Taxi Dog. I asked her what they were. "Possibly the world's first taxi services specifically conceived to cater to dog owners," said the helpful woman. Apparently people use Taxi Canine and others because not all standard Paris taxis accept dogs, especially big dogs, and even Bowser-loving cabbies sometimes make a fuss about the mess, the smell, the fleas, and so forth.

That explains why so many taxi drivers have refused to pick me up over the years: they've been mistaking me for a large, frumpy mutt, probably some kind of Saint Bernard–German shepherd cross.

I didn't believe this next item until I started getting to know the local pet world, and had several remarkable encounters of the third kind with canine-o-philes apparently visiting from another planet. To satisfy the country's countless upscale dog owners there are not only dog kennels and the like. There are also dog-friendly hotels and dog-receptive restaurants, most of them luxury properties. Parisians routinely dine out with their pets, and travel with them, too. Once, at the celebrated, centuries-old Pavillon Ledoyen restaurant near the Champs-Elysées, the movie star Jean-Paul Belmondo came in carrying two lavishly coiffed sleeve-dogs, one cupped in each bejeweled hand. Alison and I soon tired of watching the aging heartthrob—he was one of my film heroes for his roles in *Breathless* and *That Man From Rio*—but we, the wait staff, and most of the other diners at the restaurant remained fascinated throughout our hideously expensive meals by Belmondo's eerily doll-like dogs and the perfect fit they made with the mirrored, gilt décor. It harks back to an earlier age of decadence, the Ancien Régime.

It's a fact that the Michelin red *Guide France* identifies establishments that do *not* welcome *toutous* or *clébards*—French colloquialisms for "doggie." It is assumed, therefore, that all other hotels and restaurants in the land will throw open their doors at a dog's approach, and perhaps even provide a comfortable basket so that old Hector or young Troika can settle in under your starred table, or nestle at the foot of your Queen-Marie-Antoinette–size bed. I have never been able to confirm rumors of gastronomes ordering starred meals for their animals and feeding them surreptitiously with the approval of the chef.

Certainly, Parisian butchers stand to attention when they see a dog owner. As our local meat wizard on Rue Saint-Antoine, the late, great Monsieur Lefebvre, put it so poetically, most of his Parisian dog-loving clients nourish their animals as well as, and often better than, their own families. "Scraps?" Lefebvre gasped when I spoke the dreaded word signifying something cost-free, in other words, a product he couldn't sell for a profit. "No, no, they want filets, rib steaks, ground round . . ."

Oh, and should your pooch get tired after touring the City of Light, or in case you need to slip off with your human friends *sans chien,* you can park your precious pet at any of several dog day-care centers, such as City Canine or CaniCrèche. Playgrounds, canine company, and professional entertainment are provided with TLC.

Le shopping has become a worldwide leisure activity so it came as no surprise to me to learn that the dog fashion business is big business here. At the top of the gift scale there are real diamond-studded collars or lavish leashes from Chanel, Gucci, and Hermès, as you might expect. But what about a dog carry-case from Louis Vuitton starting at about fifteen hundred dollars? When out for a stroll with Randy one day I heard from a fellow dog-sitter about a website called toutouboutique.com, with fabulous leashes, clothes, collars, dog couches, and more. At the BHV department store's new doggie boutique, La Niche, in the Marais, you'll also find everything for your darling, from rubber chew toys to luxurious canine outfits costing hundreds of dollars. Two other luxury dog-accessory boutiques also operate out of the Marais, a flea-hop, skip, and a jump from where we live. I surprised and even shocked myself one day when, instead of looking for a welcome-home gift for Randy's owners—a bottle of champagne or suchlike—Alison and I actually trolled the stores looking for that perfect gift for him, Randy, which we knew would in turn please them. Dog-mania is insidious.

That was when we found out that in Paris you could at the time experience a real doggie-department-store extravaganza at Le Printemps, that venerable establishment I usually associate with people's grandmothers. Le Printemps became a dog-lover's paradise, one of the hot spots in town where you could buy Oh My Dog! perfumes and pelt-care products, or Good Doogy good-luck charms, by a company called Dog Generation. While browsing there we found out that, just in case Randy was feeling neurotic or depressed because his owners had left him in our hands, he could see the in-house vet-psychiatrist for a session. I buttonholed a Madame Titus coming out of the canine shrink's office and was assured by her that the therapy session was not mere doggerel.

"Titus is much calmer now," she said deadpan, stroking the heavy jowls oozing slime from his massive head. So, apparently, was she. Sadly, the service was shortlived, and eventually Le Printemps discontinued its experiment with dog fashion to re-center on human beings.

"You must absolutely be in touch with Le Chien du Monde," insisted a certain Madame Quantum we befriended in the Bois de Vincennes on Paris's eastern edge, and saw many times thereafter one summer. This boutique, apparently, was *the* source for custom bejeweled collars ($250 to $1,300) or silk canopy dog beds (about $2,600), and, what was better, said Madame Quantum, all profits went to worthy animal-welfare causes. The only rub was, you couldn't just pop out to the shop—it wasn't in Paris. "You know, the Riviera is where people live who are really passionate about dogs," assured Madame Quantum. "We keep an apartment in Cannes . . ." For the dog? "Well, not just . . ." The boutique in question turned out to be in Nice. "The weather is so much better down there, so much healthier for your *toutou,* isn't that right, Quantum dear?"

As we walked Randy through the *bois* later that day, Monsieur Odalisque, the affable owner of an aging German shepherdess we'd gotten to know, told us that the time had come to immortalize his beloved companion. "*Vous savez,*" he sighed, "Odalisque will not live forever . . ." So he had arranged for a renowned animal portraitist to capture Odalisque while her canines and incisors were still in place.

"Why is that important?" I asked dimly.

"So she can smile," replied Monsieur Odalisque.

The pet painter, it transpired, ran a shop called Pour Sourire, meaning, literally, "for a smile," and was noted, said Monsieur Odalisque, for her ability to transform a snapshot, even a digital one, into a cheerful oil painting, for a mere five hundred dollars and up.

Several months later we bumped into Monsieur Odalisque

again near the Lac Daumesnil, a favorite lacustrine rendezvous among Bois de Vincennes dog-walkers. He'd changed his hairstyle and now led on a new red leash a yapping puppy whose name, we learned, was Underdog. We shared with him the sad news that Randy had recently gone to the boneyard in the sky. "Odalisque too is gone," he confided. Apparently the excitement of having her portrait taken had proved too much. Monsieur Odalisque, now Monsieur Underdog, had accordingly telephoned Taxi Canine and requested that they arrange for cremation and transport of Odalisque's ashes in a decorous dog funerary urn—one of the many services they provide. "They drove us to the pet cemetery in Villepinte," he recalled. This graveyard, it turned out, is the resting place of beloved Parisian blueblood hounds and suburban mutts, the Père-Lachaise of the capital's canine world. "It's a dog's life we live," added Monsieur Underdog, giving the leash a tug. "Now come along boy, enjoy it while you can."

Why the Marais Changed Its Spots

Je voulais parler de Paris et voilà que je raconte ma vie.
(I wanted to talk about Paris but here I am telling you
the story of my life.)

—DANIEL HALÉVY

ong before moving to it I knew the Marais: as an adolescent
I'd read in the crime novels of Georges Simenon about this
patchwork of neighborhoods on former marshlands between
Beaubourg and the Bastille, Temple, and the Seine, in the 3rd and
4th arrondissements. Simenon's Marais was a dark, sinister place
of dilapidated townhouses, where prostitutes plied their trade and
murderers lurked in the shadows.

On my first visit to Paris, in 1976, I walked across the Marais blissfully unawares. It struck me, if memory serves, as a kind of landlocked Marseilles, Genoa, or Naples—without the wharves and longshoremen, naturally. The seedy edginess thrilled me. There were greasy-spoon restaurants where unshaved louts swilled cheap red and smoked corn-paper Gauloises, and hives of shady traders in courtyards stuffed with cubbyhole stores, factories and crafts shops. It was *The French Connection, The Day of the Jackal,* and Simenon's *Ombre Chinoise* rolled into one.

In 1986 I moved from a maid's room in the stultifyingly symmetrical 17th arrondissement, near Place des Ternes, to a two-room apartment above a lampshade factory in a courtyard behind Sainte-Marie, the cupola-topped Reformation church designed by seventeenth-architect François Mansard. Not that I cared two francs about Mansard at the time. The Bastille district and its ramshackle movie theaters and provincial Auvergnat restaurants was only two hundred yards away. From Sainte-Marie I eased a year or so later into my wife's apartment near the church of Saint Paul, where we live to this day.

Headquartered in our building was a packaging materials manufacturer called Relda. The courtyard doubled as a parking lot and loading dock. Trucks came and went merrily from dawn onward in clouds of murderous diesel smoke. Workers wearing blue outfits, the badge of the working class, pushed carts or hand trucks across the scarred, oil-stained cobbles, and seemed to revel in the deafening thunder. Our outwardly fierce, full-throated concierge Madame Gambaro kept the peace, directing traffic with mop in hand, as if plucked from a 1950s movie, or a still photo by Robert Doisneau. Meanwhile the plaster of Paris with which our building is held together turned back into gypsum powder and rained from the cornices framing the courtyard's seventeenth-century carriage entrance. The timbers holding up our stairwell sagged. Drop by drop our cellar filled with water from leaky pipes, some of them feeding the communal toilets on each landing. The last major documented remodel turned out to have been done in 1784.

Today the cobbles of our courtyard are sparkling clean, scrubbed daily by Madame Gambaro's affable successor Maurice. The factory and cars are gone. Tour groups file in, admiring the award-winning, beautifully restored cream-colored façades, the trellised honeysuckle, flowering shrubs, and leafy paulownia tree with its snap-dragon-like mauve-and-white blossoms. Gone are our wonderfully useful old gray shutters, too: the architects in charge of beautifying the Marais claimed there had been no shutters here originally, in 1640, and that ours had been added only in the 1840s. They had to go. The building is eerily quiet by day. By night, however, when the new Marais's cafés and restaurants get into swing on the pedestrian-only square we overlook, it's *bobo*-a-go-go—a bohemian bourgeois playground. The bunker-buster noise of merrymaking makes the cruddy old Relda packing factory seem benign.

The story of our building is worth telling for the simple reason that it's typical of dozens of other spots in the Marais—and elsewhere in Paris. The seedy neighborhood I discovered in Simenon, and stumbled across entranced in the 1970s, has undergone a basement-to-eaves remake. Museums, libraries, and administrative offices fill landmark mansions. Postcard perfect, it's a fictional place lined wall-to-wall by designer boutiques and eateries devised to please shoppers and tourists. Organ grinders and faux Dixieland bands delight visitors—and peripatetic journalists—while inciting inhabitants to homicide. So renowned had the neighborhood become by the turn of the millennium that *National Geographic* felt moved to dispatch a reporter to chronicle Paris's great "Bohemian Rhapsody."

Why the transformation? Easy: real estate speculation and necessity. What would you do with hundreds of acres of prime property in central Paris, stuffed with storied townhouses, most of them imploding like our building? You'd probably demolish or restore everything. The Marais got a dose of each.

Besotted by my adopted home, for years I pored over every book I could find about its history. I interviewed local experts and longtime residents not just to write articles. Mainly I was trying to come to grips with what was happening, a fascinating, in some ways horrifying, process.

In the beginning, the Marais was a swamp fed by the seasonal swellings of the Seine. Its past is therefore understandably murky. The area's pre-Roman inhabitants paddled across it in canoes netting fish and swatting mosquitoes (whose descendants entertain us to this day). The Romans engineered a raised roadway—nowadays called Rue Saint-Antoine—through the bogs, and some time around AD 700 monks started building the church of Saint-Gervais, which happened to be on a natural mound. They also reclaimed abutting land. The city walls of Philippe Auguste and Charles V eventually embraced these monastic islands.

Here's something most visitors don't know: to build the *hôtels particuliers*—the grand townhouses—of the Renaissance and seventeenth-century Grand Siècle for which the Marais is known, many medieval buildings were razed. The 1590 Maison d'Ourscamps in Rue François Miron near city hall, for instance, and plenty of other landmark mansions, rise atop monasteries and residences that probably looked a lot like the turreted, fortified Hôtel de Sens in Rue de l'Hôtel de Ville. It's one of Paris's remaining pair of "medieval" townhouses, completely rebuilt in the mid-1800s by zealous restoration architect Viollet le Duc. Several of the grandest Marais properties, including the Carnavalet (the Paris Historical Museum) and Lamoignon (the Paris Historical Library) are from the 1500s. They predate Place Royale, a square known nowadays as Place des Vosges. It was a revolutionary urban redevelopment scheme, initiated in 1600 by King Henri IV and still considered the Marais's centerpiece. The square itself was laid out atop the fourteenth-century foundations of the Hôtel des Tournelles, abandoned in 1559 after Henri II's accidental death there, and demolished soon after.

"If you come back to Paris in two years," wrote a certain Monsieur Malherbe to his friend Peiresc on October 3, 1608, referring to the Marais's new royal square, "you won't recognize it." You could say the same thing today to someone who hasn't seen Place des Vosges or the Marais in a few decades.

One of the lessons those dusty history books teach is that periodic change isn't the exception, it's the norm. With his proverbial panache, Henri IV did to the former marsh what Napoléon III's prefect Baron Haussmann would do to inner Paris some three hundred fifty years later: he flattened the medieval snarl to erect a comfortable modern city in its place. Suddenly the new, improved Marais was the rage. The Duc de Sully and Cardinal Richelieu commissioned townhouses near Henri IV's pavilion. Scores of sycophants followed suit. By the time epistolary queen Madame de Sévigné began penning her famous *Lettres* from the Carnavalet, the royal square and its surroundings were synonymous with riotous parties, debauchery, and the pursuit of grandeur.

The climax, so to speak, came when a spirited sixteen-year-old Louis XIV lost his virginity to the famously light-legged Catherine Bellier, ambitious wife of wealthy Baron de Beauvais. Bellier was a middle-aged, one-eyed, utterly unglamorous lady-in-waiting to Anne of Austria, Louis XIV's mother. Soon the vigorous young king was eating out of Catherine's hand. The queen-regent, glad to be in homely company, was particularly fond of her, and listened carefully to her advice. Consequently many bags of gold began pouring into the Bellier-Beauvais coffers: anyone who wanted to approach Anne or Louis wisely applied to them. By 1660 the astute lady-in-waiting and her happy cuckold husband had knocked down four medieval houses and built one of the neighborhood's more sumptuous residences, the Hôtel de Beauvais, also in Rue François Miron.

Changing fashions, the shift of the court to Versailles, and the Revolution of 1789 started the Marais's decline. The industrialization that followed changed the silk and affluence of old to soot and effluence. Townhouses were divided into tenements and factories. Workers poured in from the provinces. The Marais became a teeming swamp of the great unwashed. By the early 1900s this quagmire seemed to be standing in the way of progress. Out came the steam-rollers. On came World War I and the slamming of brakes. In the early 1920s boom, Le Corbusier teamed up with a carmaker named Voisin and devised an ingenious plan to bulldoze the Marais (and abutting Beaubourg neighborhood) and replace its buildings with a freeway a hundred yards wide flanked by eighteen high-rise towers. Inertia and the Second World War shelved the scheme until the 1950s, when postwar developers re-floated it and brought in the heavy equipment. Seventy percent of the Marais was condemned as unfit for human habitation. Some of the best townhouses would be saved, according to planners, by dismantling and regrouping them near the Seine in a Marais Village theme park. Some homeowners fearing expropriation or anticipating speculation allowed already deteriorated buildings to crumble. A white knight finally arrived in 1962, when the Marais as a whole was declared a historic monument under the so-called Loi Malraux, a law named for then-minister of culture André Malraux. "An isolated architectural masterpiece," Malraux proclaimed, "is a dead masterpiece."

His radical strategy was to free the Marais of "parasite constructions" and "pustules," an original way to describe the often handsome extensions and glass-and-iron workshops grafted onto historic buildings or dropped into their courtyards. The problem with delousing the neighborhood proved to be that people lived in the parasites and worked in the pustules. Eight thousand apartments and ten thousand jobs hung in the balance. The search began for a compromise to keep the Marais lively, with a balance of well-off and working-class residents. But the laws of the market prevailed. Between 1962 and 1982 the neighborhood's population halved to thirty-five thousand. Light industry and crafts headed to cheaper quarters. When the City of Paris and the French government began converting restored Marais townhouses into museums or administrative office buildings, the rents and real estate values took wing. In the eighties the gay community and *bobo* DINKs began arriving. The fashion boutiques, nightspots, and tourist traps followed in what's now a familiar process worldwide.

The boosters of gentrification have a rejoinder for anyone affected by what they regard as "poisonous nostalgia" for the shabby old Marais. "The neighborhood has come full circle" they say. "It is once more an enclave of the rich just is as it was under Henri IV, Louis XIII, and Louis XIV in the Grand Siècle, France's greatest historical moment."

History tells a more nuanced tale, full of inconvenient truths. I once spent several days under the painted timbers of the Paris Historical Library, tangling with curmudgeonly curators while sifting through dusty documents, many judged too fragile to handle. What I discovered is, practical-minded Henri IV, in his 1605 letters of patent, wanted rental apartments, workshops, and boutiques in his Place Royale. He wasn't creating an enclave for the rich. Henri was merely trying to enrich himself. Another telling tidbit is that before the Revolution, most Marais townhouses had a storefront on the ground floor to generate income. Rich nobles' apartments were on the floor above, the so-called *étage noble,* while the bourgeois or less affluent nobles lived above them. Servants or the poor occupied the uppermost stories, which were less desirable in pre-elevator days. Flanking the townhouses were purpose-built craftsmen's lodgings. This organic style of urbanism meant that all classes lived and (some) worked side by side.

The French have a wonderful expression for window shoppers: *lèche-vitrines.* It means, literally, "window lickers." Wearing my hair-shirt I went out on one of my masochistic reconnaissance missions not long ago on a car-free Sunday and, as usual, found myself three-deep in *lèche-vitrines,* their tongues out. Together we cruised narrow Rue du Roi-de-Sicile, Rue des Écouffes, Rue des Rosiers, Rue Mahler, Rue Pavée, and a few short blocks of Rue des Francs-Bourgeois—the Marais's drunken parallelogram of a heartland. This time around I counted nearly 150 fashion boutiques for grown-ups, and several for children (those for dogs lie farther afield), up again from my last unscientific survey.

Much loved, the mock nineteenth-century, pre-aged storefronts beckon. Erstwhile bakeries smell not of baguettes but of another kind of dough. Many of the kosher delis and grocery stores in the century-old Rue des Rosiers Jewish district (distinctly less Jewish by the hour) some years ago began swapping their pickles for bangles and sequined belts. Longtime residents have cashed in and moved out. With enviable panache, some self-styled "pioneer" boutiques from the 1980s and the "second-generation" places from the 1990s or early 2000s now grumble that their image is being tarnished by new commercial settlers. Mass-market clothing shops, chain stores, and discounters have planted their tills in the last square yards of the Marais's fertile floor space. Who can blame them?

Paris's gay community began colonizing vibrant Rue Vieille-du-Temple and surrounding streets a quarter-century ago. Now gay bookstores, bars, restaurants, bakeries, hotels, cabarets, cafés, and clubs do a brisk trade day and night. Estimates are the Marais has more than four hundred gay businesses. Many gay shop owners and their patrons earnestly believe they created, and now maintain, the neighborhood's perpetual "animation," as if it had been on a respirator before they arrived. Residents interested in something as banal as shut-eye, particularly those few remaining souls who work office hours, are hemorrhaging. But sleep deprivation and real estate speculation are hard to fight, especially when the powers that be are on the side of the merrymakers.

Ironically I washed up here with the first wave of proto-*bobos*. When I lived behind Sainte-Marie on Rue Saint-Antoine, half a dozen greengrocers still sold their fruit and vegetables from battered wooden wagons on the sidewalks. The last wagon concessionaire, a wizened woman named Madame Jaïs, boasted when she retired that she was a thirty-five-year veteran. Her day started at three a.m. and she stayed out, selling cabbages or melons, until eight p.m., six days a week. Who could be surprised to see her go, with no one to follow? Conveniently, the local authorities transformed the grocery stalls into parking places, and actively discouraged tradespeople from carrying on their businesses.

It's hard to lament the passing of such former neighborhood icons as Génie Burger, the king of grease (it became a Benetton shop, which soon morphed into a shoe boutique, which morphed into an interior decoration shop, and is now probably selling hand-held devices or candy). But even for those with a historical perspective and a wry sense of humor, it's worrisome when the long-established specialty food shop becomes a Chinese take-out joint, the dry-goods store is reborn as a chain baby accessories boutique, the poultry shop with some of the best chicken in town becomes a second-rate sandwich joint, the florist's withers into yet another Kookaï (which has morphed several times since), and both the local fishmongers metamorphose into cellular telephone stores—all in a few months. Bat an eye and the flash-in-the-pan boutiques change. The ecosystem's rules seem to be that once the useful shops of yesteryear have sold out, the infinitely replaceable chains and could-be-anywhere sellers of the desirable but useless continue to roll over. Anyone who witnessed the mom-and-pop disappearing act in America back in the 1960s and '70s is familiar with the scenario.

One of France's cult crime-novel writers moved into our building in the early eighties. Tellingly, in the late 1990s he set a series of best-selling books not in the Marais but in the adjacent 11th arrondissement, around the roughshod Oberkampf and Roquette districts. Ironically now the 11th has been thoroughly "tarted up," as our English friends put it. The real estate agents promote it as "an exciting new extension" of the Marais.

Nostalgia is big business in Paris, but it's also a subtle poison, usually concocted with vague notions and selective memory. Good news—the "news you can use as you shop," to quote muckraking reporter Mark Hertsgaard, a fellow San Franciscan—is what makes the world go round. So I try to view the Marais's current incarnation as a first-time visitor would. It's certainly a cleaner and quieter place than it has been for a long time, at least in daylight. The hard work and imagination of many business owners must be admired. Their shops, restaurants, and hotels are brighter and more attractive to passersby than were the utilitarian stores and fleabag holes-in-the-wall of pre-gentrification days. The museums—the Picasso, the European photography museum, the Jewish history museum, and others—are magnificent. The restoration jobs done to what were ruins are remarkable. No wonder some of my new *bobo* neighbors honestly believe that those blue-uniformed, corn-paper-Gauloises-smoking ignoramuses of a few decades ago are better off in the suburbs. The Marais was wasted on them.

Happily, there is continuing cause to rejoice as the Marais heads into the 2010s. The three supermarkets, plethora of gourmet convenience stores, gift shops, and hundred-odd chain stores on and around Rue Saint-Antoine haven't yet killed off our pair of outstanding cheese shops and trios, respectively, of independent wine merchants and bakeries, or the wonderful family-run Au Sanglier, whose devoted chefs make some of the world's greatest pâtés and premodern cooked dishes to go. Whenever I feel a hint of poisonous nostalgia for the place Georges Simenon described as a "backdrop for a Court of Miracles . . . swarming with a wretched mob," I head up to my old office neighborhood in the unwashed, unsung and, frankly, unaesthetic 20th arrondissement. There Algiers meets Beijing via Zanzibar—though the *bobos* aren't far behind. What does the future hold for the Marais? There might be another French Revolution. More likely, the *bobo* bubble will burst one of these decades. In the meantime the next Marais museum should probably be dedicated to "recent yore."

Night Walking

*In the evening, on the way to visit La Marquise, I intended
to walk through the Saint-Séverin graveyard; it was closed.
I took the little ruelle des Prêtres and I listened at the gate. I
heard some sounds. I sat down to wait in the doorway of the
presbytery. After an hour the cemetery gate opened and four
youths went out, carrying a corpse in its shroud . . .*
— NICOLAS-EDME RESTIF DE LA BRETONNE,
Les Nuits de Paris ou Le Spectateur nocturne, 1788

Night had fallen. Lights began snapping on, illuminating
room-by-room the interior of the Île Saint-Louis mansion. Alison and I stood outside, leaning on the parapet
above the Seine, and glanced from the dark river to the mansion's
twinkling windows. Tuxedoed men flanked by women wearing

gowns mingled under a painted ceiling. Family portraits stared down at the merrymakers, at the maid carrying a silver tray, and out to the quayside where we loitered. A *bateau-mouche* cruised downstream, its lights flooding the tableau vivant above us. One by one the tuxedos and gowns placed their emptied champagne coupes on the maid's tray and filed out. Chauffeur-driven limousines whisked them away. The maid peered down, spotted us, and pulled the shutters closed with a frown and a snap of both wrists.

By silent accord Alison and I moved on, no longer looking at the river but lifting our eyes instead to the mansions on the island, drawn to their lights like proverbial *papillons nocturnes*—a poetic way to say "moths." Around the corner from the townhouse a lamp winked on in a cozy mezzanine with low ceilings. There were leather-bound books and brass wall sconces illuminating small oil paintings. We could just make out a liquor cabinet and a stag's head. Someone moved, casting shadows across the walls. We wondered if the owner was smoking a cigar—as if Alfred Hitchcock, his profile silhouetted, had arisen from the grave.

Soon streetlamps flickered on around us, pooling yellowish light across the stone sidewalks that ring the island. Farther east, facing the Tour d'Argent restaurant, we heard a piano and glanced up to another tiny mezzanine built above a carriage door. A straight-backed piano teacher with her hair in a bun instructed her pupil in what sounded like "Für Elise." The girl shifted on her stool and played a single bar over and over again before advancing clumsily, battling Beethoven. She wore a hair-band and a long dress with pleats and seemed in that instant the distilled, awkward essence of French bourgeois girlhood.

As we made our way from one pool of lamplight to the next, rounding the island counterclockwise as we often do, we imagined a life story for the girl, for her piano teacher, for the cigar-smoking man with the stag's head in his apartment, then for the maid with the silver tray and each of the merrymakers from the mansion on the island's tip.

The *bateaux-mouches* babbled by with commentary in four languages, their floodlights splashing on the façades. Their beams exposed the requisite lovers hidden along the Seine, and revealed interiors with Pompeii-red wallpaper or gaudy chandeliers, decorated ceiling beams, stucco incrustations and seventeenth-century chimney pieces. Glitzy and loud, the tour boats and their searchlights nonetheless transformed banal parked cars or sidewalk benches—and strollers like us—into elements of a magic-lantern show.

The scene flowered in my mind. I began to realize why, in my years in Paris, I have unconsciously loved night walking.

For one thing, daylight flattens and hardens Paris, emphasizing the smog-blackened gray of its plaster façades, the straightness of its boulevards, the maddening symmetry imposed upon it by Baron Haussmann and Napoléon III during the Second Empire.

Night lighting, instead, brings out the bends and recesses, the jagged edges, the secret interiors, the sinuous quality of the Seine, the flying buttresses and other medieval escapees of modernization.

There are practical reasons, too, why nighttime strolling seems to me the finest way to experience Paris nowadays. The later the hour, the thinner the traffic, the cleaner the air, the more quintessential the scenery and atmosphere, stripped of superfluous color and noise. When the cars and trucks and buses and guided groups fade away—unless they're part of a Paris by Night tour—the city's magic steals back. Garish Pigalle seems bizarrely wonderful with its sizzling neon signs and fluorescent teeth flashing meretricious smiles. Seen from afar, the Eiffel Tower becomes an eerie glowing skeleton that kicks into life periodically, with swarming, swishing explosions of blue and silver light. Even the Panthéon's leaden dome appears to hover weightless over the jigsaw puzzle of tin and tile roofs. In winter, when the weather drives Parisians indoors, the nighttime streets and sidewalks are for the taking, and the innocuous voyeurism is unparalleled.

Ever since I had my first twilight epiphany on the Île Saint-Louis more than twenty years ago, I've not only been walking more and later at night: I've also been searching in literature for references to fellow night-walkers. It seems that *noctambulisme* has a long and noble history in Paris. A strange-sounding word, in English it simply means "sleepwalking." But in French a *noctambule* is a night owl, someone who literally walks about—very much awake—in the darkness, a denizen of the night, a night-walker, stalker, or prowler. To serve such creatures, the RATP transit authority accommodatingly created the Noctambus: Paris's late-night bus service whose symbol is an owl.

Everyone knows that Paris is la Ville Lumière—the City of Light. A century or more before it earned that moniker a restless writer named Nicolas-Edme Restif de la Bretonne pioneered the Parisian nighttime prowl. He recorded his adventures from 1786 onward in *Les Nuits de Paris ou Le Spectateur nocturne,* a rambling account of 1,001 nights spread over a period of many years. I was gratified to learn that Restif de la Bretonne's first and favorite night-walks also began on the Île Saint-Louis when he lived nearby on Rue de Bièvre. Physically at least, the isle must have been much the same then as it is today: most of the townhouses were already 150 years old (they were built in the mid 1600s), the traffic was sparse, the quays cobbled. In Restif de la Bretonne's day oil lamps with reflectors called *réverbères* hung from the center of the streets casting a feeble glow. As in the rest of central Paris, public lighting on the Île Saint-Louis today is a mix of handsome 1800s lamps and more recent units. The resultant glow entices not only *papillons nocturnes* but also lovers of the island's Berthillon ice cream.

In my reading and walking I've confirmed that no other city cultivates so zealously its nighttime ambience, a sort of luminous identity card spelling out the words *Ville Lumière.* Ever since the term was coined more than a century ago (probably inspired by the 1900 Universal Exposition), artifice is what the City of Light has been all about. Several hundred technicians, engineers, and lighting designers work full-time creating Paris's magical nighttime kingdom. They follow a master plan that covers the lighting of everything from pedestrian crossings to façades, monuments, and bridges. Lampposts are staggered at studied intervals and heights to produce a luminous blanket. Nothing is left to chance.

Restif de la Bretonne may have invented the genre of night-time sketches, but to many French people the literary night belongs to Charles Baudelaire. The inveterate noctambulist distilled his shadowy world most notably into *Les Fleurs du Mal*—flowers of evil nourished, with poetic license, not only by the sun but also by the flickering gas lamps of the Second Empire, lamps that lit the wide new sidewalks of Haussmann's boulevards and the cafés and theaters and railroad stations that sprang up on them, where people came and went at all hours of the day and night in what had become the world's first modern metropolis. Coincidentally Baudelaire lived on the Île Saint-Louis, at 22 Quai de Béthune (in the Hôtel Lefebvre de la Malmaison), and, later, among the hashish-smokers of the Hôtel de Lauzun (at 17 Quai d'Anjou).

Being able to walk safely at night, under lamps on paved surfaces, was a novelty Baudelaire didn't take for granted: paradoxically for him it meant the death of his beloved, dark old Paris. Today, many of the cannon-shot boulevards that Baudelaire tramped along, ambivalence in his heart, have been around for nearly 150 years and people now think of them as the quaint old quintessential Paris. I don't, and rarely include them (with the exception of the boulevards Saint-Germain, Saint-Michel, and Montparnasse) in my nocturnal itineraries. Though some of the grand cafés and theaters of the Second Empire and Belle Époque are still around, the Avenue de l'Opéra, Boulevard Haussmann, and dozens of arteries like them strike me as about the worst places in town for an amble. Even skillful illumination fails to give them charm.

Here's something else I've deduced: whether you have prurient inclinations or not, noctambulism inevitably induces voyeurism. Outside, in the dark, you can't help peering up at the apartments, into countless doll's-house tableaux enacted nightly, seemingly for your delectation. Exhibitionism may be part of the equation. Parisians are often unself-conscious and I sometimes wonder if they get a thrill by *not* drawing the curtains.

Beyond the Île Saint-Louis and its mansions, the most exquisite doll's houses I know for nighttime viewing are found on and near Place des Vosges, centerpiece of the Right Bank's Marais neighborhood. The square's thirty-six identical pavilions—all built in the first two decades of the 1600s—offer remarkable architectural detailing, and a chance to indulge your curiosity. There are bull's-eye windows in the slanting slate roofs, plus arcades and ceilings with painted timbers. At times, the back-lighting reveals the fabulous art collections of famous auctioneers and the rich families who've lived there for decades or centuries.

When the window-shopping culture-vultures who cruise the Marais by day bed down for the night, and the trendies cluster along Rue Vieille-du-Temple and Rue du Roi-de-Sicile, many of the area's quiet residential streets provide endless permutations for the intrepid *noctambule.* A head looms in an arrow-slit window on a tower jutting over Rue Saint-Paul. Curtains flap in a ghostly old building—until recently a squat—in Rue Pastourelle. A flash system pops and models pose in a third-floor apartment in Rue de Turenne, where a fashion photographer works into the night. Mystery awaits around every corner.

The Palais-Royal is another nocturnal treat, its long, moodily lit arcades physically unchanged since the days of Restif de la Bretonne (though what you now hear echoing are not the clogs of prostitutes or the boots of assassins, but the taps of the well-heeled tripping home from fancy restaurants like Michelin-starred Le Grand Véfour). The ghosts of Jean Cocteau and Colette flit among the perfectly aligned rows of rectangular linden trees, up and over the balconies with their giant urns and slate roofs pierced by wide-screen skylights.

One of my favorite night circuits wends from the Palais-Royal via the colonnaded Bourse (the stock exchange), through ill-lit passageways and alleys to Rue du Faubourg-Montmartre, whose hollow-eyed façades look like craggy cliff dwellings. The road changes names as it mounts in an arc past the church of Notre-Dame-de-Lorette—homely by day, almost pretty by night—and Place Blanche to the famous hill crowned by the marvelously obscene Sacré-Coeur basilica.

Over the centuries many French and foreign writers have contributed to the literature of noctambulism. In the 1920s and '30s, Louis-Férdinand Céline (*Voyage au Bout de la Nuit*) trotted obsessively to and fro between Paris and the suburb near Levallois where he lived, ruminating on the horrors of contemporary society. When he wasn't searching for outdoor urinals or gazing at his navel, Henry Miller was taking (or describing) his so-called "obsessional walks"—a kind of revelatory nighttime ramble—around Place de Clichy and Montmartre, under the night-lit silhouette of Sacré-Coeur and its "savage teat" cupolas.

When I walk around Montmartre I can't help thinking of Amedeo Modigliani, nicknamed "Modi," which sounds like *maudit* and means, in French, "cursed" or "luckless." Modi may never have written about the night himself—he used his pencil for other endeavors—but his lustful wanderings are the subject of many a biography. It seems that if the perpetually thirsty and penniless genius couldn't be found painting or sculpting in one of the Montmartre hovels he occupied, he was usually leaping from bed to bed, or mooching a drink in Place du Tertre.

This square and the streets fronting nearby Sacré-Coeur are a zoo from dawn to past midnight, and if you're into high kitsch then be my guest. In the dead of night, though, they emanate a hauntingly beautiful sadness. Nearby roads like Rue des Saules and Rue Saint-Vincent, instead, wrap around the back of the hill to a small vineyard. I like to wander there and down the arm-span-wide Allée des Brouillards—Fog Alley—which crosses an area once called Le Maquis, a no-man's-land filled with ramshackle huts

and studios. At night you can still spot the occasional artist's atelier in this eminently desirable neighborhood, illuminated from
within, or catch keyhole views of the city from streets that tilt and
turn, like Rue Lepic. About a decade ago Paris's lighting engineers
began transforming a series of Montmartre outdoor stairways into
"light sculptures," a new expression of environmental art that taps
into the enchantments of the night and helps keep tired tourists
from tripping in the dark.

Cost-free, nonpolluting, and surprisingly safe, the best thing
about noctambulism in Paris is its inexhaustible variety. Another walk that fills me with wonder follows the curving Canal
Saint-Martin from the Seine, along Boulevard Richard Lenoir, all
the way to La Villette and the beltway edging town. On cobbled
sidewalks under towering plane trees you pass the Hôtel du Nord
(*Atmosphère! Atmosphère!*), drawbridges, mossy locks, and the cir-
cular La Rotonde customs house designed in 1789 by visionary
architect Claude-Nicolas Ledoux. Or wander around Belleville,
an unsung neighborhood in the 19th and 20th arrondissements,
with unexpected views from the Parc de Belleville and plenty of
un-gentrified urban edge.

When in the mood for tamer surroundings, I walk from the 24/7
cafés of Montparnasse across sleeping Saint-Germain-des-Prés
to Notre-Dame on the Île de la Cité, then onward to the mossy
Marais. Or I ride out to Passy in the posh 16th arrondissement
to loop around hilly Rue de l'Alboni lined by towering Art Déco
buildings. Afterward I follow watery Rue des Eaux, Avenue Marcel Proust and Rue Raynouard, to see how the richest one percent lives. Emerging from Rue Benjamin Franklin and the spotlit
monument to that lusty old American revolutionary, I'm unfail-
ingly enchanted by the view from Trocadéro of the Seine and the
sparkling Eiffel Tower. But my favorite night-walk will always
remain that slow, meditative troll around the Île Saint-Louis,
guided by the words of Restif de la Bretonne and Baudelaire, and
the lights of the *bateaux-mouches*.

Grave Situations

Naître, mourir, renaître encore, et progresse sans cesse telle est la loi. (To be born, die, be reborn again, and thereby progress unceasingly, such is the law.)
— Inscription on the tomb of Allan Kardec at
Père-Lachaise cemetery

The potatoes atop the tomb of Auguste Parmentier at Père-Lachaise cemetery appeared to be staring with greenish potato eyes at passersby. It wasn't the first time the spuds had been piled there.

A hundred yards away, in Division 92, near the crematorium, a prim woman glanced nervously around before surreptitiously stroking the lumpy pants of long-dead Victor Noir, his prodigious parts already polished by many hands. Another hundred yards east, a teenage boy applied pink lipstick to his lips, puckered, and kissed the tomb of Oscar Wilde.

North of the crematorium's smokestack, a man with leather patches on his jacket leaned over Marcel Proust's gravestone. He tore a page from *Swann's Way,* recited lines from memory, like a prayer, then slipped the page under crossed twigs left by someone else.

My office used to be a one-minute walk from Père-Lachaise, a quiet refuge of looping lanes on hillsides in eastern Paris, and for twenty years I was a habitué. During those years I never quite got it: Why the potatoes, torn pages, strokes, and kisses? Then one day the penny dropped. Parmentier, an agronomist, buried in a neoclassical tomb in Division 39, taught Europe to grow potatoes, and by the early 1800s his efforts had largely eliminated famine. Farmers, botanists, or chefs, perhaps, were still sending him thanks, two centuries later.

Victor Noir, a youth killed dueling in 1870 with Prince Pierre Bonaparte—Emperor Napoleon III's cousin—had been immortalized in bronze with startling realism. Few knew that Noir had been a journalist and politician aged a mere twenty-two when he died, or that his funeral drew one hundred thousand mourners. It wasn't his history but his anatomy that mattered. For the last 140-odd years his manliness has been a cure-all among believers for infertility and impotence. Daily, dozens of barren women and men not even Viagra can help caress evergreen Victor Noir.

As to Wilde's kisses and Proust's pages, the adolescent boy, like the tweedy reader, obviously intended to give thanks to a trailblazer, recognize artistic genius, and also commune with Oscar and Marcel. That was the key to understanding one of the stranger Paris phenomena: communing with the dead.

Hundreds of the tombs of France's great and good draw millions of busily curious visitors. They leave flowers and take photos, saluting Chopin, Colette, or Baron Haussmann. But it's the graves of several score dead men and women—some unknown to the general public—that are pilgrimage sites, summoning acolytes to the city's three main cemeteries. Stranger still, many of those leaving messages or tokens, or taking away souvenirs, seem perfectly normal. They are professors and ballerinas, musicians, philosophers and teachers, not to mention butchers, bakers, and cell phone makers.

The bestselling novel and subsequent movie *Midnight in the Garden of Good and Evil* may have made Savannah's Bonaventure Cemetery famous overnight. But few other places outside Paris draw so many grave pilgrims bent on communion with lost souls. In this, as in other realms, the city stands out. Not long ago I decided to try to discover why, and make a short list of cultish tombs at Père-Lachaise, Montparnasse, and Montmartre.

A first stop for many is Jim Morrison, long a star attraction at Père-Lachaise. To me, the graffiti-scrawled enclave, littered with whisky bottles, surrounded by riot-control fencing, and often guarded by police, is less compelling than the graveyard's other shrines. From the 1970s to '90s, Morrison fans snuck in after closing time to hold druggie vigils or orgies, and one of them stole his bust. Nowadays the grave attracts mainstream visitors who've seen the movie. The passion and conviction are gone, perhaps for the better. Ditto Edith Piaf, whose tomb in Division 97 was long visited by fans of the singer. It's been mobbed since the biographical movie *La Vie en Rose* came out in early 2007, and the spot's gentle magic is gone.

One wet morning recently, after paying tribute to Parmentier, Noir, Wilde, and Proust, I headed to Allan Kardec's sepulcher, a neo-dolmen-menhir in Division 44. Fred Flintstone would have approved. For obscure reasons, the pre-Celtic peoples of Europe erected dolmens—flat fieldstones propped up by rocks—or upright menhirs. Perhaps, I thought, the Father of Spiritism wished to commune with his nameless ancestors.

Kardec lived from 1804 to 1869. Photographs show a portly sharper, but the bronze bust in the shrine evokes an intense quester. Kardec's real name was Hippolyte Léon Denisart-Rivail, and his Spiritist creed gleaned timeless secrets through conversations with ghosts. It's claimed Arthur Conan Doyle and Victor Hugo were secret admirers. Kardec's adepts believe to this day that spirits live and can be reached via mediums. Inscribed on the tomb is the device: *Naître, mourir, renaître encore, et progresse sans cesse telle est la loi.*

The belief in eternal rebirth explains why believers who encircle or touch the holy site, amid cascades of fresh flowers, often appear to be speaking. Their lips and eyelids move. So many of them lean against the dolmen—the cemetery's most-visited grave—that posted notices discourage the practice. One day the shrine may topple, doubtless to be rebuilt again. And again.

Intrepid Spiritists know the addresses of Kardec's successors. Shadow an adept like a gumshoe, as I did, and you might find yourself at the lesser dolmen of Pierre-Gaétan Leymarie, nearby in Division 70. He directed the journal *Spirite,* captured spirits photographically (charging twenty francs for six snapshots), and ran the Spiritism show after Kardec "dis-incarnated." Once Leymarie had also dis-incarnated, Gabriel Delanne (1857–1926) stepped in. His mortal coil reposes in Division 44. The tomb is banal, but perpetually covered with flowers, and often is encircled by silent Spiritists.

Rufina Noeggerath, aka "Bonne Maman" (1821–1908), is another, an Indian who, by a chain of extraordinary events, headed the Kardec congregation and left her body in Division 94. She continues to aid those with bad vision, it's said. If they're anything like me, few are capable of finding her tomb (its address is 82P1908). When I visited, spectacles and black patches had been left on the grave, and a glassy turquoise eye, the kind for warding off evil spirits. I shivered, thinking of my own patch and three sets of spectacles, and the evil-eye sign many superstitious folk have made when they see me.

Perhaps the most beloved spirit-seeker's grave is that of Anne-

Marie Le Normand. It lies, hidden, some twenty feet off Avenue Principale, in Division 3. Le Normand excelled at Tarots, thrilling 1800s socialites until she joined the ethereal crowd in 1843. On her simple gravestone "Mademoiselle" is carved—she dallied often and never married. Alongside the fresh flowers I spotted a low-relief cherub, a silver-plated cross, and a cryptic message on onion-skin paper. "Tell her I still love her," pleaded the writer, in French, "you know who, dear Anne-Marie."

Creepy? The prize at Père-Lachaise goes to admirers of Étienne-Gaspar Robertson (1763–1837), a self-styled "Phantasmagorist," who wowed, terrified, and hoodwinked the credulous with his early magic-lantern shows. He still boasts cult status. His secret was smoke, mirrors, tulle cloth, and lenses—to magnify the ghostly images he produced. Tiered and towering, his tomb on Avenue Casimir-Périer, in Division 8, crawls with winged skulls, demons, and demonic owls, plus panels of flying skeletons and astonished spectators. It isn't on the celebrity maps. One day, I was surprised to see the sepulcher gleaming white and clean. Who paid for the restoration, 170-odd years post-mortem? As if in answer, I found a plastic rat and rubber bat at the monument's base. A guard said that, once, adepts of black magic gathered here at night to perform Satanic rites. Heightened security—thanks to Jim Morrison—and razor wire on walls put an end to that.

In honor of Serge Gainsbourg, I rode the Métro from Père-Lachaise to Montparnasse Cemetery. I didn't meet the famous ticket-puncher—*Le Poinçonneur des Lilas*—for whom the cult singer's best-loved tune is named. Technology eliminated Paris's ticket punchers about thirty-five years ago. They live on in song, and in the many messages written on Métro tickets left at Serge's tomb. Gainsbourg's address is good, in the middle of this flat, neat graveyard, full of military heroes, literati, and red-blooded bourgeois. He lies in Division 1 off Avenue Principale and Avenue Transversale, with his parents, Olga and Joseph. Not bad for a guy born in 1928 as Lucien Ginsburg, son of impoverished

Russian Jewish immigrants. He died an ostensibly rebellious, chain-smoking, venerated drunkard, in 1991. The debauched persona he created—the cause of his early death—explains the beer bottle caps and cigarette butts, and the unopened packs of Gitanes, the brand of coffin-nail he preferred.

The profusion of objects—stuffed teddy bears, plaster caricature busts, wooden animal cutouts, lighters, and a big plastic jar full of tickets and messages—makes Gainsbourg's a possible winner in the Paris hit parade of tomb-top clutter. In the jar are bar and restaurant receipts. I read one message. "We had a good one, thought of you, and had another and another." Presumably the puppets, bird house, flattened glass marbles, and other tokens left for Serge refer to his lyrics. For those unfamiliar with them, a sheet of music and words in a plastic cover is at hand. I watched as a couple lifted the sheet and sang under their umbrella.

The cemetery's other *poète maudit*—the rebellious bard of a bygone Paris—is of course Charles Baudelaire. He rates not only a modest family tomb—in Division 7—but also a magnificently bizarre cenotaph poised on Avenue Transversale between Divisions 26 and 27. On the tomb were Métro tickets in imitation of Gainsbourg, plus pebbles, rubber bands, and a handwritten letter on Best Western Hotels stationery. "Cher Baudelaire," it read, "merci pour tes vers, une prof de lettres." Why a lady literature professor would write the author of *The Flowers of Evil,* I couldn't imagine. "Oh, he listens," said a French teenager staring with saucer eyes at the tomb. "He helps us."

Baudelaire's cenotaph—a monument sans corpse—is a triumph of Art Nouveau. It shows the poet as a mummy, wrapped in cloth, while another, crazed-looking Baudelaire effigy towers above, riding a giant bat with folded wings. Near the mummy was an overturned flowerpot—for flowers of evil? I lifted it and found a copy of *Spleen 4*—from the oral exam of the nationwide *Baccalauréat* examination, for high-schoolers. *Ah! Seigneur! donnez-moi la force et le courage de contempler mon coeur et mon corps sans dé-goût,* it reads. The invocation was two-fold, I realized. Baudelaire was being asked to intervene not just to give his passionate readers the strength to contemplate their hearts and bodies without disgust, but also to help them pass the rigorous *Bac* exam.

A newish holy site in Division 3 attracts fans from Buenos Aires, who leave behind airline tickets, pebbles, marbles, and more. The tomb is that of Argentinian novelist Julio Cortázar (1914–1984). Someone had carved a hopscotch pattern on the white marble grave. Others had contributed a black cat cutout, and half-burned candles. Here, too, were letters, many of them sun-bleached or washed by rain, and written in languages I couldn't understand.

Near the exit, I stopped by Jean-Paul Sartre and Simone de Beauvoir's abode. They lie together in Division 20. Surprisingly, two messages were addressed to the long-suffering, deep-thinking Beauvoir, without a word or token for JP. I couldn't help wondering if the philandering existentialist philosopher's Maoist ravings in later life had soured memories of him. Perhaps, if I'd been carrying a copy of *The Roads to Freedom* trilogy, I might've torn out a page and left it behind. "Thanks, JP," I would've written, "your books changed my life (and just look at me now)."

Underrated in charm and quality of defunct residents, Montmartre proved a rewarding finale, the perfect crepuscular venue to end a daylong graveyard crawl. While seeking the facilities, on Chemin des Gardes, I happened upon Montmartre's lamented songstress, Yolanda Gigliotti, alias Dalida. Though inauspiciously sited near the bathrooms, her glitzy sepulcher was thronged. Graying swingers wearing headphones lurked nearby, mouthing the words to tunes I never knew, but probably should've. Gigliotti was of Italian parentage—like many "French" heroes—but was born in Cairo. She became "Miss Egypt" in 1954, starred in innumerable B movies, and eventually migrated to Paris. Chronically unhappy, she committed suicide on May 3, 1987. Her origins explain the pharoah-like gray-green granite and life-size statue, heavy on the gold. Her tragic death seemed a good enough reason for her fans to look downbeat.

There were no notes or tickets for Dalida, just official commemorative plaques. As I was departing, though, I witnessed something curious. A visitor laid a letter on the tombstone, set a rock atop it, and left. Seconds later, a maintenance man snatched the letter and stuffed it into a plastic garbage bag—where I could see others. "Not allowed," he said, wagging a finger, when I asked him why. "Montmartre isn't Montparnasse or Père-Lachaise, you know!"

Plenty of Montmartre celebs attract visitors. Some leave tokens—for singer Jean-Claude Brialy, or Alphonsine Plessis, both in Division 15. Plessis was the real-life courtesan Alexandre Dumas fils used to model Marguerite Gautier in *La Dame aux camélias*. Dumas himself, laid out like a pope, has a broken toe and nose—plucked off, perhaps, by souvenir hunters. But by far the most startling was a tomb in Division 22, near the kitsch, be-ribboned bronze bust of ballet legend Vaslav Nijinski. A mound of toe shoes covered the mossy slab. On it was carved the name "Taglioni." Some of the shoes were rotten, others burned, still others fresh. Dozens of them spilled onto the leafy cemetery floor. I scanned my memory, came up empty, and decided to wait.

Eventually, an elderly gent mosied over. He'd been cleaning a tomb nearby. "Taglioni?" he asked. "A great Romantic ballerina, died in the 1880s. Every dancer in Paris has come here since, to leave her first pair of toe shoes, a rite of passage." The mound was distressing and I said so. The man sighed. "Marie isn't even buried here. Her mother is. Scrape off some slippers and read the inscription. Marie is in Marseilles. But try telling a ballerina . . ." I pondered this tidbit, waiting in the rain. When the sun began to set, a whistle blew, breaking the spell. No ballerinas had tiptoed by. I was glad. To each his quirky fantasy.

The Janus City, or, Why the Year 1900 Lives On

If you love life you also love the past, because it is the present as it has survived in memory.

—MARGUERITE YOURCENAR

*Paris is a museum, and that is a privilege. But if it wants to
be loyal to its history, it needs to innovate, to dare—it needs
to move into the twenty-first century.*

—BERTRAND DELANOË, Mayor of Paris

I t was a mild morning by Paris standards: five degrees Centigrade. The previous night's storm had blown itself out, like the
countless Réveillons de Saint Silvestre, those midnight New
Year's bashes that on this occasion linked December 31, 1899, to
January 1, 1900.

Had you arisen early, before the capital's bleary revellers,
and ridden to the observation deck at the eleven-year-old Eiffel
Tower's top, you would have gazed down on a strangely familiar city. Familiar in its layout of cannon-shot boulevards lined by
Haussmann-style apartment buildings, its Arc de Triomphe, Gar-
nier Opéra, and Bastille Column, its topography of sinuous river
and gentle hills topped, at Montmartre, by the great white wedding cake of the new Sacré-Coeur basilica.

Familiar, yes, yet wonderfully, disconcertingly different.

Once Parisians had awakened to that first day of the twentieth century, hungover from champagne, absinthe, and ether (or
exhausted from serving the privileged classes who fêted through
the night), the boulevards and the Champs-Elysées had begun
swarming, as they always did.

They swarmed with a cacophony of carriages—tens of thousands of fiacres and cabriolets jolting over the wooden or stone
cobbles. Steam-powered, electric, or horse-drawn streetcars
lurched among the waves of hurried workers, of *boulevardier*
hucksters and strolling *flâneurs* populating this metropolis of more
than three million. Nearby on the river, the first *bateau-mouche,*
named *Le Vieux Mouche,* chuffed from bank to bank, avoiding
barges and small freighters, using the Seine as another of the
city's thoroughfares.

Had you brought binoculars with you to the Eiffel Tower, you might have spotted pairs of society gentlemen removing their redingotes and top hats, preparing to duel on the Île de la Grande Jatte or, perhaps, in one of the lavishly landscaped *bois* edging Paris—the Bois de Boulogne or Bois de Vincennes. Duels were still de rigeur for the offended gent. Even the sensitive, the hypnotically intellectual Marcel Proust fought one.

Looking to the left or right of Sacré-Coeur, on rutted lanes like the Allée des Brouillards, you might have caught sight of a yoked water-bearer bent under the weight of buckets, for running water was not yet available to all. Or maybe you would have seen a lamplighter turning off a *bec de gaz* in the many neighborhoods not yet served by electricity.

Had you sniffed at the air you would have smelled the plumes of noxious smoke curling from factories scattered across town, in the courtyards of crumbling palaces—everywhere, in fact, except perhaps in the fashionable 7th, 8th, and 16th arrondissements. There the mansions of the *grandes familles* and the *nouveaux riches* vied to outdo each other in ostentation and ornament.

You would not have had to look far to find the city's sprawling slums. Work was still under way on January 1, 1900, to clear the gypsy encampments and shantytowns from the Champ-de-Mars at the Eiffel Tower's base. The undesirables had to be removed in haste, en masse. The areas in the shadow of Eiffel's freshly re-gilt tower were being landscaped and beautified, part of that greatest of turn-of-the-century Paris events, the Exposition Universelle 1900.

Indeed anyone glancing down from the Eiffel Tower—symbol of that other great world's fair, of 1889—would probably have concentrated his attention not on the damp, wintry city but on the vast work sites of the Exposition Universelle.

Paris had not wanted to host the exposition until a rival plan was put forth by the Germans. But national pride soon prevailed over common sense. By the mid-1890s Paris was piled end to end with rubble and pocked, over an area two and a half miles wide, with holes.

The holes had been dug to build the foundations for dozens of new buildings and fair pavilions, most of which were soon to disappear, with the notable exceptions of the heavily gilded Pont Alexandre III, and the Grand Palais and Petit Palais, the Exposition's centerpieces.

But the most spectacular holes had been burrowed lengthwise to accommodate the new, electrified *Métropolitain*. The city's first subway line linked Porte-Maillot in the west to Place de la Bastille on Paris's eastern edge, and was considered one of the marvels of the civilized world. "What an age! What a century! What a triumph of engineering! *Nom de Dieu!*" exclaimed English chronicler John F. MacDonald, tongue firmly in cheek. "What miracle could compare to this one—*le Métropolitain?*"

Electricity was still a novelty in 1900, a metaphor for the positive elements of modernity, and it became the theme of the Exposition, which drew 50.8 million visitors over a period of six months. The fair's lighting and machinery were powered entirely by dynamos housed in the wildly gaudy Palais de l'Electricité. The huge colonnaded building glowed with five thousand multicolored fairy lights. Its crown was the Fée de l'Électricité (the Spirit of Electricty) riding in a chariot that showered colored sparks and flames. La Ville Lumière, the City of Light, was born, both as Paris's nickname, and as a self-conscious word-concept meaning "the spiritual and material beacon to the world."

"The city was at that moment," wrote Nigel Gosling in *Paris 1900–1914: The Miraculous Years,* "the vessel which held the whole of western civilization within its twenty arrondissements."

On this drizzly dawn of the twentieth century, Paris did not know it was living in the Belle Époque. That nostalgic name was coined later, once the years of the Third Republic, stretching without a European conflict from the end of the Franco-Prussian War and the Commune (1870–71) to the beginning of the World War I

(1913), were over. The Third Republic was an "empire without an emperor," as the saying then went, for the vast majority of Frenchmen a suffocating, hidebound, class-conscious world on the brink of profound change.

In the year 1900 no one yet spoke of Art Nouveau, either. Originally the term designated the avant-garde fabrics and furnishings designed by William Morris and others in what people called the Arts and Crafts or the Liberty Style. Many were displayed in Paris by Siegfried Bing in his celebrated boutique, Salon de l'Art Nouveau, which gave the style its French name.

Even the term *fin de siècle* meant just that—"end of the century." Still to be invented—by later generations—were the compound adjective's iffy connotations: delirious decadence, tortuous mores and manners, an attitude and worldview that matched the riotous, creeping tendrils of the period's politics, social strictures, art, architecture, and literature.

On that cool January morning of 1900 most Parisians were simply too busy staying alive in their own age to worry about what *fin de siècle* might mean. Even the writer whose work now exemplifies the period for us, Proust, was then only twenty-eight and had barely begun writing his elegantly sinuous, fin-de-siècle prose.

Then as now, everything and its opposite were possible. Paris at the turn of the last century, as writer Hubert Juin notes in *Le Livre de Paris 1900,* was a "Janus city." Like the twin-headed Roman god of thresholds, of beginnings, it looked backward to the nineteenth century and forward to something it vaguely and uneasily thought of as *la modernité.*

Today's living memory stretches back to the 1920s, perhaps as far back as World War I, but even a centenarian could not remember for us the mood and events of the year 1900. So while much of the physical city of fin-de-siècle Paris remains, in this twenty-first century of ours we are cut off from personal recollections. We must rely on documents to usher us into this recent past.

To try to get a feel for what it was like to wake up on January 1,

1900, and to throw open the shutters on this strangely familiar city, I headed to the Bibliothèque Historique de la Ville de Paris, the city's historical library, housed in the sixteenth-century Hôtel de Lamoignon in the Marais. After the ritual to-and-fro, I convinced the head librarian to allow me to peruse several newspapers printed that New Year's day more than eleven decades ago. Alas, *Le Temps* had disappeared and *Le Petit Journal* was too fragile to touch. But if I was very careful I could have a look at *Le Figaro*.

The leather spine of the huge volume containing the year's *Figaro* had crumbled. The brittle newsprint had an orange cast and reeked of antique dust. Fittingly, that first day of a workaday century was a Monday. The paper's front page featured six columns. Two on the left were occupied by "Le Soldat-Labourer," an editorial on France's colonial empire. The empire stretched then from Africa to Asia. The editorialist asked, "Will we be able to administer our domain so that our growing wealth and power will not, in future, occasion our ruin?"

A small item in the fourth column titled "Hors Paris" gave news of the steamboats sailing from Marseilles to Sudan or Tonkin. "Les Échos" informed Parisians that the high-pressure weather system would continue, with temperatures in the capital of five degrees Centigrade, sixteen degrees Centigrade in Biarritz, and minus fourteen degrees Centigrade in Moscow. "A Travers Paris" announced the successful crossing of the Sahara by Foureau-Lamy, recounted the prime minister's Christmas shopping spree; and listed the heads of Paris's five academies. Finally, the Automobile Club de France, recently formed, made a membership appeal to owners of *voitures sans chevaux*—horseless carriages.

Much of the paper's far right column concerned the latest discoveries at the Institut Pasteur in the field of blood cells, aging, and sclerosis.

At last my eye fell upon the half-page, column-five piece titled "L'an 1 du XXème siècle." The writer's principal concern was to determine whether this was the first year of the twentieth or last year of the nineteenth century. His reasoning was as follows: if you count from the birth of Jesus Christ, the last year of the first century was 100, not 99, so that AD 101 (and not AD 100) was the first year of the second century. Therefore 1900 was the last year of the nineteenth century. "To say the contrary is as absurd as saying the thirty-first of December is the first day of the next year," he concluded. "If only it were true that 99 was 100, then 2 times 99 = 198 and not 200, and so forth, so that at the end of 1,000 years the world would be 10 years younger!"

Amusingly, in John F. MacDonald's *Paris of the Parisians* (published in 1900), which I came across later that day, the essay "Nouvelle Affaire!" detailed this same debate raging in Latin Quarter cafés throughout early 1900. Habitués were divided into two hostile camps, "new-century men" versus "old-century men." All discussions began with the challenge "What's your age, sir?" If you stated you were thirty, one group would agree while the others would shout, "Ah no, you're twenty-nine!"

I flipped to the January 2, 1900, issue of *Le Figaro* and discovered a report on a mathematician who, at an unnamed café, calmly demonstrated that the old-century, new-century debate was simply a question of *arithmetic* or *chronology*. The article ended, "and the two men came to blows . . ."

Pure silliness? Probably not. Old-century men were inclined to look back with horror or delight to the Dreyfus Affair; the Panama Canal scandal that ruined countless French shareholders; the loss of Alsace and Lorraine to Prussia; the Commune (seventeen thousand dead in Paris in a matter of weeks, most of them rebellious poor); the fall of the Divine Right of Kings and the end of Enlightened Emperors; the rise of organized labor; the composition of salons and café-society rivalries; the death of Delacroix and Victor Hugo.

New-century men spoke of the Exposition, of electricity, of horseless carriages, of the Lumière Brothers' moving pictures, of further colonial domination and economic expansion, of Cézanne, Caillebotte, and Jules Verne.

But that is too neat a picture. These were the anything-goes days of *le parti opportuniste*—a political party whose credo was to leap at every opportunity that arose (only later was the term "opportunist" freighted with negatives). Some monarchists were in fact progressive, and some progressives were anti-Semites and distrusted democracy. Then as now the political left and right blurred.

In the same way that many Parisians of 1900 looked back fondly on the days of the Ancien Régime or the First and Second Empires, conveniently forgetting the misery and bloodshed, today the distorting lens of nostalgia does not encourage us to look clearly at the disconcerting complexity of that 1900, turn-of-the-century, fin-de-siècle Paris.

Belle Époque? Yes, for the happy few, most of them men: the world was a man's place. Even rich or noble women could not vote. A single woman lawyer, the first in France, was admitted to the Paris bar in 1900. Working women, men, and children alike were lucky if they spent only sixty to seventy hours a week in sweatshops and factories. Newspapers and popular magazines gave advice to the middle classes on how to manage their servants, how to keep them from stealing, moonlighting, or indulging in prostitution.

Prostitution was a way of life for servants, dancers, models, and seamstresses—the quaint figures of all those Degas canvases we now love—because with their salaries they could not feed, house, and clothe themselves. Today most people have forgotten that in 1900 *le mal du siècle* was not some philosophical unease. It referred to syphilis, incurable then, the scourge of everyone from Émile Zola's fictional heroine Nana, to countless real-life men and women of all classes, including Gustave Flaubert and Friedrich Nietzsche (both died of it). Sexual repression and licentiousness literally went hand-in-glove: some titillating 1900 models for object-women reached above the elbow, with thirty-two buttons on each glove.

It was in the Belle Époque that the upper classes in particular, frustrated by the stifling customs of the Second Empire and Third Republic, began experimenting openly with their sexuality. Orgies, Sapphism, pederasty, and cross-dressing became fashionable not only with the so-called *hors nature* but also among heterosexual women and men. Absinthe, ether, and alcohol—as captured by Toulouse-Lautrec, Picasso, and others—were the drugs of choice both in private and at the city's cafés, bars, and music halls.

As regards the quality of life in what we now think of as the quiet, genteel Belle Époque, Hubert Juin provides a fascinating statistic. On a single day in 1900 some 60,000 vehicles, 70,000 horses, and 400,000 pedestrians crossed Place de l'Opéra. In the course of the year, 150 people were killed and 12,000 injured by horses and streetcars in Paris alone. Readers of Proust will recall how in *Swann in Love* the desperate Swann wishes his debauched demimonde lover Odette de Crécy (mistress of men and women alike) would conveniently die in a traffic accident, so dangerous was it merely to step down from her carriage. Street cobbles were made of wood not for aesthetics or safety but in a mostly unsuccessful attempt to attenuate the nightmarish noise of metal-rimmed carriage wheels.

The Seine? A picturesque river dotted with sailboats, indeed, but also an open sewer: garbage collectors dumped their loads into the river from the Pont des Arts, and the untreated effluent of millions flowed into the river's brown currents.

It was this mixture of wealth and misery, of forward-looking optimism and retrograde nostalgia, that somehow transformed Paris in 1900 into a crucible of creativity and a magnet for the world's greatest talents.

With that thought in mind I resolved to revisit a handful of my favorite 1900 Paris locales. Near a café called Le Paris-London, on Place de la Madeleine, I took the spiraling staircase down to the famous subterranean Art Nouveau *toilettes publiques,* a lavish cavern of carved wood, brass, and mirrors, with floral frescoes and stained-glass windows in each *cabinet.* I awoke the sleeping *Madame Pipi,* as the French still coyly call bathroom attendants, and once I'd tidied up as a fin-de-siècle gentleman would've, I set off for one of my regular Paris haunts, the Musée Gustave Moreau.

Built in the mid-1800s, this house-atelier of the enigmatic Symbolist painter (much admired by everyone from Klimt to Picasso) has remained largely unaltered since Moreau's death in 1898. Prominently displayed was the jewel-like, gold-embossed rendition of the temptress Salomé—perhaps Moreau's most famous painting, an icon of what fin-de-siècle men thought of dangerous, Siren women.

A half-mile away from the museum, in Rue du Faubourg-Montmartre, I peeked into Chartier, surely one of Paris's most handsome turn-of-the-century restaurants, specifically designed for a working-class clientele. Beneath an immense skylight hang brass chandeliers with white glass globes. There are brass coat racks and carved panels, bentwood chairs, vast mirrors, and kitsch paintings. More than a century after it opened, the same kind of food is still on the handwritten menu, presumably because Parisians and visitors still like it.

Another quarter mile east is a second Belle Époque gastronomic institution, Julien, built for the 1889 Exposition Universelle. With its lapis lazuli peacocks, stained-glass skylights, and rampant floral-theme plasterwork it's the prototype of the period's architecture. Here, too, the food hasn't changed much and neither has the bustling, jovial atmosphere.

It was too early to have dinner, but a coffee at Angelina, on Rue de Rivoli, seemed like a good idea. Unchanged since 1903 (except for a few Art Déco lamps from the 1930s, and periodically refreshed upholstery), this straight-laced temple of *gourmandise* used to be Coco Chanel and Marcel Proust's hangout, though the plaster-encrusted mirrors now reflect a distinctly New World and Asiatic clientele.

While sipping my coffee I thought about all the places in Paris I could visit if I continued my whirlwind 1900 tour. There was La Pagode, the crazy movie theater made from a Japanese pagoda and opened in 1896, and of course the 1900 Musée Grévin with its theater. Forget the waxworks housed there; the Palais des Mirages, a mirrored hall hung with sculpted elephant heads and snakes, with Fée de l'Électricité lighting, was rescued from the 1900 Exposition Universelle and has been displayed there ever since.

What else was there from the year 1900? The daunting list of sights seemed to stretch forever, from the BHV and Au Bon Marché department stores to thousands of buildings lining the streets. The list was as infinite, in fact, as the city's seemingly endless turn-of-the-century boulevards. Baron Haussmann's creative destruction of Paris may have begun in the Second Empire (1852–1870) under Napoléon III, but it was still under way in 1900. No, there was no easy way to draw a line and say, here the nineteenth-century ended, and here the twentieth began.

Hungry by now, I decided to ride the Métro again, down to the Gare de Lyon, and dine there at Le Train Bleu. Both the train station and its luxurious upstairs restaurant were built, like the subway, for the 1900 Exposition Universelle. Unlike the subway and station, however, Le Train Bleu, a landmark, really has not changed.

A dizzying pantheon of plasterwork putti, overflowing amphorae, and fruit-and-floral garlands clings to the heavily gilded neo-Rococo ceiling. Brass, cut-crystal, and carved wood, framed by painted panels showing destinations served by the trains on the tracks below, round out the décor of the dining room, which is a hundred yards long. I settled into a comfortable booth and, after tucking into a Belle Époque dish of *sole meunière* washed down with cool Sancerre, everything became clear. Why were locals and visitors obsessed with 1900 and the Belle Époque? The answer was easy: because many Parisians are still living in the period.

As we see the portals of the latest fin de siècle receding in our rear-view mirrors, the two-faced god of thresholds seems to be staring fixedly at a bygone Paris, unwilling or unable to shake off the past. Perhaps Janus is merely reminding us that in this old Europe of which Paris is still the cultural capital, to look forward we must first look back.

Life's a Café

[T]he sympathy we felt for the young idlers in the Flore
was tinged with impatience: the main object of their non-
conformism was to justify their inactivity, and they were
very, very bored.

—SIMONE DE BEAUVOIR, *La Force de l'âge*

At about six o'clock every morning but Sunday, Madame
Renée or her husband, José, would drag the banged-up
tables and chairs out of their café and set them up on the
cobbled *terrasse* under our bedroom window.

At anywhere from eleven p.m. to two a.m. they would muscle
them back in again. Renée did this all her working life and even
when still in the womb: her mother ran the café before her. A few
years ago Renée and José retired, selling the place to a nearby

restaurant. The chair-and-table tradition continues, with thumping music added.

Alison and I have lived above the café for more than twenty-five years or approximately 18,250 chair-and-table draggings. We don't feel particularly privileged. There are roughly ten thousand cafés in Paris, which I think should consider renaming itself the City of Caffeine and Nicotine. Up and down the scarred asphalt sidewalks, and across the quaint cobbled squares, café owners do the same dawn and midnight furniture dance for Paris's 2.2 million inhabitants.

That could be enough, you might say, to make us hate Renée, José, their successors, and Paris café owners in general. Never. Well, maybe once in a while we'd love to pour boiling oil from our window, and sometimes I do lean out and shout abuse in several languages. But what would Paris be without its cafés? They're the stomach, lungs, liver, bad conscience, and, yes, the soul of the city. You buy tobacco in some cafés (*tabacs*), gamble on pari-mutuels or lotteries in others (PMU/Lotto), philosophize, scribble, or surf in yet others (*philocafés, cafés littéraires,* web bars), and drink and eat in all, sometimes well. Romance buds, hatred flares, revelation dawns, violence erupts, fortune smiles upon lucky winners, and smoke gets in everyone's eyes—on outdoor terraces. Puffing indoors has been banned since 2007.

If nothing else, cafés animate the city, that's to say they keep it awake with noise and mostly legal stimulants. They've been around for centuries: Paris's first, Le Procope, now a travesty of a café, was founded by the Sicilian Francesco Procopio in 1686. Though there are fewer of them today than, say, twenty years ago, cafés are unlikely ever to disappear. Admittedly the coffee in them is often bad, which is one reason why Starbucks, Columbus Café, and a myriad of other New World–style competitors are gaining ground.

"For the coffee? Good heavens no, I don't go to a café for that," remarked a friend of mine, a café connoisseur. "Coffee is simply the cheapest thing you can order while occupying a table for an hour or so . . ."

It was mid-morning. My friend and I were in the Café Jade on Rue de Buci in the Saint-Germain-des-Prés neighborhood. I always met this particular friend—recently deceased—in a café. An English woman who lived in Paris more than fifty years, she did her entertaining, held meetings, reviewed scripts, edited manuscripts, and generally enjoyed life in cafés. As we chatted about the institution of the café she took a hummingbird sip at the black tar passing for espresso in her cup. It was not her cup of tea, so to speak, but then the tea in Paris is usually even worse than the coffee.

She nodded at the goings-on: waiters whirling among the mushroom-shaped tables, a mixed clientele of aging regulars from the neighborhood, loners, mavericks, tourists, Sorbonne students, and a businessman seated outside on the shaded *terrasse,* shouting into his cellular telephone. Shops were open around the corner so the street swam with colors and movement. Our table was an eddy in this stream: in safety we snapped up snatches of foreign and French conversation, feasted on the sight of passersby, and drank in the kitchen smells of simmering food.

"That's why one comes to a café, isn't it?" asked my friend. "For this—the life, the human contact."

Once the haunt of Paris inevitables like Jean-Paul Sartre, Picasso, Hemingway, et al., the Saint-Germain-des-Prés area may have lost most of its *intellos* (intellectuals), artists, and retinues of sycophants. But its dozens of cafés live on. Contrary to what most visitors think, the Deux Magots and Café de Flore are the exceptions to this rule. Exquisite tourist traps, they are embalmed, mummified, and as such are tremendously popular with non-Parisians.

My friend and I hadn't really meant to meet at Café Jade, a hipster hangout nowadays. Until the new millennium it went by the name Café Dauphin. Since it was never our regular café, we'd both forgotten about the changeover. Gone are the Dauphin's booths with their slippery, pumpkin-colored moleskin seats. The Jade first morphed into a retro-theme spot with faux-antique wooden everything, and a salmon-colored neon tube curling across the ceiling. But in recent years it's gone minimalist, with gray or black everything, and giant lettering that spells out the names of artists, writers, and thinkers who used to haunt the neighborhood but no longer do, either because they're dead or wouldn't be caught dead among the current generation of neo-poseurs.

It's ludicrous to lament the passing of the old Café Dauphin and its hideous 1970s décor, uneatable food, and black-tar coffee. But as my friend pointed out, the décor, food, and coffee are marginal considerations for habitués. It's the feel of the place that counts, the atmosphere, the spidering relationships between waiter and client, waiter and *patron, patron* and client, client and client.

This web is spun over months, years, even decades. More than anyone, perhaps, photographer Robert Doisneau captured this microcosm of Frenchness in his grainy black-and-white images. They are images that have become icons and clichés, like berets, baguettes, *pétanque* bowlers, and ripe Camembert.

Cheesy cliché or not, today most Paris cafés are still family owned or managed and many are handed down the generations, webs and all. Long taken for granted, these supremely democratic social institutions are a focus of official attention, in part because they are disappearing, in part because a few actually serve decent food and have lured the restaurant critics. Cafés are now reviewed alongside their siblings, the bistros and brasseries. The stumbling café revival got a boost a decade ago with the annual Bistrots-en-Fête, a two-day event held in late September. This contemporary Bacchanal featured dancing, feasting, and drinking, often to excess, and was so successful that it was copied all over France, before disappearing from the radar screens in Paris. It was no longer needed: the Parisian *movida*—a never-ending bohemian bourgeois party—had kicked in by then, transforming cafés into daily party venues.

At the opposite end of the spectrum, the high-fashion-lifestyle industry adopted the café concept, wedding it to Food-in-Shop, that paean to consumerism pioneered in the late twentieth century in London and New York. Nowadays chic Parisians buy their DVDs then linger at the Virgin Café in the Virgin Megastore on the Champs-Élysées; they unburden their pocketbooks at Emporio Armani surrounded by fellow X-rays lapping up foamy lattes; or they toy with the accessories at Lanvin on swank Rue du Faubourg Saint-Honoré before lunching in the modish Café Bleu. Do-it-yourself types head for the hardware section in the basement of the celebrated BHV department store, home to Bricolo Café, which is set in a mock-early-1900s *bricolage* (hardware) shop.

Another twist on the caffeine scene got started in the 1990s at Café des Phares, the first and still most popular "philosophy café" in town. It is perpetually packed by bespectacled *intellos* and posturing *philosophes* carrying tomes by Pascal, Descartes, Camus, Sartre, Deleuze, Baudrillard, and Foucault, and has spawned dozens of similar hangouts.

Such places are a long way from the Procope of the 1600s or the standard nineteenth- and twentieth-century café type run by what's known as the Auvergnat "mafia." For a hundred years or more most Paris cafés have been in the grip of Auvergnat families. The "mafia" supplies everything from furniture to mortgage loans, lettuce to coffee beans. Here's how the system works: starting in the 1800s the Auvergnat came to the capital from the impoverished Auvergne region centered on the Massif Central. They transformed cafés from their earliest Italianate incarnation into havens of the working class, serving food and drink while carrying on their main business activity of selling coal or wood for heating.

This "mafia" is really a mutual aid society, and has nothing to do with organized crime. The rub is that most of the coffee blends the Auvergnat supply their brethren are undrinkable, but everyone has always taken them and those who discontinue do so at risk.

I decided to accompany my English friend to her afternoon café meetings at her then-favorite among the Odéon quarter's "literary venues." It's called Les Éditeurs, meaning "The Publishers." Several venerable publishing houses continue to operate in the vicinity, and donate many of the books that line the café's shelves. Les Éditeurs even awards its own literary prize. Like Café Jade and countless others, Les Éditeurs also underwent a radical remodel at the turn of the last century. It was transformed from a kitsch Alsatian eatery. Now it boasts wooden tables and comfortable plush armchairs, tasteful prints, and of course groaning bookcases. French writers and editors actually do meet here. Les Éditeurs has been more successful than most in shedding the moleskin and linoleum and reinventing itself.

As I sipped my fine Italian coffee upstairs and listened to the pens and fingernails scratching away or tap-dancing across touch screens, I reflected on the fact that most of the working writers I know in Paris, whether French, Italian, British, or American, are café habitués. Each has his own list of favorite cafés. Few—precisely three, including my English friend—would ever do serious work in a public venue. I suspect that most of those handsome ink pens, leather-bound pads, laptops, and hand-held devices are used for e-mailing; online banking; writing letters home to Peoria, Sorbonne course outlines, shopping lists—and tragically unpublishable masterpieces.

I said good-bye to my English friend and rode the 96 bus across town. My aim was to get some serious work done. En route I attempted to count the cafés we passed. There were about a thousand, I reckoned, between Odéon and Boulevard Beaumarchais, at which point a pierced belly button and an open *Le Monde* closed off my view.

Any student of life will tell you that gluttony takes many forms, including the occasional desire for self-punishment. With that in mind I chose to get off the bus and have yet another coffee, albeit this one a *déca* (decaffeinated). Across the street from the bus stop nearest Rue d'Oberkampf and Rue Saint-Maur is Café Charbon. To fully appreciate this establishment it's essential to know several Parisian slang words. *Branché* means hip, cool, hot, trendy, and so forth, though in the 2010s *branché* is no longer *branché,* having been replaced by *tendance, trendy, cool,* and *underground.* In fact *branché* is *démodé* and is just as often used nowadays as a pejorative, because it suggests a lack of authenticity and an excess of *frime,* as in *frimeur,* another highly pertinent term. A *frimeur* is a poseur of a peculiarly pernicious variety, the kind who stars in the very worst of current French cinema, or builds architectural nightmares favored by state-subsidized latte liberals, known here as the *gauche caviar. Frimeurs* are the stock in trade of Café Charbon.

The place has had several incarnations over the last 130 years or so, including a pocket theater and an industrial workshop. But it was never an authentic Auvergnat café selling coal (*charbon*) and wood, as the name suggests. Everything in and about it is strangely marvelous, bona fide 100 percent *frime.* There are War of the Worlds praying mantis–style lamps. The counter is zinc (or, more likely, tin). The floors are covered in broken tiles, just like those of an authentic Auvergnat café circa 1950. It is, in short, a retro decorator's dream. The faux element is so well done that most regulars actually think the place was once powdered with coal dust and filled with blue-collar Potato Eaters in funny hats.

Happily the Café Charbon's hardcore *frimeurs* don't show up until after their office jobs, mostly at architectural firms, so a mid-morning or mid-afternoon visit is a treat. I sat in the dark recesses of the place and observed the sneaker-shod, un-uniformed waiters groove with the hipsters perched in booths or poised in front of huge mirrors. Several watched themselves billow smoke from mouth and nostrils, like Stalin-era coal plants. This particular *frimeur* activity is now pursued exclusively on sidewalk terraces which, as is the case at Café Charbon, usually open directly onto indoor nonsmoking areas. It's a *branché* way of subverting the smoking ban and is therefore widely considered *cool, tendence, trendy,* and *très underground.*

Jazz played on the radio. The waiter did not pester me to consume or move on. I had a table all to myself, with plenty of room, and enough of a draft to keep me from choking on the blowby from the terrace. Strangest of all, the coffee was good. Needless to say it was imported Italian coffee, and had no more to do with Auvergnats and their daily grinds than did the faux-everything décor.

Perhaps I was experiencing the future of French cafés, I told myself. I hoped not.

Having ingested enough stimulants to keep me awake until the next day's chair-and-table ritual, I was too jittery to get anything done at my office. Besides, by the time I got there it was aperitif hour. Dispensing *l'apéro,* as my French friends call it, is another important function of the café. How could I have overlooked it?

Alison agreed to meet me back in the Latin Quarter on the glassed-in terrace of Brasserie Balzar, an old favorite of ours and about a million other locals and visitors. Every table was taken. We couldn't get in for dinner.

"It must be the atmosphere," said Alison, indicating the brasserie's Art Déco interior, the mirrors and cozy tables pushed up to moleskin banquets. "The food certainly has never been great, but who cares?"

We quaffed several ruinous rounds of beer, eavesdropped on an adulterous couple, and decided it would be all right to continue toward dinner at another of our troughs, Les Fontaines, near the Panthéon.

Les Fontaines is the antithesis of Balzar and happily has so far been overlooked by most paratrooper-correspondents and bona fide reviewers. It has tacky décor but good food. The view of other portly, savvy, ecstatic regular diners obscures the sagging, scarlet vinyl banquettes and jaundice-hued lighting. Les Fontaines is less uncomfortable now than it used to be twenty years ago, but is still noisy, a favorite of French provincials resident in Paris. Its menu features the kind of devastatingly caloric, premodern delicacies that make squeamish eaters squirm. On its wine list are more quaffables by the carafe or the glass than many upscale restaurants offer.

My liver needed a crutch after the chicken heart salad, the pâté, the rabbit kidneys with mustard sauce, the tender sweetbreads and creamy wild mushrooms, the strawberry pie, and all that chilled Brouilly. There just wasn't room left for a coffee. So, we decided, what the heck, let's finish the evening at what used to be Madame Renée's, now known with a growl as "That café underneath our windows." But by the time we got there it was after midnight and the owners were locking up early. "Shucks," I exclaimed to one of them, "you won't be waking us up tonight." Alison and I yawned in tandem, said good night, and woke up as always to the table-and-chair dance the next morning. In Paris, life's a café.

ACKNOWLEDGMENTS

For their encouragement, enthusiasm, generosity and wise counsel, we would like to express our deep gratitude to Diane Johnson, Steven Barclay, Mark Eversman, and Donald George, with a special thanks to our skilled and cordial editor, Charles Conrad at Broadway Books, and to Barrie Kerper, for placing PARIS, *PARIS* in his hands.

We warmly thank our friends, relatives, and colleagues Susan Aurinko, John Baxter, Jenna Ciongoli, Lauren Dong, Diane Downie and Paul Shelley, Daniel Eastman, Marie-Pierre Emery, Penelope Fletcher of the Red Wheelbarrow bookstore, Laura Furman, Anton Gill and Marji Campi, Anne Harris, Erica Heller, Odile Hellier of the Village Voice bookshop, Paul and Mimi Horne, Elizabeth and Nevin Kuhl, Janet McDonald, David Malone, Julie Mancini, our wonderful agent Alice Martell, Nicolas Mengin, Kimmo Pasanen, Elaine and Bill Petrocelli of Book Passage, Russ Schleipmann, Rick Simonson of Elliott Bay Books, Jay Smith, Gloria Spivak, Paul Taylor, Becky and David Tepfer, Robert Tolmach, and Barbara Torgoff.

Mille mercis to Jane Roberts, Bernard Metais, Elvira Schwartz, Melissa Kling, Nora Delanay, Elaine Uzan Leary, Jennie Luening Malloy, Barbara Bouquegneau, Marie Teixeira, Misa Bourdoiseau, Margaret L. Baldwin, Nicolas Cardou, Joe Rivlin, and the many other members and employees of the Federation of Alliances Françaises, USA, who so kindly helped us early on.